The Balancing Act

The Balancing Act

Rediscovering Your Feelings

Barbara Killinger, Ph.D.

KEY PORTER BOOKS

Canadian Cataloguing in Publication Data

Killinger, Barbara
    The balancing act: rediscovering your feelings

ISBN 1-55013-648-8

1. Narcissism – Popular work.   2. Narcissism – Treatment – Popular works. I. Title.

RC553.N36K55   1995   616.85'82   C95-930378-2

The publisher gratefully acknowledges the assistance of the Canada Council, the Ontario Publishing Centre and the Government of Ontario.

Key Porter Books Limited
70 The Esplanade
Toronto, Ontario
Canada M5E 1R2

Distributed in the United States of America by National Book Network, Inc. 1-800-462-6420

Design: Jean Lightfoot Peters
Illustrator: Leah Gryfe
Electronic Assembly: Heidy Lawrance Associates

Printed and bound in Canada

95 96 97 98 99 5 4 3 2 1

Table of Contents

1. *Flat Feelings — Tipping the Balance: One Couple's Experience* — 1

2. *The Thinking and Feeling Functions: Understanding What Makes You Tick* — 13

3. *Misunderstandings: The $64 Question — What in the World Went Wrong?* — 25

4. *The Workaholic Trap: Personality Changes on the Gerbil Wheel* — 43

5. *Narcissism: Mirror, Mirror on the Wall, Who Is the Fairest of Them All?* — 75

6. *The Narcissist's Family: The Birth of Narcissism and Its Generational Legacy* — 95

7. *The Journey — Stage 1, Awareness: Learn to Internalize Your Feelings* — 109

8. *The Journey — Stage 2, Rescheduling: Problem-Solving. Now or Later, That Is the Question!* — 137

9. *The Journey — Stage 3, Non-Controlling Communication: Unplugging Our Ears, and Staying on Our Own Side of the Fence* — 157

10. *Feeling and Thinking Language and Behaviour: "I Thought We Spoke the Same Language!"* — 175

11. *Problem-Solving Through Creativity: The Logical Circle* — 201

Appendix 1 — *Learn to Internalize Your Feelings — A Summary* — 221

Appendix 2 — *Additional Functions from Jung's Theory of Psychological Types* — 227

Quiz — *What Is Your Level of Narcissism?* — 243

Bibliography — 247

Index — 251

*I dedicate this book
with much love to my children:
Kathy, Michael, and Suzy*

ACKNOWLEDGMENTS

This book honours the memory of my parents, Eva and Cuyler Henderson, who lived a balanced and admirable life together, and gave their children a legacy of stability and love. Family and friends offered support through their curiosity about the contents and title of "this one." Clients, as always, enriched my understanding and insight as we journeyed together to re-establish a healthy equilibrium in their lives. Maria Quilici's assistance at home freed me to write. Many thanks to my agent, Beverley Slopen, for her cheerful spirit and helpful advice; to my editor, Jennifer Glossop, for her wise counsel and sensitivity; and to my publisher, Anna Porter, for her vision, and for her continued interest in my writings.

1
Flat Feelings — Tipping the Balance

One Couple's Experience

*"A lot of folks don't know what's cooking
until the pot boils over."*
MORNING SMILE, *THE GLOBE AND MAIL*

SPINNING OUT OF CONTROL

A sunbeam slants across my desk, and the morning sun warms the room. Yet an anxious, tense feeling hangs in the air.

Peter, a darkly handsome fifty-year-old entrepreneur, sits rigidly upright and immobile, some distance from his wife. He casts the occasional furtive glance at Sally as she tearfully describes the state of their marriage. Peter's face registers little emotion. His brow is deeply furrowed, his cheeks sunken. Ridges stretch up from his tense jaw. His eyes look flat, vacant, and haunted.

In contrast, Sally's eyes, although darkly circled, shine brightly through her obvious pain. She is articulate about her experiences, and describes the last few years as an absolute nightmare. Her childhood sweetheart has disappeared into this stranger whom she hardly knows.

"I know I'm depressed and not myself," Sally confides. Then, in a more desperate tone, "I feel numb so much of the time. I don't even know who I am any more!" Sally's voice catches, and tears spill down her cheeks. "It's as though Peter's rages have absolutely traumatized me. I just can't cope with all this chaos. He's Dr. Jekyll one minute, Mr. Hyde the next." Sally fights for control, and then almost apologetically completes her thought. "Quite frankly, I'm just as worried about myself as I am about Peter!"

Sally is not alone in feeling traumatized. Peter's anxiety level is sky-high. His prized family business is threatened by bankruptcy. He frets continually that his colleagues and business associates will ask embarrassing questions. He has poured his heart and soul into this firm.

Peter started working for his father part-time at the age of twelve. Even before that he tagged along when his father went into work Saturday and Sunday mornings. "I think now that I was just trying to get this man's attention. My father," Peter explains, "had ice in his veins!" As is so often the case, a workaholic father has produced a workaholic son. When Peter took over the family business, it was the proudest day of his life. It was also, unfortunately, the beginning of a long, slow decline for Peter. Not long after, things started to go awry.

Sally and Peter are typical of the workaholic families I see in my practice. Workaholics like Peter gradually become one-sided and emotionally crippled. Their obsession with work becomes a relentless, compulsive drive to achieve the control and power necessary to gain others' approval. A successful public persona allows them to enjoy the accolades that hard work brings in our society. Workaholics are perfectionists who need to control *all* the variables to ensure that things gets done "right," in their own way. Unfortunately, other people must be controlled to achieve this. Work is the arena in which they shine, but soon long hours, overscheduling, and frantic rushing become the norm. The adrenalin high is their "fix," the drug that frees them from emotional pain. Anger, hurt, guilt, and fear are repressed, and the addiction eventually controls their lives. The workaholic cannot *not* work without getting anxious.

At the end of our first session, I describe to Sally and Peter the therapeutic journey we will take together. Both of them are out of touch with their feelings and emotionally out of control. Our chief task will be to restore their Feeling function so that their psyches will be in balance once again. Both Thinking and Feeling are necessary to make wise decisions. Our journey will take them "from Numb to Joy."

IDENTIFYING THE IMBALANCE

While both Sally and Peter tell me they are numb and confused, Sally alone acknowledges her flat feelings. Peter thinks he is just fine. He's here, he tells me, "only because Sally tells me she's thinking about leaving." He then lets me know that "something's wrong with Sally. She's crying all the time, and for no good reason." Sally is still conscious of her feelings; Peter is not.

A few minutes earlier, I had asked Peter how he was feeling about his wife's unhappiness. His expression turned quizzical. As happens so frequently in my office, Peter turned to Sally, searching for an answer. He needed her to bail him out. It was clear that Peter did not know how he felt. Pointing out this dynamic is one way to help the couple to recognize the emotional dependency that occurs when feelings no longer register.

It is scary not to know how you feel, or what you want. Ironically, the strange truth is that negative feelings still work. Anger and envy, for example, surface quite unexpectedly and often are revealed in alarming thoughts. One client hesitantly admitted that he secretly felt superior when he found out a colleague had cancer. "That's not very nice, is it?" he queried, checking out my reaction. Anxiety soars as self-doubt and insecurity make decision-making increasingly difficult.

Sally, under prolonged stress, is suffering depressive symptoms brought on by despair. She tries to suppress her anger as she fights for self-control, but feelings of helplessness and outrage surge. She has worn herself out trying to keep some intimacy alive in this troubled marriage. Sally, a people person, needs harmony in her relationships. Without inner peace, she is prone to extreme psychological and physical distress. She tells me that she has suffered from a series of illnesses that her doctor tells her are all induced by stress.

Disillusioned, and emotionally fatigued, Sally now avoids her friends. "I just don't have anything left to give," she explains.

In fact, both partners have become socially isolated. For the past year, when invitations come, Peter's typical response is, "I'm not going. It's more trouble than it's worth!" In fact, people have become a nuisance. Peter has even stopped attending the business functions the couple never missed before.

Days, nights, and weekends, Peter frantically drives himself. Every avenue must be exhausted to salvage his empire. Failure, for Peter, is unthinkable! So much is at stake — family pride, his reputation, and lost jobs. He knows he can't afford to give in to his panic. He therefore overcontrols, and increasingly he pushes others beyond limits so that at least some short-term goals are met. Peter will do almost anything now to block out painful reality, but the adrenalin rush that work used to give him no longer covers his anxiety. Bouts of binge drinking are becoming more frequent. He flies into a fury when Sally confronts him, and denies that he has a problem with alcohol. Peter, flipping in and out of denial, still believes he is firmly in control.

Sally doesn't see all this hyperactivity at Peter's work. In her presence, Peter's rounded shoulders spell defeat. She has noticed that he is increasingly lethargic and oblivious to his surroundings. Simple everyday distractions set off episodes of black moods or extreme irritability. Peter has become like a petulant child, dependent on Sally to run everything. Ironically, Peter was always very protective of his independence.

Riddled with a mixture of guilt, shame, resentment, and insecurity, Peter lashes out at Sally in ugly rages. Sally increasingly can do *nothing* right. Instead of recognizing his own chaos, Peter projects his anger outwards. Fear is contagious. Living in such an unpredictable environment, Sally and the children grow increasingly anxious and "hyper" themselves.

Rapid mood swings are common symptoms of extreme anxiety. Sally tells me she is so terrified of risking one of Peter's temper tantrums or rages, that she immediately gives in. Anything to keep some semblance of harmony. Peace at any cost is expensive. It means that Sally sacrifices her own needs. Like all martyrs, she feels victimized and bitter. "Nowadays, I cry at the drop of a hat. The slightest provocation, and I'm a bowl of jelly. It's getting that I can't remember what I used to be like!"

Peter has pushed Sally to her limit. Railing against being a powerless puppet, Sally finds her rage erupting into hysteria. Her usual sensitivity and thoughtfulness go out the window. "When I let go, I'm incredibly short and sharp. I lecture and preach, and exaggerate things. All the junk I've been storing up for weeks just comes pouring out." Sally looks chagrined. "I'm really losing it. I've never behaved like this in my entire life."

Peter, on the other hand, appears to have forgotten his angry outbursts completely. He reassures me that he handles all his anger internally. Peter then turns on Sally. "You just admitted you exaggerate." He then explains to me, "Really, I'm sure she makes up a lot of this stuff."

WHO'S AFRAID OF VIRGINIA WOOLF?

We are all probably afraid of anger. Behind negative feelings such as anger, envy, jealousy, and hate lies fear. When Sally says, "I'm really losing it," she no longer feels safe. Not only have Peter's unpredictable outbursts threatened her security, she no longer trusts her own restraints.

When Peter denies his hostility, he avoids taking responsibility for his negative feelings. Instead, he sees Sally as the angry one. A destructive merry-go-round I call the Terrible Twist illustrates this projective technique so frequently used by workaholics to control and put down others. A typical exchange goes like this.

In the morning, on the way out the door, Peter tosses over his shoulder, "I'll be home about 6:30 tonight."

By seven o'clock that evening, Sally's feelings have progressed from hurt to frustration. By eight, her rising anger gives way to worry. She has visions of Peter in a car accident, or worse. A disturbing panic rises from her gut.

At 8:30, Peter comes rushing in the front door and is met by Sally, tears streaming down her cheeks. No apology, no explanation are offered. Sally's confrontation triggers Peter's rage.

"You're acting like a spoiled brat," he screams. A litany of Sally's faults ensues. It ends with the ultimate and all too familiar refrain: "You're always ruining our evenings! No wonder I don't come home any more." Yet again, Sally is made out to be the culprit. Not only is Sally deeply hurt by this twisting of the truth, but she is furious and frightened. Her sense of reality is shaken. Her inner turmoil escalates. Eventually she withdraws into silence, and sinks further into depression.

Peter interprets Sally's withdrawal as rejection. In defiance, he stubbornly resolves not to tell Sally any details about his failing business. "Sally asks too many questions," he protests. Peter, too, protects himself with his own armour of silence. Sometimes he sulks for days.

While both feel frightened and abandoned, Peter handles it by running on an even tighter schedule. He avoids thinking about Sally. Sally can't turn herself off so easily. When hostility builds up unchecked, it eventually erupts like a volcano. Anger spews forth in the form of ridicule, caustic sarcasm, and smouldering resentment. Bitterness turns into defiance. Temper tantrums give way to acts of destructive rage. Drivers cut off other drivers or go too fast, refusing to follow the rules of the road. People play the devil's advocate, and argue just for the sake of arguing. People humiliate others, destroy their own and others' security. The ultimate act of rage occurs when someone commits murder or suicide.

When hostility goes underground, feelings are cut off and denied expression. The person shuns personal responsibility and instead acts out in passive-aggressive ways. Those affected by such behaviour feel victimized, rejected, even abandoned. No healthy resolution is possible without true dialogue.

Peter and Sally had little insight into the magnitude of their anger. The following quiz helped them identify their own passive-aggressive styles of anger.

When others speak, do you
  1. Tune out and block out what is said?
  2. Avoid looking at the speaker, and look elsewhere?
  3. Remain silent to avoid giving any part of yourself?
  4. Get bored easily, yawn, sigh, or grow restless?
  5. Rehearse what you are going to say, instead of listening?
  6. Distract yourself by doing something else?
  7. Send signals indicating you are in a rush?
  8. Interrupt others in mid-sentence?
  9. Refuse to state your position, or refuse to respond?
  10. Often bring the conversation back to your own interests?

Do you typically
  11. Neglect to follow through on promises?
  12. Put off unwanted tasks as long as possible?
  13. Tell others what they want to hear, instead of telling the truth?
  14. Say yes when you mean no?
  15. Agree to do something in less time than is realistic?
  16. Use sarcasm, ridicule, innuendos, or put-downs?
  17. Promise things you cannot possibly deliver?
  18. Act impulsively, without thinking?

THE EFFECTS OF DEPRESSION AND ANXIETY ON FEELINGS

Both depression and anxiety deaden feelings and cause people to feel numb and flat.

Sally's symptoms indicate that she is suffering a reactive depression, a state brought on by an external situation and relieved when that situation is removed. Her idealistic dreams for her marriage have been frustrated at every turn. Sally is unwittingly carrying Peter's disowned feelings of vulnerability, inadequacy, need, and unresolved guilt, as well as her own stored-up anger. Naively oblivious of her best interests, Sally has become a martyr-victim — the good co-dependent in relationship with an addict. She sacrifices her true Self to maintain a semblance of harmony in the home. The more Peter abdicates his personal responsibilities at home, the more overly responsible Sally becomes. She is left fully in charge of intimacy in their relationship. Deep inside she carries the fears and concerns of the whole family. Women like Sally are too often taught to be nice, sweet, cute, silent, self-effacing, and self-sacrificing.

As depression settles in, Sally is zapped of all energy. As Clarissa Pinkola Estes writes in *Women Who Run With the Wolves,* "A woman may try to hide from the devastations of her life, but the bleeding, the loss of life's energy, will continue until she recognizes the predator for what it is and contains it." Desires, goals, and hopes slowly ebb away under such circumstances. Lifeless thoughts, feelings, and desires provide no energy for dreaming or action. Naivety takes the place of intuition.

Intuition is the soul's spokesperson. It is quick, curious, and adventuresome. It takes risks and is a powerful ally for justice and fairness. Its role is to measure and weigh information, to sort through extraneous material to discover the essence or core meaning of an idea. It sees the forest, but does not get lost among the trees. It anticipates and forewarns us of people's motivation and intentions. It draws maps to tell us the best and wisest direction in which to proceed. It fuels us with enthusiasm and vitality, and gives wings to our imagination.

Sally's fatigue is a symptom of the hopelessness she feels. She has lost weight, and her sleeping patterns are disturbed. Sally falls asleep in exhaustion, but sleeps fitfully. At four o'clock, she is wide awake and thrashes about until she falls into a deep sleep, only to be awakened again from disturbing dreams. Her concentration is shot. She gets distracted easily, and after reading a newspaper, she can't retain what she has read. Loss of memory and forgetfulness are common. It is harder and harder to motivate herself to do even routine chores.

Sally feels mentally, physically, and emotionally drained. Much of the time she feels "like a zombie," as she phrases it. Not only is she avoiding friends, she sees very little of her extended family. Tears brim easily, and crying spells are more frequent.

When the couple do have sex, which is rare these days, Sally does not initiate it. Her libido is low, and she has lost confidence in her desirability. She realizes she is distancing herself from problems. Motivating herself to do anything has become difficult, and she finds that often she just doesn't really care what happens. Irrational angry outbursts and cynicism frighten her. "I'm so pre-occupied with myself! And so negative about everything. It feels as if I'm permanently wearing dark glasses."

Sally has no trouble recognizing the severity of her depression. She knows that depression is a dangerous cycle that spirals down-wards. The worse Sally feels about herself, the less she is motivated to take any action that might make her feel more effective. Her insecurity and immobilized feelings threaten to undermine her self-worth.

Sally is anxious to get started on her journey back to health. Peter, on the other hand, may falter along the way. His worka-holism is an insidious addiction, and recovery will be slow and frustrating for him. Peter's symptoms revolve around anxiety. Panic attacks rather than depression are his major concern. He needs to be aware, though, that once his anxiety attacks lessen, denial may close in again. Peter's soul and Self are in jeopardy, but he lacks the insight to know this. Peter's real problem, as we will learn later, concerns his high levels of narcissism.

Repeated failures have threatened Peter's perfect persona. Repressed anger breaks through the layers of denial and surfaces in an eruption of rage. Panic attacks rupture the fragile ego tem-porarily to warn of excessive stress. Anxiety Peter can recognize!

Egged on by Sally, Peter reluctantly tells me that, more and more frequently, he finds himself breaking out in sweats. At first it was in the middle of the night. "I'd wake with a start and sit bolt upright. I couldn't breathe, and it felt like a paddle was press-ing against my chest."

No, he didn't think he was dreaming. He doesn't think he dreams much. "I felt dizzy and disoriented — almost claustro-phobic. My pyjamas were soaked!" According to Sally, he would rush from the bedroom and frantically pace up and down the living room until his anxiety subsided. Only then could he begin to breathe normally again.

Peter was terrified when these episodes began to occur at work. One day when he was chairing a meeting of the shareholders, he felt his hands go clammy, and beads of sweat appeared on his brow. He could feel his shirt growing damp. "I wonder if they can tell!" Then he worried, "If my panic shows, I'm a goner. They'll lose *all* confidence in me!" This group had already been witness to one of his outbursts two weeks before.

Peter's flights from reality are of grave concern. Not only is his memory terrible, but as Sally explains, "I sometimes worry that he has early Alzheimer's. He not only doesn't remember where I've told him the kids are, he asks me the same question moments after I've answered him the first time." Sally adds, "Peter doesn't seem to remember anything he doesn't want to be responsible for."

There is a danger that Peter's episodic psychotic breaks, where reality and fantasy blur, will become more frequent and severe. The breakdown syndrome of workaholism leads towards a disintegration of the ego. Peter needs to recognize how urgent it is that he gain insight and learn new skills before strong denial shuts off his chance for a full recovery.

CRISS-CROSSING JOURNEYS

Sally and Peter have one common path — their mutual need to get back in touch with their feelings — but different dynamics drive them. Sally, suffering from a reactive depression, is likely to recover from her depression fairly quickly once the trauma of the current situation is corrected. A more difficult task for Sally will be confronting her co-dependent role in this marriage. She has tried to keep everything and everyone around her in harmony, but in doing so, has sacrificed her own sense of self. She needs to learn that giving in is not true generosity, but a form of dishonesty that leads to a loss of integrity.

Peter faces a more difficult recovery from workaholism and narcissism. His will be a long, arduous journey, full of many setbacks and frustrations. Peter's feelings are deeply repressed because his level of anxiety prevents him from facing the numerous fears, guilt, shame, and insecurity that haunt the workaholic throughout life.

There is much background information to understand before we are ready to learn the techniques and skills necessary to get Feeling and Thinking back into balance. Chapter 2 prepares us with an explanation of how Thinking and Feeling function in the psyche. Chapter 3 goes on to explore the misunderstandings that occur when Feelers and Thinkers communicate. It also examines the Shadow side of these functions, which often wreaks havoc in people's lives.

Workaholism, until recently, has been little understood. Chapter 4 is devoted to exploring why feelings are lost when a person progresses through the breakdown stages of workaholism and turns from Dr. Jekyll into Mr. Hyde. Narcissism plays a key role in workaholism, and its self-serving focus profoundly affects all family members. Both workaholism and narcissism are also passed down from parent to child. Chapter 5 explores why narcissism is so prevalent a problem today, and explains its developmental roots and tell-tale characteristics. Chapter 6 demonstrates the dangerous legacies that narcissism brings to the family through a return to Sally and Peter's story.

Chapters 7, 8, and 9 take us through the techniques involved in restoring feelings and becoming a more effective problem-solver. Chapter 10 explores the differences between Feeling and Thinking language and behaviour. Our journey will conclude with a creative technique called *The Logical Circle*, which will help us form intelligent and wise decisions.

2
The Thinking and Feeling Functions

Understanding What Makes You Tick

*"The true portrait of a man is a fusion of what he
thinks he is, what others think he is, what he really
is and what he tries to be."*
DORE SCHARY IN *HEYDAY*

PSYCHOLOGICAL TYPE — A BRIEF OVERVIEW

Understanding our personality is of utmost importance if we are
to gain insight along our psychological journey towards a balanced
life. In the early 1920s, C. G. Jung, the Swiss psychologist, developed his theories of psychological differentiation. In *Psychological
Types,* Jung stated that "type differentiation often begins very early,
so early that in some cases one must speak of it as innate." He dis-
tinguished four basic functions that the conscious psyche requires
for adaptation and orientation. One or two functions tend to be
dominant, while the others remain inferior or undifferentiated.

According to Jung's theories, *ideally* all four basic functions
should contribute equally: "thinking should facilitate cognition
and judgment, feeling should tell us how and to what extent
a thing is important or unimportant for us, sensation should

convey concrete reality to us through seeing, hearing, tasting, etc., and intuition should enable us to divine the hidden possibilities in the background, since these too belong to the complete picture of a given situation."

YOU CAN'T HAVE ONE WITHOUT THE OTHER

Once we perceive information, it can be used to make decisions, form an opinion, or reach some conclusion. How we make decisions or judgments will differ depending on our dominant type. Therefore, one of the most relevant questions in getting to know yourself is, Is your dominant function normally Thinking or Feeling? Healthy functioning, of course, requires a good balance between both functions. In Jungian theory, if one function works but the other does not, the strong imbalance eventually produces neurotic or pathological behaviour.

Depression, for example, is a sign of imbalance in the psyche. Depressed people become emotional easily, but they are often out of touch with their feelings and unable to make wise decisions. Similarly, when a person is ruled by an obsession, the dominant Thinking function becomes fuzzy and confused because it is overused and distorted by anxiety. Judgment is always affected when Thinking or Feeling do not function well. Behavioural changes will become increasingly evident as this imbalance between Thinking and Feeling widens.

For instance, Thinking without feelings of compassion and empathy to temper its wisdom allows one to justify and rationalize deceit and to condone unethical behaviour. Uncensored, wilful thinking permits one to commit dangerous, even evil acts, such as premeditated murder and suicide. The defenses of intellectualizing, rationalizing, projecting blame, dissociation, and compartmentalization, as described later in Chapter 7, can all be used to justify and excuse insensitive and destructive dysfunctional thinking.

Similarly, Feeling without Thinking to guide and inform it leads one to remain naive, irresponsible, even ignorant. Hysterical, childish behaviour results when one is hypersensitive and overreacts to situations. Denial, moodiness, temper tantrums, rages, and extreme stubbornness are signs of unhealthy feelings.

Wisdom and maturity develop when both Thinking and Feeling functions inform our decision-making. Marcel, a thirty-year-old client on a leave of absence because of his workaholism, told me one day that he had started getting flustered the day before. "My mind was racing, and I was cooking up all sorts of ideas about what I was going to say to my boss, when I suddenly realized that my thinking had become obsessive and irrational." He looked pleased with himself as he continued: "I stopped and asked myself what I was feeling at that precise moment. I felt justifiably angry because of what I had just experienced. I decided then to just let myself huff and puff for a while." Then Marcel added, "It really works, you know. All of a sudden I didn't need to be frustrated any more." There is wisdom in making sure that both emotions and intellect get equal energy and time.

THINKING AND FEELING

Before you learn my techniques for getting in touch with feelings, it is essential to know whether you are naturally a Thinker or a Feeler.

Thinking and Feeling functions link up the information acquired through Sensation and Intuition, and use it to make decisions, form judgments, reach conclusions, and develop opinions about both people and things. Each function has its special strength and its own liabilities or negative, Shadow side.

Feeling and emotion should not be confused. Emotion is a complex that includes Thinking and Feeling functions, but also sense impressions, gut reactions, impulses, etc.

Thinking is essentially impersonal. According to Isabel Myers in *Gifts Differing*, "Its goal is objective truth, independent of the personality and wishes of the thinker, or anyone else" (p. 65). Thinking is most useful for impersonal problems, such as drawing up building plans, interpreting a legal document, or analysing whether information is true or false.

Feeling is best used when handling people and their problems, interpreting human motives, and facilitating a co-operative,
mediatory, team model where both the welfare of the people
involved and the agenda are considered equally important. People
remain motivated if they feel part of the decision-making process.

If a Thinker and a Feeler go to a store to purchase a rug, you
will hear the Thinker say, "I think we should get this one. The
quality is good, it's a practical colour, and the tight weave will be
serviceable."

The Feeler's response might be, "Yuk, I couldn't walk on that
rug every day without getting thoroughly upset!"

Both are equally valid responses. The Thinker makes decisions
based on logical, rational, practical thinking. The Feeler makes
decisions based on what he or she appreciates or values. Unfortunately, in our society and within the individual, thinking often
devalues and overruns feeling values.

Thinking

Thinking is reflective and objective. It asks the reasons for doing
things. Thinking analyses and weighs the available evidence. It
considers cause and effect, and it stays objective when exploration
uncovers unpleasant facts or discovers something is wrong. It
wants proof, validity, and reliability. Therefore, Thinkers give
more credence to things that are logical, scientific, and observable. They prefer to wait until results are in before stating their
impersonal findings.

Numbers, facts, and figures are highly valued. Thinkers' executive skills include an ability to organize facts and ideas in logical
sequence, and to be objective when hypothesizing or developing a
theoretical approach. Thinkers are best at impersonal jobs. Sur-
geons operate with an objective distancing. Strong Thinkers are
able to fire employees with relatively little trauma, and rationalize
their motives for doing so — "It's necessary because it's best for the
welfare of the organization." Technicians, scientists, researchers,
lawyers, engineers, analysts, and judges tend to be Thinkers.

Thinkers have focused awareness. Consequently, they find it

difficult to concentrate on more than one thing at a time. Don't expect a Thinker to read the paper and listen to what you have to say. They heartily dislike interruptions because their inner processing of information gets distracted. They lose their train of thought.

Thinking processes information by sifting through objective information and drawing a conclusion. This package, the Thinkers' own version of the situation, becomes their reality. Unfortunately, logic and reason are no guarantee of being right. Yet Thinkers, convinced of their argument, may be difficult to challenge. Openness is not one of their virtues.

Thinkers can react emotionally with some intensity, but their emotions are less visible and therefore not communicated. People often see Thinkers as cool, aloof, inflexible, arbitrary, and even ruthless, because objective data ignore personal information and values. As Jung puts it, "He may be polite, amiable, and kind, but one is constantly aware of a certain uneasiness betraying an ulterior motive — the disarming of an opponent, who must at all costs be pacified and placated lest he prove himself a nuisance" (p. 241). Thinkers are competitive, and their tendency to take the one-up position is usually met with resistance, distrust, and resentment in the sensitive listener who feels belittled or talked down to. The used-car salesman's pitch typifies this manipulative manoeuvring.

Thinkers, because of their competitive nature, tend to be envious and jealous. They are skeptical, judgmental, critical, and pessimistic. They see half-empty rather than half-full.

Thinkers are poor communicators because they package information in their heads prior to speaking:

1. Thinkers can clutter up their communication with adjuncts, qualifications, retractions, saving clauses, doubts, etc., but forget to tell you the subject of their discourse.
2. Thinkers tend to be blunt, short, or sharp in their delivery, and often neglect to give the listener enough information about how they reached their opinion.
3. Thinkers can take too long and be overly intense about an idea that intrigues them and forget to focus on the relationship with the listener.

4. Thinkers tend to lecture and preach, and thereby bore the listener because there is no exchange of views.
5. Thinkers can fail to personalize and own what they are saying. Instead they talk in generalities, referring to people in general. Or they use theoretical rhetoric to prove their own point.
6. Thinkers enjoy being "historical," bringing up facts and experiences from the past to support their present argument. Elephant memories infuriate the listener, who often has no recollection of the event, or totally disagrees with the information presented as evidence of the Thinker's being "right."

Thinkers appear to be listening because they do not interrupt. In reality, they are often lost in thought, rehearsing what they are going to say next. Their focus is arrested on one of the thoughts that interested them personally.

Thinkers can be domineering, opinionated, and prickly. Outsiders often see them as inconsiderate, insensitive, and arrogant. They can make Feelers feel that they have been "run over by a bus!" If teaching, their thoughts are concerned with the material, not the presentation of it or whether the student understands. The first day of my return to school after a fifteen-year absence, I watched in fascination as about a hundred students exited in droves past the professor, in the middle of a Psychology 101 lecture. He didn't miss a beat and remained focused on his lecture notes. I was amazed that he didn't seem interested enough to ask the students why they were leaving. Asking for feedback is rare for a Thinker.

The more Feelings are cut off, the more Thinking will become rigid and unbending, shut off from outside influences, and from reality itself. Rigid Thinkers tend to take everything personally, and fall back on emotionality and touchiness. If challenged, such Thinkers lash out, or withdraw into passive-aggressive anger. Their personal retorts can be vicious and highly irrational. Gradually, their isolation increases as people withdraw because they are afraid, or do not trust that the Thinker is capable of being empathic or compassionate.

Tragically, as Jung states, "His originally fertilizing ideas become destructive, poisoned by the sediment of bitterness. His struggle against the influences emanating from the unconscious increases with his external isolation, until finally they begin to cripple him" (p. 244). As a Thinker grows more out of touch with subjective reality, his thinking becomes fanciful and irrelevant to facts as they are. A wall builds up around the person as secrecy and privacy become even more important. Chaos is building up inside, but no one must know!

Fairness is important for Thinkers. It often seems as though they place things on scales, ensuring that one thing balances another. "If I get this one, then you can have that one" is the exchange. Truth, principles, policies, and laws are valued. Thinkers, however, tend to distrust and ignore decisions made by feeling. Feelings are deemed flighty, unreliable, and totally illogical, or off-the-wall. As Isabel Myers concludes in *Gifts Differing*: Thinkers "contribute to the welfare of society by the intellectual criticism of its habits, customs, and beliefs, by the exposure of wrongs, the solution of problems, and the support and research for the enlargement of human knowledge and understanding" (p. 68).

Men slightly outnumber women Thinkers (60 to 40 per cent). In my practice, I find that Thinkers who marry Feeling types often create difficulties because they tend to problem-solve or "fix" a spouse whose thinking they consider inferior. In turn, Feeling types distrust the Thinker's cut-and-dried method of discussion. Although both these types just "know" what ideas, which people, and what course of action they value and appreciate, Thinkers want to argue and debate with others to prove that their way of doing things or their thoughts are best. Thinkers contradict each other, each one claiming "the truth," while for Feelers it is enough that something is "valuable" to them.

Feeling

Feeling, above all, values harmony. Feelers make decisions based on a personal value system and on a subjective appreciation of a person or object.

Feelers excel in the social arts because they are sensitive to human interaction. They tend to be well-adjusted and reasonable, and get what they want easily. They are accepting, agreeable, and usually have lots of friends and acquaintances. Feelers are generally good at sizing up and judging the positive and negative sides of people. Feeling is naturally uncritical, trusting, and optimistic. Feelers like to agree with others, if possible. They give people the benefit of the doubt at least until evidence to the contrary is acknowledged. Therefore, Feelers can be naive and subject to others' manipulation. However, feeling itself can become mechanical and calculating if the person neglects to nurture and genuinely care for himself or herself. As a result, Feelers may eventually become neurotic.

Sacrifice is easy for Feelers because they have diffuse, open awareness. Their attention is naturally directed outwards towards others. They can do several things at once, and still pay attention to the actions and behaviour of family members, friends, and things going on around them. If other-directedness comes at the expense of nurturing the Self, Feelers can become victims or martyrs. Such people lose the Self in the service of others and may become bitter, resentful souls who don't feel appreciated for all their efforts. In truth, they are apt to lose their own feelings and become manipulative and controlling people. They give or "give in," but their giving has strings attached. There are unstated expectations about what the other person "should" give back to them. Giving in, by the way, has little to do with real generosity!

Because harmony is so important to them, Feelers tend to avoid conflict. Anger can go underground if not expressed. It becomes passive-aggressive in nature and turns into a slow-burning fuse. Eventually this anger turns destructive, both to the Feeler and to those who eventually have to deal with the Mount Vesuvius rages that erupt when the Feeler finally explodes. Withdrawing, sulking, not speaking, not listening, and so on serve only to delay problem-solving, or inhibit resolution of problems.

Further, Feelers risk building up enormous resentment and self-pity if they feel totally unloved or unappreciated. They may give all their energy to others, yet fail to be assertive and stand up for their own needs. Such victims, unfortunately, often fall into despair. Some even contemplate suicide because they feel helpless to change their circumstances. Usually depression becomes a serious problem because their repressed anger remains beneath their consciousness. Feelings of sadness and bitterness are experienced instead. "Smiling depressives" look happy while telling you horrific details of their life, completely out of touch with their own anger. "No, I'm not an angry person," he or she will insist. Anger would mean that they were out of harmony, an unforgivable sin.

Extraverted Feelers like to talk through their thoughts, to eliminate possibilities and to brainstorm ideas through to a conclusion. Thinkers believe that Feelers ramble, repeat themselves, go into too much detail, or talk too long during this process. When two Feelers are talking, they often interrupt each other, add facilitating or supportive comments, and share experiences. The conversation continues, despite the additions and qualifications, with no apparent problem. Sharing and affirmation are very important.

Feelers, especially Extraverted types, are naturally tenderhearted, diplomatic, tactful, sensitive, and thoughtful. They make friends easily and are able to put themselves in others' shoes. Feelers are enthusiastic, accepting, supportive, and interested in what others do and think. Feelers ask questions and draw out others.

Introverted Feelers, however, resemble Thinkers, as they keep feelings tucked safely inside. They are more shy, timid, secretive, and private. They tend to have one or two close friendships. They may open up after a time when they get to know you. Friends and relatives complain that they don't say nice things, even "I love you." Their response to this complaint is often utter surprise. Because they do care deeply and often passionately, they find it hard to believe that others don't know this. In fact, the assumption that others are as perceptive and thoughtful as they are leads Feelers to suffer great disappointment. They expect similar behaviour from others and are devastated when it is not forthcoming.

Misunderstandings occur frequently between Thinkers and

Feelers because of the way caring is shown. Thinkers value doing things for others, such as fixing appliances or cutting the grass. They think problem-solving for others is "helpful." However, Feelers value affirmation and confirmation from others. They love to hear phrases of endearment and support from loved ones. Typical complaints from a Thinker sound like this: "It's not what you say but what you do that counts. You don't appreciate all the things I do for you. You just want my pay cheque." Or, "You can say you love me a hundred times, but if you turn me away sexually, that's not okay with me. I want a wife who thinks I'm important, who will look after me."

The Feeler rejoins, "It's not what you do but what you say that is important to me! I need a sensitive, gentle husband who wants to share and laugh, and who tells me he cares." Or, "How can you expect me to want to be sexual with you when you're so neglectful and thoughtless of my needs. You never say 'I love you,' even though you know it would make me so happy." Until both Thinking and Feeling are developed within the individual, this dilemma will remain unresolved and irresolvable.

For Feelers, honesty is innate. If they tell a lie, Feelers suffer great dissonance until the truth is out. Small children will tell a fib, but then, after much suffering, will tell you, "You know what I told you the other day? Well, I really wasn't over at Susan's house!" Ironically, Feelers are sometimes tactful, rather than honest. Hurting other people's feelings is to be avoided because they well understand the pain involved when that happens to them.

Oversensitivity, taking everything personally, is not a healthy response. One must be truly sensitive to *both* oneself and others. Being assertive and firm is therefore important for Feelers. They need to develop the ability to stand up for their own values and to understand the process by which they develop their ideas. Otherwise, they will feel as if they have been steamrolled by a dominant Thinker. Harmony-lovers become demoralized, passive, depressed, and anxiety-prone unless they develop their own objective thinking. A healthy skepticism is in order when Feelers learn to ask these questions:

1. Is this information or opinion really true about me?
2. Is this person attributing something to me that he cannot recognize in himself? Is this a projection?
3. Is this person's blunt, sharp delivery making me defensive? Am I really able to hear what is being said as a result?
4. Do I really understand what she is telling me, or are details left out that might help me figure out what she means?
5. Do I expect him to say thank you graciously, when he really doesn't know how to say it that way?

Isabel Myers, in *Gifts Differing*, points out that Feelers "contribute to the welfare of society by their loyal support of good works and those movements, generally regarded as good by the community, which they feel correctly about and so can serve effectively" (p. 68). Women Feelers who marry Thinkers too frequently take on the disowned feelings of vulnerability, insecurity, and inadequacy of their publicly superefficient husbands. They feel sad, get depressed, and act out anxiety for both of them. Their empathy and compassion spill over because ego boundaries are unclear. They thereby overburden themselves by carrying the whole family's problems.

Sadly, to the outside world, the passive, irresponsible husband appears together and strong, while his wife is labelled neurotic! She is told that "Everything is her fault," and too often she learns to believe it.

This victim spouse becomes a parent, guardian, and jack-of-all-trades who handles the full responsibility for home and children. Slowly, the loving, nurturing wife loses her true self in the service of others. Depressed, angry, bitter, and resentful, she finally asks for support outside the family. The status quo is so entrenched that neither member of this couple can grow because they are trapped in the angst of a dysfunctional family.

WHY THINKERS AND FEELERS HAVE TROUBLE UNDERSTANDING ONE ANOTHER

Now that we have some idea about how Feeling and Thinking function, we will go on to explore how they cause problems in our relationships with others. We will look at the different communication patterns of Thinkers and Feelers, and examine a controlling tactic that is highly destructive to others' feelings, especially those of their Significant Other.

We will also learn how our least-well-developed Inferior function turns against us to undermine our best functions. If negative thinking is your Inferior function, for example, then taking the time and energy to develop your positive thinking will be to your advantage. Otherwise, the negative, Shadow side of your personality will become dangerous and do harm to both yourself and others.

3
Misunderstandings

The $64 Question: What in the World Went Wrong?

*"What Evil Lurks in the Hearts of Man,
Only the Shadow Knows!"*

CONFUSING, CONFUSED, OR TRAUMATIZED?

Poor communication is the number one reason people give for the breakdown of a relationship. Communicating well is an art that can be learned, but it takes much patience, tolerance, and skill. It also helps to know the different ways people communicate. For example, do they share their thoughts and feelings, or is everything kept safely tucked inside?

In this chapter, we will discover why Thinkers and Feelers have difficulty communicating with each other, and why "The Terrible Twist," a controlling tactic, is so destructive.

We will also learn why the Inferior function is the dark culprit behind many of our upsets and rows. When this Shadow aspect of ourselves roars to the surface unannounced, atypical personality changes occur that surprise us and others. Nobody wins when the Shadow is at play.

CONVERSATIONS BETWEEN THINKERS AND FEELERS

Thinkers and Feelers process information and make decisions in different ways.

Two Thinkers
Andy and Bruce are both born Thinkers.

TWO THINKERS IN CONVERSATION

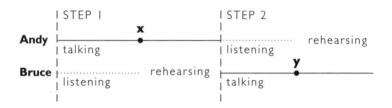

STEP 1: Andy is talking to Bruce. Bruce listens until Andy says X, an idea that happens to interest Bruce.

At this moment, Bruce goes inside his head and processes this information.

Bruce begins to formulate his own version of X and starts to rehearse what he is going to say when Andy finishes speaking.

Because Bruce is preoccupied with his own thoughts, he hears little else that Andy is saying.

Andy finishes talking.

STEP 2: It is Bruce's turn to speak, and he now responds to Andy.

Bruce tells Andy what he thinks of Andy's idea, X.

Andy, meanwhile, is unaware that Bruce has heard only part of what he said.

Andy listens to Bruce, until Bruce says Y, an idea that gets Andy's attention.

(A similar process ensues as Andy becomes preoccupied with

his own thoughts about *Y*. He starts rehearsing what he wants to say to Bruce when he finishes talking.)

Andy and Bruce appear to be listening to each other, but it is selective listening based on what each is particularly interested in. Each Thinker has focused awareness, ($\wedge$), so Thinkers function best when they are able to concentrate on one thing at a time. Some real listening does occur, but since both Andy and Bruce hear only snatches of each other's thoughts, true understanding is inhibited.

Although Thinkers tend not to interrupt each other, when they become emotional about a subject and want to get their point across, they can interrupt or both talk at once.

Two Feelers
Cindy and Diane are both strong Feelers.

TWO FEELERS IN CONVERSATION

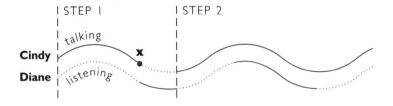

STEP 1: Cindy is talking through her problems, sorting out what she thinks about a subject.

Diane listens, until she hears Cindy mention that she has experienced *X*, an upsetting situation.

Diane then jumps in with a brief story about a similar experience of *X* in her own life. She shares this with Cindy.

STEP 2: Cindy continues talking about her own experience of *X*. Diane breaks into the conversation several times, and once even speaks at the same time as Cindy. Cindy stops momentarily to let Diane finish her thoughts. Then Cindy continues with her story, while Diane listens.

STEP 3: While Cindy is speaking, she is thinking through her own thoughts. Verbalizing helps her clarify her thinking. Diane acts like a Greek chorus, affirming, sympathizing, supporting, and questioning Cindy's ideas until she finally comes to some resolution of her own problem.

Interruptions are no problem for this pair. Both have the Feeler's diffuse awareness, (∨). Both are able to concentrate on several conversations at once and still keep track of their own viewpoint. Clarification comes for Cindy as she works through her ideas. It is helpful to have Diane's support, and she enjoys sharing ideas and opinions along the way. Cindy needs acceptance and affirmation.

A Thinker and a Feeler
Andy is the Thinker, and Cindy, the Feeler.

THINKER AND FEELER IN CONVERSATION

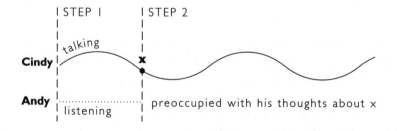

STEP 1: Cindy is talking through a relationship problem with Andy.

She goes to some length to explain her thoughts to Andy.

Andy listens until Cindy says X, something someone said to her that she found upsetting.

STEP 2: Since Andy thinks this thought, X, is somewhat bizarre, he tries to figure out why Cindy is so upset. X wouldn't bother him at all!

STEP 3: Eventually Cindy realizes there is a blank look on Andy's face. Cindy stops, and verbalizes her anger towards Andy because he isn't listening to her. This is important stuff to her.

STEP 4: Andy tells her that he thinks her statements about X are ridiculous and totally illogical. "How could you possibly get upset about that?" he asks.

STEP 5: Cindy explains to Andy that X was only a tangential thought. It really has little to do with the relationship problem she is trying to solve. "And why are you talking about X anyway? It's got to be the least important thing I said," she adds in frustration.

Cindy gets very upset because, as she says, "He never just understands my point of view. He always has to add his own two cents!" She feels belittled and offended that Andy didn't even try to listen. "It's obvious you haven't the faintest idea what I'm talking about!" Cindy exclaims. "Why don't you ever just simply listen to me?"

In addition to her initial problem, Cindy now has the problems caused by sharing her thoughts with Andy. Cindy will soon learn not to "think out loud" to Andy. By doing this, she unwittingly stops sharing, and thereby lessens her own generosity, a precious Feeling function. Andy does his own thinking and tends not to share his thoughts until he has reached a conclusion. Certainly, he doesn't talk while he is thinking. Doing two things at once is not Andy's strength.

With communication breaking down, soon neither understands the other. Eventually both cease to even care, and little energy goes into talking or listening. Feelings have become too painful and raw, and they just shut down. Communication, for this couple, occurs only when it is necessary to discuss superficial, impersonal, "safe" topics.

Andy is most interested in ideas, things, goals. Cindy's interests centre around relationships and people. No wonder their focus is directed towards different things. Send these two to a movie, and listen to the conversation after. Andy will extol the virtues of the film's technology. Cindy will try to figure out all the relationships between the characters. She will worry about what happened to so-and-so, and why the heroine didn't see what was coming, and so on.

Solution

STEP 1: Cindy needs to stop when she sees a blank or far-off look in Andy's eyes, and ask, "Where did I lose you?"

STEP 2: Andy also needs to take responsibility when he stops listening.

At the time he goes inside to start processing X, he needs to warn Cindy, "Can you hold on for a minute? I'm trying to figure out why you would be so upset when so-and-so said X. I can't listen and try to figure this out at the same time."

STEP 3: This gives Cindy a chance to reply that X was only an aside.

It isn't important, the way she sees the problem.

She herself may be puzzled about why she brought X into the conversation. The reason may be an unconscious one, in which case she won't be able to figure it out immediately.

If she does know why she mentioned it, she will be able to explain why she digressed onto that particular tangent

STEP 4: Both Cindy and Andy can then resume the conversation, with both of them involved, until Cindy discovers her own solution.

Andy will be able to ask her questions along the way if he finds he is getting lost again.

STEP 5: When Cindy has reached her own solution, Andy can clarify his understanding by rephrasing her conclusions about what she is going to do to settle her relationship conflict.

"So you've decided to phone Mary and explain this to her?"

The goal for this couple is to develop mutual listening skills. Their differences must be understood and appreciated rather than scorned. Otherwise, there will be the familiar arguments about who is right, or challenging questions such as, "Why did you say such a stupid thing?" Such divisive tactics mean no one wins.

THE TERRIBLE TWIST

The Terrible Twist is a controlling tactic that I described in my book *Workaholics: The Respectable Addicts*. Communication becomes highly destructive with its use, and the recipient of the message is left devastated. Feelers especially need to be aware because Thinkers are naturally competitive, and being "one-up" is very important. They are, therefore, more prone to project blame as a defense mechanism.

STEP 1: One person does something that the other person feels is thoughtless, such as coming home for dinner two hours late without any warning phone call. He or she finally arrives, with no apology or explanation.

STEP 2: The waiting person, having experienced first anger, then hurt, and eventually fear, is extremely upset and says so: "I was worried sick that you'd been in a terrible accident. Where were you, and why didn't you have the courtesy to call me?"

STEP 3 (The Twist): The first person becomes highly annoyed at this rebuke. The precipitating behaviour is totally ignored, as if it hadn't happened.

"It's all your fault!" shouts the accused. Then, the crowning insult: "See, you're spoiling our evening again! It sure doesn't make me want to rush home." And then, to wound even further: "I can't stand your snivelling. Why don't you grow up?"

Such a devastating interchange would traumatize anyone, but since Feeling types are highly sensitive, they are more vulnerable to such abuse. If something goes wrong in a relationship, Feelers tend to take more than their share of responsibility. They try even harder to make it work. The natural other-directed focus of Feelers makes them put other people's happiness before their own. Feelers tend to be pleasers who, in order to keep harmony in the family, sacrifice their own inner harmony. The loss of Self is a very real danger for people exposed, over time, to this very dangerous projection of blame technique.

After my book on workaholism was published, many wives across Canada and the United States phoned to tell me that their eyes had been opened to this terribly abusive tactic. A typical comment: "Thank heavens I finally understand what is actually going on. You know, I really thought I was going crazy!"

One completely demoralized spouse told me, with touching gratitude, that my book actually saved her life. She had planned her own suicide because she had begun to believe her husband's often repeated charge, "It's all your fault!" Her feelings of guilt were too painful, so she became numb and mute. Initially, she had defended herself at every turn, but he used whatever she said and twisted it back against her. She gave up trying to defend herself because her husband could argue rings around her. She had lost her will and felt totally powerless. The Terrible Twist is a lethal weapon in any power struggle.

This woman and all people exposed to this tactic need to develop their own clear-cut thinking and to learn to be completely objective at such times. When you recognize the Terrible Twist, simply say in a firm voice, "I don't agree, and I don't appreciate your comments. I'll talk to you about this later, when I'm not so upset."

Withdraw from the situation, and try to write down the exchange in a diary or notebook. This action will help you to be objective, especially when you see the words in black and white.

Then, when you are calm, ask yourself this crucial question: Was his original behaviour insensitive or inconsiderate? If you are convinced it was, choose a time when you are both in a more positive frame of mind. Follow through on your promise to return to discuss the previous situation.

Make sure there is no blaming or judging. Clearly state that your goal is that you seek a solution together, so that similar incidents do not occur again. The conversation might go like this: "It's important to me that we are both reliable and loyal to one another. I suggest that we both make a commitment to call if one of us is going to be later than we promised." Make sure to ask, "Would you be willing to meet me halfway on this?"

If the answer is positive, you might add, "I appreciate that. By the way, I'd love to hear any of your ideas about how we could make our relationship run more smoothly."

Dysfunctional communication is a sign that there are serious problems in the relationship. Often, the Inferior function, working overtime, is one of the culprits.

THE INFERIOR FUNCTION — OUR PHANTOM SHADOW

The Inferior function is largely unconscious and therefore is our least-well-developed function. When we get upset, our emotions flood to the surface. We become irritable and sometimes fall into dark moods. Unfortunately, others are often on the receiving end of our unexpected and atypical negative reactions. The Inferior function is autonomous. It has a life of its own! When you over-react to something, "act out" with anger, or "act in" with depression or anxiety, it is a sign that you are in the grip of its power.

The Inferior function, according to Jungian theory, whether it be Thinking, Feeling, Sensation, or Intuition, typically possesses five qualities:

1. It is *primitive,* not well formed, or barely developed.
2. It is *childlike.* We often act in a petulant, childish manner when under its influence.

3. It is *negative,* and causes us to withdraw, become grouchy or
    short-fused, or feel out-of-sorts. Negativity takes different
    forms, depending on which function is inferior.
4. It is *stubborn*: it digs in its heels and has a habit of hanging
    around for a long time.
5. It is *rigid* and resolute. Each of us develops patterns of attack,
    one of which is blaming others, regardless of what happened.
    The Inferior function often runs on automatic pilot, with-
    out any help from us.

No one can reason with us when we are caught in the Inferior
function's clutches. Our Thinking or Feeling cease to operate, so
we become increasingly immobilized. We are possessed and lose
all objectivity. Our judgment is distorted.

To counteract its negative influence, we need to develop our
opposite functions. Then we will be in better balance psychologically. A Thinker, for example, needs to develop his Feeling function so that he may be more diplomatic and gracious. Otherwise,
we risk becoming both bored and boring! Without a well-balanced
personality, we become lopsided. Our joy and zest for life fade as
our repressed energies are consumed by unresolved problems and
irresponsible behaviour. It is not fair or responsible to expect our
loved ones to carry our disowned craziness or angst!

WHEN THINKING OR FEELING IS YOUR INFERIOR FUNCTION

To illustrate the workings of the Inferior function, we will look at
the situation when this function is Thinking, and when it is
Feeling. My clients Sally and Peter will serve as examples.

Sally — the Feeler

Sally is an Extraverted (E), Intuitive (N), Feeling (F), Judging (J)
(ENFJ) personality. Her dominant function is Feeling; her auxil-
iary or second-best function is Intuition. Her third function is
Sensation, and her Inferior function is Thinking.

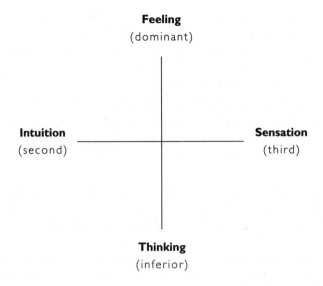

Feeling
(dominant)

Intuition
(second)

Sensation
(third)

Thinking
(inferior)

A thumbnail sketch of an ENFJ is offered by Coleen Clark in her Myers-Briggs booklet: "Compassionate, caring, idealistic, responsive, charismatic, sociable. Good at organizing & leading people. Need & give affirmation. Need & create harmony."

Jung's theory suggests that if Sally is exposed to ongoing stress from her deteriorating marriage, her Inferior Thinking will become activated. It will start to sabotage her best function, Feeling. Recall how Peter, as he became increasingly frustrated at the loss of control in his life, projected his anger onto Sally by criticizing and putting her down. This tactic served to make him feel superior, at least temporarily. Eventually, Sally could do nothing right in Peter's eyes because she had begun to challenge his controlling behaviour. She had become the "enemy," someone to defeat.

Sally, in response, grew increasingly defensive. She became supersensitive and overly emotional, taking things too personally. Any time she flooded with emotion, her Inferior Thinking surged up. Instead of withdrawing as she usually did, she would lash back at Peter.

Note that *negative thinking* is skeptical, critical, judgmental, and pessimistic — "half-empty." It is competitive, and therefore prefers to be right. It excels at one-upmanship. Jealousy and envy motivate the making of comparisons about who is better. Negative thinking gets argumentative, picky, and prickly. It has a short fuse, and its messages are delivered in a clipped, blunt, sharp staccato. Its opinionated statements are not open for discussion.

Negative thinking leaves out essential information, yet is flustered by the listener's puzzlement. It lectures, preaches, and goes on and on, boring the listener because there is no exchange of views. It rarely asks questions of others, and it listens poorly. It gets too intense about its ideas. It turns "historical," bringing up supportive evidence from two weeks, three months, or four years ago. It repeats itself. It fails to personalize and own what it is saying, preferring instead to talk about "people" in general. It uses theoretical rhetoric and quotes from authoritative sources. Quite frankly, it is a roaring pain!

This type of behaviour from the ordinarily nurturing, kind, and gentle Sally has a tremendous impact. It is expected from a Thinker who is in a bad mood. It is shocking and totally disorienting coming from a Feeler. No wonder Peter becomes even more distrustful and confrontational with Sally.

Sally needs to make a concerted effort to develop her positive thinking. Effective thinking is rational, logical, sensible, pragmatic, and realistic. It analyses and takes an objective, impersonal look at the facts. It is fair and consistent, and values truth, principles, policy, and laws.

Peter — the Thinker

Peter is an Introvert (I), Intuitive (N), Thinking (T), Judging (J) (INTJ) personality. His dominant function is Intuition; his second-best function is Thinking. His third function is Feeling; and his Inferior function is Sensation.

INTJs are described by Coleen Clark as "Independent, reflective, organized, organizing, intellectually astute, skeptical, theoretical, analytical, insightful. Have a private need to control. Good at improving others' ideas but forget to stroke."

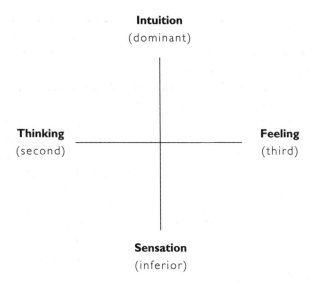

Intuition
(dominant)

Thinking
(second)

Feeling
(third)

Sensation
(inferior)

Peter's Inferior Sensation is working overtime because his obsession with work has immobilized his Thinking. Because of his workaholism, his positive Feeling and Intuition are repressed and thus not effective. No moderating diplomacy or tact is coming from his Feeling side.

Note that when *negative sensation* is dominant, Thinking becomes dualistic and concrete. Peter sees only two options: black–white, right–wrong, dominant–submissive. He gets lost in obsessive detail. Myopic, he fails to see the big picture any more. He increasingly feels overwhelmed by too much detail or stimuli, and any distractions bring confusion and anger. He is so concrete in his Thinking that abstract subtleties are lost on him. At such times, he seems almost childlike and naive.

When sensation is negative, selective listening — hearing only what one wants to hear — becomes problematic. I call it the "3 out of 5" syndrome, meaning the person hears or sees only the details that he wishes to hear. To illustrate, a woman once moved in with a man she thought was intelligent, rich, and witty — the three things she wanted to see. This decision was made after knowing him only a few months. The man, it was discovered, was dabbling in some high-flying business ventures. Not only was he totally absorbed in his work, thinking of little else, but he was still emotionally involved with his first wife, despite numerous liaisons since his separation several years before. The important information, the "book ends," as I call them, were forgotten. She ignored his workaholism and his constant talk about his ex-wife because this gentleman was extremely charming and persuasive when he wanted something. She had been swept off her feet!

Peter needs to develop his *positive sensation*. He needs to develop his creativity and imagination, his ability to see possibilities in the future. He needs to use his objectivity, to stand back and sort out what details are the most important. He might ask Sally to work with him on brainstorming, and appreciating the symbolic and metaphoric once again. Peter, as an Intuitive type, used to be good at this. Most of all, he needs to learn to appreciate sights, sounds, touch, smells, and tastes — to develop the sensory aspects that provide much pleasure in life. They ground us to the earth and to nature, acting as a constant source of inner nourishment to our souls.

Peter is experiencing double-trouble. Not only is his Inferior Sensation function causing problems, but his positive feelings are barely functioning. He is numb, and feels flat and empty. As he says, "I always feel as if something is missing." Peter is battling depression, and his chronic fatigue is the result of his endless pumping of adrenalin. Remember, *negative feeling* is moody, resentful, and grouchy. It feels hopeless or helpless. It gets overwhelmed, and feels useless and paralysed. It concentrates on all the things that are wrong or have been done poorly. It generalizes until it sees everything going wrong. It feels sorry for itself.

Negative Feelers are self-focused and self-absorbed, and have no ability to empathise. They withdraw and shut themselves off from the world at large. They become silent and often sigh. They look down and lose eye contact. They slump forward, feel exhausted and heavy. Anxious, they hold their breath and lose concentration. Thoughts get jumbled, and nothing seems funny or fun any more. An empty, sick feeling lies in their stomach.

Peter is not available emotionally, either for himself or for others. He is supersensitive to rejection and avoids situations where he is vulnerable. He, like Sally, takes everything personally, but he is also quite paranoid. Peter's high anxiety makes him afraid of life itself.

Peter needs to develop his positive feeling. *Positive Feelers* are sensitive, thoughtful, considerate, and warm. They are generous, tactful, gentle, gracious, diplomatic, and conciliatory. They are creative and resourceful, and content if harmony prevails. They can be quietly assertive, if necessary.

It's no wonder that Sally and Peter have grown miles apart. Sally's negative thinking responds to Peter's negative feeling, and on both a conscious and an unconscious level, these functions hook one another. A destructive discourse, or passive-aggressive withdrawal, inevitably follows. No constructive problem-solving is possible at such times.

LOVE YOUR SHADOW

When the Shadow is at work, it sounds like this: "I don't know why I just did that!" Or, "My wife told me: 'It's not what you said, it's the way you said it.'"

The Shadow, a term used by Jung, has three parts. First, the negative Shadow consists of all the unfavourable aspects of ourselves that we have repressed or disowned, often for adaptive reasons. Second, the positive Shadow contains our admirable, but often hidden strengths, which have remained largely undeveloped. For example, if we are Introverted, a great deal of our Extraversion lies dormant, waiting to be brought up into our consciousness.

Last, but not least, the Shadow contains the *wisdom* of the Collective Unconscious. Jung used this term to describe the innate information and knowledge carried deep within each individual. There are many collectives that influence our behaviour. Our society, for instance, offers laws, rewards, and punishments that filter through to us via newspapers, radio, and television. Family values are taught by example and words. Similarly, the collective affiliations we identify with — our schools and our spiritual, financial, and business institutions, for example — all strongly influence our choices. Which partners we choose, what friends we gravitate to, and which work setting we select can be influenced by age, race, status, and historical or political factors.

Carl Jung offers this good advice: Love your Shadow. Nourish it, protect it, and you will stay safe. But first the Shadow must become conscious. Jung warns that considerable effort is needed to recognize the "dark aspects of the personality as present and real. This act is the essential condition for any kind of self-knowledge, and it therefore, as a rule, meets with considerable resistance" (*The Portable Jung,* p. 145).

Strong will and insight are necessary to challenge our Shadow. Only when we hear our Shadow voice, or alert ourselves to our own atypical and often bizarre behaviour, can we monitor when and how we project unwanted emotions onto others.

We may eventually come to tolerate and even nourish and "love" our Shadow side. However, others will not like it at all! That is because the Shadow is usually projected. As John Sanford, in *The Invisible Partner*, points out, "When something is projected we see it outside of us, as though it belongs to someone else and has nothing to do with us" (p. 10). The good news, ironically, is that only unconscious contents are projected. Projections cease when our faults become conscious. Only then can we attempt to transform them each time they manifest themselves. It is then possible for us to be fully responsible for our behaviour.

Jung describes so well the consequences of refusing to see the Shadow in ourselves: "It is often tragic to see how blatantly a man bungles his own life and the lives of others yet remains totally incapable of seeing how much the whole tragedy originates in himself, and how he continually feeds it and keeps it going" (*The Portable Jung,* p. 147).

Facing up to the wasted years and the sorrow of having damaged others' lives is a daunting task. It takes great courage to say "I am sorry." Growth and maturity come when we allow ourselves to take the necessary steps to make amends.

UNDERSTANDING THE PROBLEM

Before we begin to find out what we can do so that we don't keep negativity going round and round in circles in our life, an understanding of what went wrong is essential. How did we get out of touch with our feelings? Have we always been emotionally crippled?

In Chapter 4, we will explore workaholism. How do people know if they have become workaholics? What does the loss of balance in the workaholic's life do to his or her personality? Why do workaholics eventually suffer a loss of feelings? What are workaholics afraid of, and why do they become chronically fatigued and burdened with guilt?

In Chapter 5, we will learn why narcissism is such an important part of workaholism, and why narcissists lose their feeling values, and therefore become self-serving and lacking in insight.

In Chapter 6, we will see how narcissism spills down through generations by exploring the family dynamics in Peter and Sally's family.

We will then be ready to learn some important techniques that will help undo the damage caused when people lose touch with their feelings.

4
The Workaholic Trap

Personality Changes on the Gerbil Wheel

> *"Isn't it amazing how many people there are who long for immortality — but can't even amuse themselves on a rainy evening."*
> MORNING SMILE, *THE GLOBE AND MAIL*

THE LOSS OF A BALANCED LIFE

A quote from the author Jack Kerouac says it all: "Who wants a living — I want a life." Today, family life and work have become two worlds in conflict. There is no balance in life when the ideas and goals we pursue come to fruition but we ride roughshod over our own and other people's feelings and values. Ironically, although workaholics are overly responsible in public, they become increasingly irresponsible to their family and to themselves.

In my book *Workaholics: The Respectable Addicts,* I tried to show why workaholism is such a dangerous and life-threatening addiction. It changes not only people's personalities, but also the values they live by. It threatens family security, and often leads to family break-up. Surprisingly, it also distorts the reality of *each* family member. Along the way, workaholics always suffer the loss of personal and professional integrity.

My focus in this book will be on the workaholic's loss of

personal balance. The excessively long hours spent working, the frantic rush of the "Gerbil Wheel" existence, and short-sighted, "bottom-line" thinking are, after all, only symptoms of a deeper war being waged within the individual's psyche.

Workaholics are not addicted to work, as everyone supposes. Ironically, the term itself, as coined by Wayne Oates in 1971 in his *Confessions of a Workaholic,* is misleading. One does not have to have a "real" job. Many homemakers, and even high school and university students, become chronic workaholics.

In attempting to understand the workaholic personality, it must be acknowledged that work plays an essential role in defining the Self. Our well-being springs from a sense of accomplishment. We develop our strengths, set goals, and overcome difficult hurdles along the way. Our self-confidence comes through developing skills and mastering tasks that contribute to an entity greater than ourselves. As anyone who has lost a job will attest, without work, our personalities suffer profound emotional disorientation.

A hard worker who maintains a healthy balance between work and play, and is emotionally there for all family members, is *not* a workaholic.

RECOGNIZING THE WORKAHOLIC PERSONALITY

A workaholic is a person who gradually becomes emotionally crippled and addicted to control and power in a compulsive drive to gain approval and success. Actress Bridget Fonda describes her own workaholism to journalist Deirdre Kelly in a *Globe and Mail* article headed "Bridget Fonda: 'burned out' at 30" (October 30, 1994).

"Up until now my career has been absorbing a lot of my energies and it still is. But very soon things are going to grind to a halt for a while because I sort of feel burned out. That's the workaholic thing, the thing that makes me work until I feel I've done what it is I need to do before … I can really rest. But now what's telling me to rest is not that I feel that I have achieved my life goals but that I feel that I'm on the verge of a breakdown. I suddenly have an image of myself slowing down to a lie-down position and having the grass grow all around me. That's what I feel I want. To be dormant for a while."

A member of a famous screen family, Fonda started her film career at twenty-two. In eight years she has accumulated more than twenty film credits. She's upset about being a perfectionist because "it's not very healthy." Recently she has felt that her body has been failing her. "Acting is something I care a great deal about. It's something for which I want to do a great job but sometimes I feel that physically I'm exhausted and I can't do as good as I think I can in my head. That's why I've got to stop."

Despite these insights, Bridget is working on a new film. Kelly asks whether the race to outdo herself will ever end. "I guess that's what acting is all about … you just can't help it." She explains that horses at the track know what they have to do, and acting is much like that. "The adrenalin kicks in and you do it, you get an urge to stampede, and in the end it feels good even when it feels bad."

Good is rarely enough for perfectionists. Always to be better, or the best, is the ideal. One goal is reached, yet soon after, another is set. Goals rarely bring the expected satisfaction, because deep inside the individual is full of self-doubt. He must prove himself once again. Combine the motto "Never is ever enough" and Lord Acton's truism that "Power tends to corrupt, and absolute power corrupts absolutely," and you have a recipe for disaster.

As we saw in Peter's story, a public persona that broadcasts success is paramount for the workaholic. In fact, workaholism is really about self-aggrandizement. Ambitious workaholics become increasingly obsessed with their work performance because of a drive for public and peer approval. The public persona presented to the world is therefore about "Looking Good." Some workaholics are the Mr. Nice Guys who can't say no. Others control and misuse their power to charm and manipulate others to their personal benefit.

Many workaholics do manage to look "great" for long periods and maintain the facade of success, even after repeated failures. In a 1992 interview about my book in *USA Today* (August 13, 1992), Donald Trump was asked by journalist Nancy Hellmich whether *he* was a workaholic. "I've worked extremely hard over the last year and a half to achieve the success I have attained. There is no such thing as a workaholic if you enjoy what you are doing." This sounds like an alcoholic rationalizing that there is nothing wrong with being an alcoholic as long as you enjoy drinking!

Workaholics feel most vital and alive when they are pumping adrenalin. Getting from A to B consumes their energy. Totally focused and engrossed in their single-minded pursuit of a goal, they compulsively overschedule and overwork until an extra "fix" is needed just to stay alert and keep up the pace. Rushing becomes the norm. Coffee, alcohol, smoking, drugs are then often taken because increased amounts of adrenalin are needed to cover rising anxiety. Overstimulated, overstressed, and often overwhelmed, workaholics are no longer in control. The addiction is running their lives. Balance is a thing of the past.

Gary, a handsome, bright, and articulate professional engineer, referred by a former client who recognized his workaholism, came into my office one day looking ashen. "Look, I've got to be frank with you today." He paused. "I'm barely functioning. I'm just not getting it! Ideas are flying past me, and I don't see them!" Obviously in despair, Gary added, "I can't make even the simplest decisions any more! I don't know which way is up!"

When I suggested that he take a minimum of three weeks off to get all the adrenalin out of his system, and take care of himself before he suffered a stroke or heart attack, Gary protested. The company was in yet another crisis. Like many workaholics, Gary's company itself was a victim of workaholism.

Time out, apparently, was out of the question. When I enquired whether he saw the arrogance implied in this, he blushed. We then discussed whether anyone really was indispensable and irreplaceable.

Workaholism, as I told Gary, can be a lethal addiction. The Japanese call workaholism *Karoshi*, and warn that overwork is life-threatening, even fatal. An article in the *Toronto Star* titled

"Overwork kills many, Japanese group says" states: Labor ministry rules stipulate that to be decreed a victim of Karoshi, someone must have worked continuously for 24 hours before death, or at least 16 hours daily for seven consecutive days beforehand."

The National Defense Council for Karoshi Victims published a book called *Karoshi: When the Corporate Warrior Dies*. Hiroshi Kawahito, the group's secretary-general, reports that up to 10,000 Japanese work themselves to death every year. He adds, "We can't name a precise figure ... But when relatively young people die of strokes and heart attacks after working excessively hard, we can't really doubt that it is a case of Karoshi."

In an article in the *Globe and Mail* (March 13, 1993), "Japan gets a life," Alan Freeman reports that the Japanese government's Economic Planning Agency has a five-year plan that calls on Japanese workers to achieve a better quality of life, and "reduce the standard work week to 40 hours from 44, eliminate Saturday work and get employees to take the vacations to which they are entitled."

In North America, some families are suing companies over the stress-related death of family members. Unfortunately, we still face a wall of denial, both by the individual, and in society itself, about the fatal outcome of workaholism.

Our focus here, however, returns to the individual.

A PARADIGM FOR THE LOSS OF FEELINGS

What happens inside the psyche when workaholics narrow their focus and drive themselves obsessively? Why do they grow numb and feel flat? Why is change so threatening to these "black-and-white" thinkers?

As the obsession with work grows, it consumes ever-increasing amounts of psychic and physical energy in order to build ideas, challenge goals, and complete exciting projects and schemes. Everyday family responsibilities and people-related problems at work suffer. Soon, the spouse, child, or co-workers, ignored or taken for granted, neglected, in some cases even abandoned, begin to make demands. Stretched to the limit already, frustrated workaholics resent these "impositions," and anxiety escalates.

As workaholics become overwhelmed, changes take place in the way information is gathered and processed, and in how decisions are made. A brief summary of my paradigm for the loss of feelings, based on Jung's theory of psychological types, explains why shifts occur that affect the way workaholics function.

PARADIGM FOR WORKAHOLISM

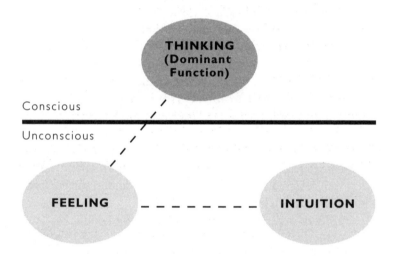

Thinking

Thinking becomes obsessive as the fascination with work grows. Clarity is lost because feelings are dulled in order to keep pain and fear from flooding the fragile ego. Feeling ceases to moderate the thinking process. Instead, obsessive ruminations are apt to completely immobilize the person. Workaholics plot strategies and devise elaborate schemes, absorbing themselves in endless details. Instead of confronting the problem, they distract themselves by going off on tangents. Anything not to feel!

Soon survival becomes the real issue, rather than competition or being first. Anything that diverts attention away from their own agenda is discouraged. It's as though workaholics wear blinkers or develop tunnel vision. All psychic energy is being drained away, and life's balance is thrown askew. Terry, a young law student, was telling me that he had had a panic attack sitting in front of the TV the night before. When I enquired whether he turned the TV off, he looked quite surprised! It had never occurred to him that his overloaded system just couldn't absorb any more stimulation. His feeling functions weren't working to tell him his body was sending off warning signals.

The rational, logical, analytical, realistic side of Thinking gives way to its skeptical, critical, judgmental, competitive, controlling side. The personality of the workaholic is radically changed by this shift. When I use Gestalt exercises in psychotherapy, directing clients to different chairs to speak for different aspects of their personality, a surprising thing happens. Inevitably, it seems that the doing and performing "Fixer," chair, which "helps," overprotects, or manipulates, demonstrates its power. It bullies and tells other facets of the personality to basically pull their socks up: do this, think that, feel as I do. Or, its sarcastic voice humiliates the other aspects of the personality that remain speechless or stumble to find a voice.

Clients are fascinated but appalled when they experience the power of their controlling side. I had to take an important call one day, which left the wife of a workaholic client stranded in her "Fixer" chair. I noticed her squirming, and as soon as I completed the call, she sprang from the chair. "Thank goodness, now I can get out of that chair!" We both laughed, and she exclaimed, "I hate that side of myself now. It reminds me of my bossy aunt." Workaholism is, after all, about controlling and gaining power. Spouses, as well as workaholics, get caught up "fixing" others.

Feeling
When Thinking's goals and ideas dominate our thoughts and personality, Feeling's empathy and compassion functions receive little psychic energy. Robbed of Feeling's support and nourishment,

we feel frightened and anxious. Like children, we start to feel bad or guilty.

The playful, humorous parts of the personality are flattened. There is no energy left to lighten up the intense and serious Thinking side. When inner fears, doubts, and guilt dominate the psyche, sensitive, thoughtful, conciliatory feelings are replaced by sullen moods and resentment. People grow quiet, become stubborn, and withdraw into oversensitivity, and thus get their feelings hurt on all possible occasions. Depression lurks in the shadows. After all, it is easier to adopt the self-pity of the martyr than to take personal responsibility.

"If I keep running on my Gerbil Wheel, I don't have time to think or confront myself," says Elizabeth, a naive but driven nursery teacher. Instead, this forty-five-year-old woman remains inside her head and intellectualizes. She also develops fantastic schemes to outwit people who she believes are jealous of her, or are "out to get her." She often becomes obsessive about romantic but imaginary encounters. If Elizabeth allowed herself to face her uncertain social skills, she would have to feel her loneliness and fears around aging. "Why should I depress myself?" she protests. Criticism is quickly disregarded. She desperately wants to see herself as perfect. Anger surfaces, but is quickly squelched to avoid an explosion.

Hard as it is to believe, workaholics like Elizabeth reach a state where *they do not know how they feel*. This situation is very difficult for family members to grasp. The spouse and children know they hurt. They are sad. They feel furious! "Can't my stupid father see what he is doing to his family?" asks Dan, a twenty-year-old arts student. Dan searches for an answer. "Surely he must know what he is doing to my mom!" Dan's disbelief will continue until he learns more about workaholism. Older children and young adults need to be involved in the therapeutic process so that healing can begin to take place. In order to forgive, children need to understand *why* a parent has been unavailable to them emotionally. It is important to break the cycle, so that this generation will not repeat the mistakes of the past.

Intuition

When Feeling stops working, so does Intuition, a sixth Feeling, which sorts out what is important. The big picture gets sacrificed to immediate gratification. Short-term, concrete goals with high visibility become important. Today's fax machines, e-mail, and car phones encourage instant decisions and quick action. Intuition needs delays and overnight reflection to reveal flaws in a plan. Constant emergencies and general chaos leave no room for Intuition's creativity and its admirable capacity for delaying gratification. "I want it NOW!" is the workaholic's cry.

Imagination, with its endless possibilities and objectivity, ceases to work as feelings atrophy. Brainstorming stops, and metaphors and some abstract thoughts go unrecognized. Instead, workaholics become obsessive over small details. They grow picky and argumentative, stuck in their own myopic vision of what is right, or even possible. Stubborn rigidity kills all creative thinking. The person becomes restless and impulsive, easily bored, and never satisfied.

Sensation

Negative Sensation eventually dominates and sways the workaholic's decision-making skills. Dualistic thinking reduces the complex to two simplistic options. If one thing is "right," that makes anything else "wrong." As Heather, a middle-aged bank manager, put it, "Black-and-white thinking is simple — I fail, or I succeed!" She laughed nervously. "It's colourful thinking that stymies me! I still can't quite believe all the options we've looked at today." It will be some time before Heather's natural intuitive skills return and work well enough for her to brainstorm effectively. It is difficult for people to comprehend that functions you once relied on have stopped working.

"Don't confuse me with the facts!" is a remark that workaholics might well use. Selective listening is a vital part of negative Sensation. This is another example of "3 out of 5" thinking, in which people focus on the facts that support their own views, and ignore often very important information that takes a contrary position.

Workaholics take little time to "smell the roses." Symphonies and theatres, which used to interest them, become great places to nod off and catch a few winks. Positive Sensation, which celebrates all five senses, enjoys the here-and-how, and trusts the observable and concrete, ceases to function well. Instead, future gains are sacrificed for immediate gratification and creature comforts. There is little satisfaction or appreciation because greed always exacts more. Obsessed with details, the workaholic forgets to appreciate the contribution that lesser parts play in the big picture. Idealism soon replaces realism.

Distortion

The workaholic's reality becomes distorted because Thinking grows fuzzy, and Feelings and Intuition are devalued and repressed. Negative Sensation becomes a powerful force in the personality. Unconscious anxiety surfaces, but unwanted feelings are disowned by the workaholic and quickly projected onto others.

Unfortunately, the spouse and the children are easy targets. Family members are less likely to fire you. Thus, spouses are criticized, ridiculed, and blamed for everything and anything that goes wrong. Children, they insist, still receive "quality time," but unconditional love and affection are scarce. The self-involved, preoccupied workaholic has little time or energy for the small, "petty" things that are important to children. Ball-games are missed. The chair at the head of the table is empty. Although children still must perform and make the workaholic proud, rarely is praise or encouragement forthcoming. Instead, "Why didn't you get 90?" stays with the child forever. The cool, aloof, and demanding parent rarely ventures out from behind his or her wall of reserved arrogance. Work is to be respected above all else. Family life must revolve around the workaholic's schedule. "Be like me!" is the subtle message conveyed.

UNDERSTANDING THE COMPLEXITY OF WORKAHOLISM

Workaholism is like a perfect tapestry hanging proudly for all to see. Slowly, almost imperceptibly, the threads start to twist and sag until the pattern becomes distorted.

Three threads are woven through the workaholic's life and help explain workaholism. Each thread is clearly affected by the other two strands. This brief summary will focus on the first thread, and the *conscious* aspects of the second thread. Together, they will show how workaholics become emotionally crippled and out of touch with their feelings. The following outlines the three interacting threads, which are covered in depth in my book on workaholism.

1. *Perfectionism* leads to *Obsession,* which leads to *Narcissism.*
2. *The Breakdown Syndrome* — conscious and unconscious factors.
3. *Denial, Control,* and *Power* — *The Workaholic Trap.*

1. Perfectionism/Obsession/Narcissism

Perfectionism
Bridget Fonda is right: the seeds of workaholism do lie in perfectionism. To achieve excellence and mastery, perfectionists try to gain control of *all* the variables that feed into a successful outcome — and that, unfortunately, includes people!

Perfectionism shapes a person's life-style. If idealistic drives and ambitions are to be fulfilled, a single-minded focus becomes necessary. Delegating and sharing are discouraged by this one-sidedness. As I wrote in *Workaholics,* Thinking dominates, and feelings remain largely unconscious.

Perfectionists believe that they are highly intelligent, even superior, and thus capable of great achievements. Although they are, indeed, often quite bright, they are also openly arrogant, ambitious, competitive, and demanding of themselves and others. Although self-sufficient and independent on the surface, they require admiration from others, or demand obedience and want their own way. Underneath this self-confident facade lies an insecurity fed by unconscious inner struggles to overcome unresolved childhood fears of helplessness, dependency, and loss of approval and affection.

Proud workaholics, torn between arrogance and insecurity, solve the dilemma by consciously identifying with only the positive attributes of their personality. Unflattering feedback is filtered out through selective listening.

NICE GUY OR GAL

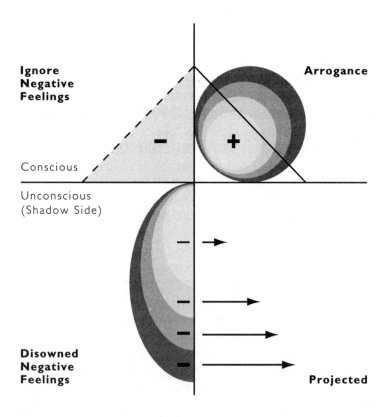

Thus, workaholics hear what they want to hear. In turn, they manipulate others by telling them what they think the other person wants to hear. Workaholics can be extremely charming when they want something!

The control necessary to maintain this Nice Guy or Gal image breaks apart as the workaholic progresses through the breakdown stages of workaholism. "I'm losing it!" is their cry for help. Like Narcissus, of the Greek myth, who was mesmerized by his perfect reflection, when troubled waters stir up the pool, the workaholic is left with a well-crafted persona, but with little sense of a true Self.

Joel, a thirty-five-year-old lawyer, told me that he felt paralysed by bizarre fears. "You may find this hard to believe," Joel projected. "I'm embarrassed even saying this. But I feel like a fraud sometimes, especially when I'm in court. It's almost as though there's a detached part of me that looks on, as if in utter disbelief. It taunts me: 'Who do you think you are!' 'You're such a phony!' 'You're going to blow this one!'"

Joel, who had graduated cum laude in his last year at law school, was now plagued with self-doubt. "Am I going crazy, or what?" he asks. The mighty often have a great distance to fall from the pedestal on which parents, classmates, or spouses have placed them. Remember, workaholics had to *do* something to get recognition in the dysfunctional families in which they were loved conditionally, and rewarded primarily for their "doing and performing" talents.

Obsession

The chief sign of perfectionism is obsession. Obsession occurs when one area of the personality receives a disproportionate amount of the psyche's energy. Ambitious workaholics, focused on distant goals, fail to attend to warning signs from the body. It isn't until the obsessive, out-of-touch workaholic experiences panic attacks that his or her extreme distress becomes conscious.

Obsessive thinking works overtime while workaholics dream up schemes and strategies that will move them from A to B faster and more effectively than others can do it. The greater the pressure to complete these often grandiose plans, the more frantic the individual becomes. Inflated egos and heady arrogance leave these people totally unrealistic about what is possible. Workaholics promise the earth, by Tuesday!

Work habits thus necessitate rushing, frantic activity, and overscheduling. After an interview with me for *Pathways* magazine, contributing editor Kim Pittaway wrote: "Speaking with Killinger helped me to recognize one of my own triggers. As a freelancer, I set my own work schedule. In the past, I routinely viewed weekends as potential catch-up time. I'd procrastinate during the week with the rationalization that I could always make it up on Saturday and Sunday." So she set aside her weekends as a "no-work" zone, and consequently stopped procrastinating during the week because she put a "play boundary" around Saturday and Sunday. Her guilt about *not* working on the weekends vanished.

Without set boundaries, work can spill into everything one does. Soon, you are caught on the Gerbil Wheel, and you can't get off. No time to think, and certainly no time to feel! Fear of failing is ever present, and anxiety fuels this relentless drive.

Severe obsessions stretch your nerves to the limit, as if on the proverbial rack. You can't stand the intensity and pain, but you can't get off either. You're hooked! You soldier on, a martyr to your cause, but soon you start to resent everything and everybody. You even begin to hate yourself. Such bad feelings, often too painful to bear, are repressed. It may look like an exciting life to people who observe and even envy the workaholic. But nothing fills the emptiness that is experienced in the pit of the stomach.

It is almost impossible to lower a person's sights once he has fallen under the curse of perfectionism. I once bargained with an extremely obsessive final-year high school student about aiming for an 85 per cent average, instead of the 98.6 per cent he had managed to attain. No talk of the Rhodes Scholar's values of doing well in a number of areas could sway this young man! Many other clients tell similar stories about high expectations but tortured lives. It's like living with your own sergeant-major cracking the whip. Going AWOL is out of the question. Perfectionists lose their badge of honour if they quit!

Compulsive acts or rituals grow more chaotic as the workaholic loses control. Counting, checking, cleaning, ordering, straightening, making lists, rewriting, all done to an extreme, are efforts to counteract inner confusion as the workaholic strives to impose order out of chaos. When a child or spouse unexpectedly interferes in a compulsive ritual, it is often enough to set off an explosive temper tantrum, or even rage.

People around the workaholic walk on egg shells much of the time, uncertain what will trigger off the next barrage. When the workaholic is an emotionally drained homemaker, it's like living in the middle of a minefield for the rest of the family. Compulsive activities can become so frantic that the person collapses, unable to function effectively any longer. "I couldn't get out of bed to start my day" is a common complaint signalling a breakdown.

An obsessional triangle of guilt, fear, and negativity locks the workaholic in a strange prison where perfectionism is replaced by an agitated compulsive need to dominate and control even the smallest detail. No wonder the psyche bounces between fear and anger as the workaholic is driven towards despair.

Bouts of rage are common at this point. The stressed psyche, worn out by the constant exercising of dominance, is totally drained. While "one-up" is acceptable, "one-down" is not! Submission of any kind, whether brought on by criticism or a challenge, sets off panic reactions. Obsessive workaholics often swing between dominance and submission. By tipping the balance either way, they can maintain a comforting, but false, sense of control.

Some workaholics act out their rage in a passive-aggressive manner. They suffer severe mood swings or anxiety attacks, and "turn off," sulk, or withdraw emotionally and physically into depression. Others let pent-up feelings build to dangerous levels. Family members are easy targets for abuse. Such explosive behaviour would not be tolerated for long in the working world, unless you happened to be the boss. After my book on workaholism was released, I received calls from all over North America from wives saying, "Thank God, I'm not crazy. I was starting to believe my husband, that it was *all* my fault. Thanks so much for writing that book!

Narcissism

Perfectionism and obsession lead to high levels of self-absorption. As fears produce obsessive behaviour, workaholics become pre-occupied with inner insecurity and try to control everything and everybody around them. Any threats or challenges to their power and ability to control must be countered to protect the fragile ego.

Narcissism is the real evil of workaholism. It is also an important problem in our society today, coming out of the greed and power-trips of the eighties and the legacy of the "me" generation. The two following chapters are devoted to understanding narcissism, in the individual and in the family.

2. The Breakdown Syndrome

Many older workaholics can trace the onset of workaholism to a situation in their lives or that of their families that occurred perhaps twenty or twenty-five years before. From that moment on, they decided they were going to be in control of their lives. In those days, wives usually stayed home and were not in direct competition, as it were. By fully supporting the workaholic's career, she unknowingly furthered the addictive habits of her ambitious breadwinner. Financial security brought the husband the recognition and power he craved, and the life-style he desired for his family.

Nowadays, the breakdown is occurring over a five- or six-year period. Our society encourages people to overwork, and greed often underlies the endless search for a more profitable bottom line. Many companies and institutions are workaholic entities that suffer many of the same breakdown symptoms as the individual.

Earliest Signs of the Breakdown

Fortunately, the earliest signs of the breakdown process are recognized by the workaholic. At our busiest times, all of us experience some of the following fears, the chronic fatigue, and guilt. It is when we get hooked by the obsession with work and its relentless rush of adrenalin flooding our system that we can be overwhelmed and immobilized.

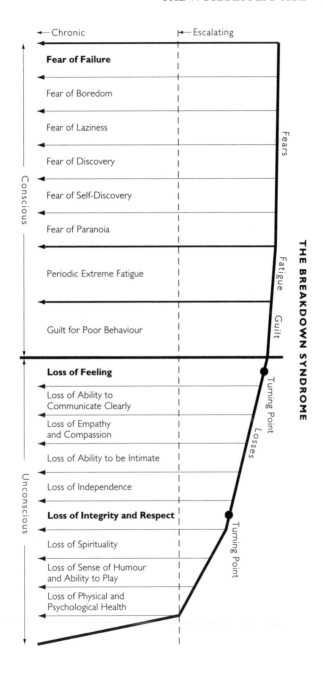

Chronic Fears

Fear can gnaw away at insecure people who depend on others to affirm their worth. Feelings force us to experience our vulnerability, but workaholics manage to fend off any negative feelings and feedback that threaten their perfect persona. Feelings are repressed and intellectualized as thinking dominates the psyche.

Fear can reach obsessive levels when people who have a strong need to control are faced with criticism or rejection. Such threats to their self-esteem force them into a one-down position on the hierarchical ladder. Therefore, in the workplace, annual employee evaluations, censorship of ideas or projects, threatened demotions, forced transfers, or the ultimate fear of dismissal generate great stress for workaholics who are beginning to realize they are less effective than they once were. These excessive fears breed rigidity and stubbornness. The modern trend for industry to reduce middle management is especially threatening to workaholics who, at the best of times, find it difficult to adjust to change. Dismissal can enrage and immobilize them. Even low productivity or disorganization of any kind can induce mounting anxiety and often panic attacks in workers, students, and homemakers alike.

FEAR OF FAILURE. G. K. Chesterton wrote: "The reason angels can fly is that they have learned to take themselves lightly." Not so perfectionists. Failing for them is the end of the world. Early years for these ambitious children are relatively free of failure because a strong need for approval drives them to excel. The work ethic is usually a powerful force in the family of origin. Narcissistic parents, who see their children as extensions of themselves, expect high levels of achievement, sometimes to compensate for their own blocked ambitions.

University years often set patterns for future habits. Faced with the brightest and the best, perhaps for the first time in their lives, these perfectionistic students struggle to succeed. Rather than face lower grades, which for them would signal failure, they burn the midnight oil in a frantic effort to "catch up." Many workaholics who achieved fame or notoriety at college, excelling at sports or scholastics, spend a lifetime trying to recapture the elusive glory of those years.

Promotions often mean that workaholics are pushed up the corporate ladder beyond their level of competency. More senior jobs often overtax their limited social skills. Arrogant, and often notoriously poor listeners, these emotionally crippled people lack the sensitivity, diplomacy, tact, and grace necessary to co-operate with fellow workers, to mediate, or to respond to others' needs.

As long as idealism prevails, the workaholic ironically faces ever-increasing self-doubt. Promotions, expansion into new markets, take-overs, and research discoveries lead to increased responsibility. Paddling faster while struggling against internal chaos only escalates feelings of impending doom as fatalistic workaholics keep battling against a harsh reality of diminishing resources. As power and omnipotence fade, workaholics work even harder. Immersed in the moment, they lose touch with objectivity and long-term goals. When life throws a curve, most of us pick ourselves up, dust ourselves off and ask probing questions about why and how things went wrong. Workaholics, in contrast, are devastated and too afraid to face an imperfect self. Instead, they deny their fears and push negative feelings out of their consciousness.

FEAR OF BOREDOM. When chaos threatens, workaholics maintain the familiar Gerbil Wheel existence rather than face up to what is going wrong. With their strong need to be right and to get their own way, they feel best when nothing distracts them from their goal-directed focus. This focus provides a sense of purpose and accomplishment. Workaholics therefore are reluctant to say no, and cram their days full by overscheduling. Rushing and being late become the norm. No time is left to feel their experiences or to contemplate where they are headed. The purpose of life is never evaluated. Narrowly focused, single-minded workaholics become what they fear — boring, shallow people. As J. B. Priestley wrote: "Any fool can be fussy and rid himself of energy all over the place, but a man has to have *something* in him before he can settle down to do *nothing*."

Long periods of relaxation are threatening, partly because adrenalin withdrawal causes severe distress. Holidays are either avoided on the excuse of one crisis or another, or replaced by brief weekend jaunts or by a week or two crammed full of activities. Workaholics rarely stay away when they are sick, or if they do stay home, they call in to the office regularly to check up on things. When it takes twelve hours to do what used to be done in eight, time off is out of the question.

FEAR OF LAZINESS. This fear of laziness, which workaholics seem willing to admit to, may be the unconscious compensating for an overly developed sense of responsibility. Life must be serious and goal-directed if workaholics are to succeed at all costs. Their persona must not be seen to be frivolous — no "vegging" allowed. Instead, workaholics do two things at once. Drivers use car phones, joggers listen to Walkmans, and commuters read the business section of the newspaper on the way to and from work. Talk to a workaholic on the phone, and you will hear papers shuffling. Silences are filled in with clicking sounds as they think things through. They start language courses "for fun," but cancel classes for more important business. If one thinks all the time, there is little time left to feel.

Laziness is not to be confused with chronic fatigue. Workaholics often become "couch potatoes," plunked in front of the TV because they are so exhausted they can barely function. Laziness shows up when the workaholic avoids personal responsibility at home or elsewhere. Psychologically, workaholics are lazy. They seem to have little curiosity about what makes themselves tick. They rarely read self-improvement books unless they are motivational ones directed towards improving your performance. Denial allows them to hang on to the illusion of the perfect Self.

FEAR OF DISCOVERY. As fears lead to confusion and turmoil, efficiency and productivity are strongly affected. Workaholics worry about the visibility of their mistakes or about low productivity. They know they are not measuring up to their peers. Rather than be found out, workaholics cover themselves by lying or neglecting to tell the truth. They withhold essential information from their staff. One client told me that when a colleague was finally let go, management found a pile of unfinished files stashed neatly underneath the couch in his office.

Secrecy and privacy become all-important aids to protecting workaholics from scrutiny. They ride on their reputations as long as possible. Carl, a well-respected business executive, was let go in a company power-play. He had built up an elaborate support system and depended on his juniors to do the things he didn't like doing. He despaired that he would ever be able to replicate his present success and high sales figures in another company. "I'm not sure I can learn all the things I need to know before I leave," he worried.

Delegating work to others who might take away their earning power is discouraged initially. Instead, workaholics will stay at the office until seven or eight o'clock regularly. The extra hours become necessary because fears block focused and rational thinking. Later in the breakdown, emotionally and physically exhausted workaholics use others in the office to do their work. Stretched to the limit, workaholics stall until work shifts to secretaries and juniors. Colleagues at the peer level must not find this out. Yet these same people continue to take on new projects in order to feel powerful and to prop up sagging egos. Mr. Nice Guys rarely say no, at least at work.

Because feelings are numb, workaholics do not anticipate the breakdown or "crash" that is lurking ahead. The workaholic will not admit that something is wrong until panic attacks, claustrophobic episodes, an irregular heartbeat, or other health troubles force a recognition of their problems. Without insight, however, workaholics rarely understand what actually is happening to them.

FEAR OF SELF-DISCOVERY. Workaholics depend on an external frame of reference to form their definition of Self. They judge their success by guessing what others perceive them to be. Their mask must therefore be one of studied self-assurance. The label "conceited" stuck to Brenda, a competent office manager. One day, however, she revealed her own self-doubt. "I put terrible pressure on myself to always stay up and cheerful. I got to believe my own myth despite repeated criticism from my staff. They told me that I was short, blunt, and sharp. Apparently, people felt I was overly critical and judgmental. I just didn't see it, until it was too late." Her eyes brimmed with the tears she hadn't allowed herself before. "I just wish I had another chance with those people now that I'm getting better. I think that now I could do a good job there."

People like Brenda who are out of touch with their own feelings cannot possibly be sensitive to others' vulnerability. Instead, they unconsciously tap into the weaknesses of others, yet remain oblivious to these same foibles in themselves. A strong fear of disapproval keeps denial, dishonesty, and secrecy alive. Hard-core workaholics avoid introspection at all costs. Projection of blame is a popular defense for people who cannot accept the Shadow aspects of themselves. "Promise me that I won't hate myself at the end of this process" is a remark that reveals the self-loathing of a Dr. Jekyll turned Mr. Hyde to his family. "When I was high on myself," Cynthia admitted, "I could do no wrong! But at three a.m., it was quite a different tale." Cynthia asked, "How could I be so blind? Why didn't I remember those screaming episodes my husband keeps talking about? The poor guy still seems so traumatized by all of this."

The journey from perfectionism and idealism to self-knowledge and wholeness is a real victory. Unfortunately, fears and laziness work against the workaholic who might otherwise gain the insight necessary to challenge and develop a strong sense of Self. It's easier to keep developing the ego, a job the narcissist devotes her life to, at least until the persona cracks. As one spouse mocked her husband's words: "Why would I want to read Dr. Killinger's book? She doesn't even know me!" The implication here is that this man is special and different. No book is going to tell him otherwise.

FEAR OF PERSECUTION. The ultimate fear is paranoia. As Dr. R. Campbell writes in the *Psychiatric Dictionary*, in a paranoid personality, the affected person is "hypersensitive, rigid and unwarrantedly suspicious, jealous, and envious. He often has an exaggerated sense of self-importance, must always be right and/or prove others to be in the wrong, and has a tendency to blame others and to ascribe evil to them" (p. 444).

Sadly, what the paranoid individual fears the most is likely to come to pass. Other people pass by them on the climb up the corporate ladder because they lack genuine "people skills." Social niceties are buried deep underneath the mask of self-deceit. It takes enormous energy for these tortured people to confront the pain of facing up to what they have done to others. Pandora's box contains self-loathing and countless insecurities, so rather than confront the Shadow aspects of the Self, paranoid workaholics avoid anyone who challenges them. Rejection is a force to be feared, so workaholics dismiss others from their consciousness by using dissociation, a defense tactic in which people and things cease to exist for the individual. Loved ones who try to help are seen as persecutors, not the true friends they are trying to be.

When turbulent feelings do surface, the workaholic often experiences psychotic breaks in which rage spills out unchecked. "While Chuck was shouting abuse at me, his face turned purple. I looked into his eyes and it was like *nothing* was there," cried Pam in despair. "He has lost his soul, I think. The poor guy!" Paranoia is a hellish state, and many workaholics who suffer frequent bouts of rage appear to be on the edge of a breakdown. The miracle is how these loners still manage to do their job at all. Their support systems gradually desert them, but they march on to their own drum.

Chronic Fatigue

Over time, cumulative fears and concerns about performance produce bouts of emotional and physical fatigue. At first, workaholics find themselves nodding off in a movie, or fighting to keep awake at the supper table. Energy is depleted after a day of rushing, missing deadlines, or frantically overscheduling. Later, these bouts of fatigue become more frequent and debilitating, and therefore more public. Chronically exhausted workaholics become the butt of family jokes. The family just gets used to the father falling asleep without warning, anywhere and at any time. The children just nod to each other or raise their eyes, and move around him. It doesn't seem to matter how many people are present, or how noisy the gathering. Father sleeps soundly in his chair until he wakes with a jolt, a surprised look on his face.

Exhaustion takes the form of hyperactivity in many workaholics. They become obsessive about exercise, and may decide to train for a marathon, rather than rest. They run their life as though on an endless treadmill. "Hyper" types jump from one activity to the next, and often have trouble winding down at night. They are scarcely aware of how tired, cramped, and tense they are.

Dr. A. Hart, in *The Hidden Link Between Adrenalin and Stress*, explains that the stress response alerts the body to prepare itself for action. Adrenalin and the related hormones act to signal the conversion of stored sugar to glucose, so the body can prepare itself for muscle activity. Adrenalin contracts the muscular layer in the walls of the arteries, and together with speeded-up heart rate, raises the blood pressure and stimulates increased respiration, so that extra oxygen is available to the body. In this state, the body fights off disease and discomfort.

As the demand for oxygen and excess energy drops, the body tries to return its systems to normal functioning. Hart writes: "It is then that headaches, diarrhea, fatigue, illness, rapid heartbeats, skipped beats, depression, and generalized anxiety are felt" (p. 72). Adrenal fatigue sets in when high levels of adrenalin are maintained for extended periods. The adrenal cortex becomes enlarged, key lymph nodes shrink, and the stomach and intestines become irritated until the system crashes in severe fatigue. Hart concludes that "the victim's sudden inability to tolerate any stress or raise any energy" is a sign of adrenalin fatigue brought on by too much stress.

"Couch potatoes" may be workaholics who are barely functioning. They stare unseeing at the TV, or escape to dens or bedrooms where no "performance" is necessary. They become very selective about what they will, or will not, do. They avoid responsibility at home whenever possible, and all their energy is reserved for the office. I suspect that the chronic fatigue of workaholism and the phenomenon known as "Yuppie Flu" are linked.

Guilt

Guilt is an uncomfortable feeling that warns us that our irresponsible or unhealthy behaviour is contrary to what we would ordinarily believe to be morally or ethically just. As the breakdown progresses, workaholics suffer frequent guilt pangs as their resentment and hostility erupt into destructive, ugly acting-out. Quentin Hyder, in *The Christian Handbook of Psychiatry*, notes that guilt is an awareness of wrongdoing as well as a fear of punishment. Both lead to shame, regret, remorse, and low self-esteem. Thus alienated from his ideal persona, the workaholic experiences loneliness and isolation, depression and anxiety.

Guilt is really self-anger, but unfortunately, workaholics project their hostility outwards, or repress it and become depressed and moody. After one distraught wife discovered her husband had picked up their young son and thrown him across the room for calling his father a name, she screamed at him to stop, and placed herself between them. "You're just getting hysterical, Elaine. Get a hold of yourself, for heaven's sake" was the projection William hurled at her. By doing so, he absolved himself of guilt. Unwilling to face rejection or feelings of inadequacy, workaholics often reject others first so they can feel superior once again. Without compassion and empathy, emotionally crippled workaholics are unable to forgive others or themselves.

Shame replaces guilt. Directed outwards, shame manifests itself in ugly moods, put-downs, sarcasm, and outrage. Directed inwards, shame means workaholics overwork and neglect to eat properly or get enough sleep. They are too busy to see their doctor when warning signals of bodily distress should no longer be ignored. Without the feeling and compassion to experience guilt and gain insight, workaholics act out their shame. Many become vindictive and punish others when things go wrong.

The Evils of Workaholism

The combination of escalating fears, chronic fatigue, and guilt are emotionally draining. So workaholics are overwhelmed by excess stimulation or demands on their time. They become agitated and frustrated when anyone threatens their ability to control everyone and everything. They still need to be "right" and have their own way — this rarely changes. Rigidity and stubbornness work together to make sure of this.

Once workaholics grow numb and stop feeling, profound personality changes begin. A series of losses occur that are largely unconscious and therefore are not recognized by the individual:

- The *ability to communicate clearly* is lost because workaholics are uncertain about how they feel. Consequently, they watch others to see how they should act and what they should say in certain situations.
- The *ability to be intimate* is threatened. When feelings don't function well, workaholics lose their ability to be empathetic and compassionate. They lack warmth and thoughtfulness. Intimacy, in fact, becomes very stressful. Workaholics can "perform" in the technical sense, but his or her partner is aware that the workaholic is not there emotionally. Sexual intimacy often ceases because both partners are left feeling frustrated, or "like an object," as one wife phrased it.
- *Independence* is challenged. When workaholics depend on others to tell them what they should feel, they cease to be the strong and independent people they once were. When they repress their own feelings, others must express their feelings for them. Ironically, they resent and often punish the spouse, child, or fellow worker they rely on the most.
- *Loss of integrity and respect* is a sad fate for these formerly idealistic people. The individual starts to do the opposite of what he or she would have done before. The Shadow side of the personality begins to influence, and eventually dominates, the psyche. "I know now why I first came to see you. My Shadow was pulling me down so hard that I could not *not* go!" said one married man caught up in an obsessive affair

with an unstable, seductive woman. Respectability and trust earned through hard work and devotion can be lost overnight.

- *Loss of spirituality* occurs because one has to love oneself before a truly generous spirit is possible. Denial and dishonesty lead to a loss of Self — the pathway to the soul and one's inner connection with God. Arrogance and selfishness discourage an open acceptance of a greater Power.

- *Loss of a sense of humour and the ability to play* occurs gradually and almost imperceptibly. Workaholics *work* at their play, always improving their skills in order to reach a better outcome or score. If they can't do well, they often avoid the activity. A genuine, hearty laugh becomes a thing of the past. In its place is the narcissist's chilling laugh or sneer, and a sarcastic, black humour.

- *Loss of physical and psychological health* occurs as the breakdown spirals downwards. Excess adrenalin and a lack of nurturing and healthy habits take their toll. Physiological responses to workaholism reported in my previous book include excess stomach sensitivity, abnormal blood pressure, heart trouble, nervousness, lack of vitality, and total inability to relax. Anxiety reactions may include disturbed breathing, increased heart activity, vasomotor changes, and musculoskeletal disturbances such as trembling, paralysis, or increased sweating. Workaholics often report a feeling of pressure in their chest, constricted breathing, dizziness, and light-headedness. Prolonged stress leads to more frequent and severe anxiety and psychosomatic complaints; partial withdrawal where a person dissociates and pretends something didn't happen; panic attacks when a fragile ego ruptures temporarily; a full retreat into a psychotic state in which reality and fantasy blur; or a complete disintegration of the ego, or suicide. As noted earlier, death from strokes and heart attacks due to workaholism, or *Karoshi*, are reported in some Japanese studies.

3. Denial, Control, and Power —
The Workaholic Trap

Denial

Denial allows workaholism to grow unchecked in the individual. Denial becomes a power unto itself. Honesty therefore must become the cornerstone of the recovery process.

Workaholics become entangled in a web of deceit and lies. Broken promises, lies, saying what others want to hear, and refusing to say no when this would be wise — all contribute to a loss of integrity and self-respect. Denial serves as a protective shield to help workaholics avoid confrontations or challenges to their power and ability to control. Rather than face the disintegration of the Self, the feeling-being side of the personality, workaholics repress the dark, Shadow side and focus only on their "perfect" image and on their accomplishments.

Impression management is the workaholic's art. The public persona that broadcasts success must be protected at all costs. Secrecy and privacy become a powerful weapon, a comfortable ally to maintain the *illusion* of perfection, to avoid dealing with the damage done to others through manipulation and deceit. The mask created by workaholics in the professions is a carefully crafted one. Self-sacrificing physicians, dentists, or health and spiritual professionals often are respected and revered by their clientele. The true Self is hidden beneath a cloak of respectability and even nobility. Workaholics who relish praise and adoration from grateful patients, parishioners, or students expend all their energies at work. They have little time or patience for their neglected families. Quality time does not replace quantity time with children who must learn to expect little or no consistency or reliability from their Jekyll and Hyde parent.

As long as denial remains strong, families and concerned friends are helpless to intervene as the breakdown progresses unchecked. Workaholics resent any criticism or challenge whatsoever, and the person delivering the negative feedback becomes the "enemy," and must be punished. Workaholics reject others lest they be rejected themselves. Denial makes projection of blame, dissociation, and compartmentalization necessary defense mechanisms.

Control

Workaholics feel safest when work and life are predictable and consistent. The more uncertain life becomes, the more they try to control everybody and everything. They carefully plan and organize down to the most minute detail, and firmly refuse to delegate work to others.

Workaholics use a quiet, manipulative type of control to retain their superiority, their one-up position. The Terrible Twist, a twisting of the truth so that the other person gets blamed for the workaholic's insensitive or thoughtless action, is a favourite way to maintain dominance over others. Outwardly solicitous workaholics avoid personal responsibility by agreeing to do something and then do nothing. Yet they manage to leave the impression that they are cool, reserved, and removed from the chaos they create. It is others who are seen as angry and hysterical because they end up responding to the projected blame. Workaholics accept high profile work that is "visible" to all, such as committees or boards, yet neglect the mundane but necessary work that keeps the wheels in motion from day to day. Self-aggrandizement is the name of this game.

Blatant, overt control is not hard to miss. If you are always right, then it is important to "help" others by telling them what they should do, say, think, or feel. Difficulties arise because workaholics lack the insight to criticize their own actions, and fail to see what their suggestions or advice do to others. Workaholics fear challenges to this control because they are terrified of rejection. Subsequent reactions produce irritability, sarcasm, bitching, shouting, temper tantrums, and rages. These outbursts become more frequent and more severe as the workaholic breaks down.

Giving up controlling behaviour is frightening for insecure workaholics who know that something is wrong, but lack the insight to recognize that their own poor judgment is creating problems both at home and at work. Support usually ebbs away at an alarming rate as people become genuinely frightened and suspicious of these self-serving and selfish individuals.

Power

The workaholic's power is driven by greed — an aggressive, instinctual need for more control, more success, more rewards, more recognition. Nothing is ever enough for these perfectionists. Power combined with a growing arrogance, accompanied by an unconscious deep insecurity which feeds anxiety, is a recipe for disaster. Greed is fed by ambition, competition, perfectionism, anger, and guilt. It starts with personal control, and spreads to control of other people, objects, organizations, and even whole industries. Strategies, one-upmanship, manipulation, exploitation, and domination are the tactics of power.

Recovery comes only when the power of love becomes stronger than the power of greed. Love encourages empathy, compassion, generosity, good will, and compromise. Its language is appreciation, support, enthusiasm, and sharing. Compassion and competition are like oil and water; they do not mix. Compassion does not deal in winners and losers. It doesn't isolate, separate, or estrange.

Competition can be constructive and creative, but it becomes unhealthy if one constantly needs to measure oneself against others and come out ahead. It is most destructive when motivated by a need to punish others and vindicate oneself. Only through gaining wisdom and exercising compassion will the workaholic ensure that personal control and power are used for good, not evil.

Narcissism

In this chapter, we learned that perfectionism leads to obsession, and that, in turn, obsession leads to narcissism in the workaholic. In Chapter 5, narcissism will be explored in depth, because high levels of it produce strong denial and loss of feelings in the individual. Narcissism therefore becomes the stumbling block that makes recovery from workaholism increasingly difficult, if not impossible. Narcissistic workaholics do not experience the guilt that others feel when they do something wrong or unthoughtful.

Shame replaces guilt; they fail to realize what their actions and words have done to others, or how they are sabotaging their own health. Instead, these individuals repress or dissociate negative reactions from conscious awareness.

While workaholism does foster narcissism in formerly functioning individuals, a different type of narcissism, called the narcissistic personality, occurs in people who fail to develop emotionally past the adolescent level.

In the following pages, we will learn how narcissism develops in the individual, and what damage is caused to the developing ego in childhood when the family is dysfunctional. We will explore how the child is psychologically wounded when the Self is confronted with neglect, abuse, or idealization. Denial becomes necessary to defend the ego from painful feelings. Feelings grow numb, and the individual learns to intellectualize instead. Chapter 5 concludes with a number of ways to identify narcissistic characteristics in ourselves and in others.

5
Narcissism*

Mirror, Mirror, on the Wall, Who Is the Fairest of Them All?

*"People who get carried away with themselves
often have to walk back alone."*
MORNING SMILE, THE GLOBE AND MAIL

Normal levels of narcissism are fundamental to the development of self-respect, self-love, and pride. We nurture ourselves each day by meeting our physical and psychological needs. In excess, however, narcissism becomes a destructive dynamic that warps our life energy and blocks psychological growth.

The chief sign of a neurotic narcissism is the loss of feeling, the loss of the *real Self,* which is the whole person and his potential for growth and development. The person instead identifies with an idealized view of what he feels he should be, and thus denies and rejects his actual Self. In the extreme, narcissism becomes a personality disturbance in which the person is overly invested in his own image or persona, in how she wants the world to perceive her. Narcissists manipulate situations and people to serve their own self-interest. Acting without feelings, they strive for power to

*See Quiz — What Is Your Level of Narcissism? on p. 243

enhance their image, often at any cost. Ironically, in spite of this exaggerated self-interest, narcissists lack a true sense of Self.

THE DEVELOPMENT OF SELF

The roots of narcissism lie within our earliest childhood experiences. A weakened or damaged Self results when there is faulty interaction between the child and those he is mirroring or merging with in the process of self-identification.

The Healthy Self

According to Drs. Heinz Kohut and Ernest Wolf, writing in the *International Journal of Psychoanalysis,* there are two types of "self-objects" in healthy ego development. Through *mirroring,* the first type, the child develops the Self by identifying with an accepting and confirming parent who affirms his "innate sense of vigour, greatness and perfection." He learns to see himself through the mirror of his parents' eyes. If he is positively reinforced for his actions, he will affirm those aspects of himself that are rewarded. Parents who value performance will reward high academic grades, winning at sports, or excelling in the arts. High achievement will be further recognized and rewarded by society. Conversely, if the child receives negative looks or criticism, he will devalue that personality trait or activity, and associate it with his own reflected negative feelings. A healthy Self develops when the child receives positive regard and respect for his *whole* person. Both strengths and weaknesses are acknowledged, and the child's "being and feeling" side is supported, along with the "doing and thinking" side. He thus becomes his true Self, an individual who is separate and different from his parents.

Through the *idealized parent imago,* the second type, the parent serves as a model of inner strength and calmness, of infallibility and omnipotence. If parents have calm voices, relaxed and yielding bodies, and offer warmth and affection through physical closeness and verbal expressions of love, the child copies these characteristics and develops a firm sense of Self. If the parents are self-accepting and at peace with their own strivings and values, the child, too, will receive unconditional acceptance for who she is. When conflicts and new challenges test the child's self-confidence and inner security, the healthy family is there to offer the encouragement and support necessary to learn life's lessons and transform them into self-knowledge and growth. The Self thus develops in a healthy environment relatively free from the high levels of anxiety created when families are dysfunctional and parents are in conflict.

Unconditional acceptance does not imply permissiveness. Children need parameters within which to develop self-acceptance and self-control. Indulgent parents who overprotect and problem-solve for their children, rob them of their chance to develop independence and self-esteem. These children have been shielded from reality, and remain naive. When they reach puberty, they are expected to assume adult responsibilities, with no real preparation for life's difficult experiences.

As John Sanford points out in *Evil: The Shadow Side of Reality*, the growing child needs to identify societal standards for behaviour and learn to control his behaviour from within. "In a permissive atmosphere a child's capacity to develop his or her own behaviour monitoring system is blunted. The ego development will then be too weak to enable the child as an adult to cope with the Shadow" (p. 56). The negative Shadow is the fearful, dark, unwanted side of the personality, which is repressed or disowned in order to protect the ego's ideal persona. Our ego ideals may be influenced on both the conscious and the unconscious level by family, peer group, school, or religious teachings.

Performance, what the child does, needs to be recognized as quite separate from the Self. The child's behaviour is commented on and evaluated, based on what the parents believe to be appropriate and acceptable. Feedback is given accordingly. The child is not labelled good or bad as a consequence of her behaviour. She can recover confidence quickly if she acknowledges challenges and failures as a normal part of life's struggles. The child feels loved and supported, not criticized or judged.

A strong Self can tolerate wide swings in self-esteem in response to victory or defeat, success or failure. Success and joy are incorporated in the self-image, as are hopelessness and despair. The healthy individual operates within a wide band of fluctuations of feelings. If life gets chaotic for whatever reason, it is normal to sometimes feel like one is on a roller coaster.

The Damaged Self

In sharp contrast, children in dysfunctional families often receive ambiguous and unpredictable messages from a parent. Their "self-object" role models are confused and confusing. A parent may be emotionally unavailable because of his or her own narcissism, alcoholism, work addiction, drug addiction, or perfectionism. A climate in which role models are self-focused, obsessive, dishonest, unpredictable, and unreliable breeds insecurity and a confused self-image in children.

In the narcissistic personality, the damaged ego is too fragile to tolerate wide mood swings. Instead, any negative aspects of the personality or undesirable feedback are quickly dismissed and repressed. Such denial often conceals underlying fear, guilt, rejection, or depression. To compensate for these perceived threats, the ego is inflated even more. Eventually, the ego gets puffed up to a state of arrogance. High self-expectations often produce hyperactivity in the child, and later in the adult, because anxiety and even self-loathing bubble dangerously just below the surface of consciousness.

Discovering how and when the Self has been damaged is an important part of life's journey. After all, we must recognize what is wrong, how we have been wounded, before we can heal ourselves. Self-knowledge and wisdom come through understanding and acceptance. Eventually we must learn to love and nurture the disowned, damaged Shadow side, which so frequently causes pain, sadness, guilt, or anger in ourselves and in others.

Unwittingly, parents often discourage the acceptance of such negative feelings in their children. Repeated episodes, innocent though they may seem at the time, can foster long-term dishonesty and denial in a child. The seeds of narcissism are thus planted in the next generation.

Alexandra, exploring the roots of her damaged Self in one of our sessions, recalled how negative feelings in her home were definitely unacceptable, even taboo. Many times, she was told by her controlling mother, "If you can't be pleasant, then you'll just have to go to your room until you can put a smile on your face!"

"I was never allowed to think for myself," Alexandra now realizes. "In fact, I sometimes wondered if I really did exist. I felt like a nuisance, someone they didn't want to deal with." Her mother wanted the children to be obedient, and to respect her. Disobedience meant that she would refuse to speak to her children for hours. Sometimes, if she was really upset, it lasted for days at a stretch.

Alexandra remembers desperately wanting to be a part of her family. "So if things went wrong," she explained, "I'd go to my mother and say, 'Mommy, I'm really sorry for whatever I did.'"

Surprisingly, at least to Alexandra, her mother would answer, "Sorry isn't good enough! If you don't know what you did, you'd better go away and think about it some more." Alexandra assured me that she honestly had no idea what she was supposed to have done.

The crucial question for Alexandra became, What do I have to do in this family to get my needs met and survive? Her answer was that "I had to deny who I really was." She could talk only about positive things; anger was never to be expressed. In fact, Alexandra felt "bad" when she was angry. Her mother kept her anger tightly controlled, although her pursed lips and frown instilled fear in her child.

Denial became an adaptive habit. Alexandra learned to tell others what they wanted to hear. After a while, little white lies became progressively easier to tell. "It never crossed my mind that I was being dishonest!" was how she phrased it.

Another problematic pattern emerged. Because Alexandra was not allowed to be angry, she learned to project blame onto others. She recalled with chagrin the many times she had set up her brother so that he looked like the guilty party. "I was quiet about it, but I was a real brat!"

Telling people what they want to hear, rather than the truth, fosters narcissism. You not only manipulate others, but you learn to kid yourself about all sorts of things. Life consequently gets very complicated and convoluted. The real Self gets lost in the confusion and chaos that the individual creates around himself. Instead, all the psyche's energy is invested in the ego, the persona that the individual wants the world to see. The centre of the true Self, the soul, lacks nourishment, and the person is left with a deep emptiness. Nothing is ever enough to fill this longing for self-acceptance, and so the person tries to get his needs met by others. The loss of Self is a personal tragedy.

THE LOSS OF FEELINGS IN NARCISSISM

Why is it so difficult to restore the narcissist's ability to feel once again? A healthy person's self-image correlates with and confirms the body's own direct experience. Even though Sally is depressed, she is connected with her body. She says, "I'm crying because I'm so damned mad!" Peter, on the other hand, often honestly does not know how he feels. In the narcissistic personality, the ego is dissociated from the body or Self. Consciousness is thus severed from its life force, the body. Ordinarily, the body's involuntary circulatory, digestive, and respiratory functions send signals to inform the mind about our emotional state. Depending on the information from this feedback, we experience excitement, happiness, depression, or sadness, and so on.

Normal Development

When development is healthy, the key function of the ego is to distinguish reality from fantasy, and to seek gratification of our needs in the outer world. The ego perceives information, co-ordinates action, adapts to reality, delays gratification, and ensures safety and preservation by avoiding injury and punishment. It selects what features of the environment to respond to, and how best to get its own needs met safely. The ego has a high degree of continuity and identity. It is capable of observing and criticizing itself, so that we may learn and persevere. The ego is conscious, or at least available to consciousness. It is the "doing-performing-thinking" action centre of our being.

The ego serves to perceive the Self, but is not the Self. Nor is it completely separate. At birth, the biological Self comes into being. The psychological concept of Self, in Jungian terms, describes the psychic totality of the personality, including both conscious and unconscious aspects. The Self is experienced through the feeling aspect of the body. It can express itself only after there is an awareness and acknowledgment of feelings. Without this expression, the Self remains largely unconscious and undeveloped. What we feel depends on what happens in the body, what information we receive from our involuntary feedback functions.

The ego controls the body's action through its will. Will can control the mind, and therefore is capable of manipulating how we feel. It also interprets or misinterprets how others feel. However, it is important to note that the will or ego is incapable of "creating" a feeling. In *Narcissism: Denial of the True Self,* Alexander Lowen suggests, "One can't truly will a sexual response, an appetite, a feeling of love, or even anger — however much one may 'think' one can ... For body happenings to lead to the perception of feeling, the events must reach the surface of the body and the surface of the mind, where consciousness is located" (p. 30). For example, the impulse of Peter's anger does not reach the surface of his body to tell him to cry or lash out. It is kept safely hidden inside until his defenses prove inadequate to handle the surging rage bubbling close to the surface of his consciousness. Only when this rage breaks through does Peter experience his anger.

Dysfunctional Development

In the narcissist, reality becomes increasingly distorted. Not only is there a lack of congruence between the desired self-image, or persona, and the true bodily Self, but ego boundaries are blurred to the point that it becomes difficult to distinguish between images of the Self and objects outside the Self. Unfortunately, these objects are often people! Peter rationalizes that if he wants to go skiing, of course the whole family wants to go. It is assumed, and no questions need be asked. The narcissist's strong will or mind can refuse to see or hear what he or she does not want to acknowledge — especially if the evidence is contrary to what the narcissist wants to believe.

Denial, of course, implies initial recognition. A decision is made to deal with a situation or to deny its existence. In time, however, *the narcissist's denial becomes unconscious.* Narcissists carry on as if everything is all right, even if their reality is different from what others perceive.

The bodies of many narcissists appear rigid and stiff. Others, like some athletes, dancers, and actors, are agile and move gracefully, suggesting that emotion is present. However, their behaviour is often without feeling. Lowen explains this phenomenon. He believes that tension at the base of the skull in the muscles that hold the head to the neck blocks the flow of excitement from the body into the head. The narcissist, cut off from bodily feeling, lives from the neck up, in the mind. It's as though a scarf were tied too tightly around the neck. Not surprisingly, many narcissists complain about neck pain or pain felt in the back but referred from pinched nerves in the neck. Spouses will often describe them as "a pain in the neck." Too frequently, the spouse also will develop neck pain because of the constant stress of dealing with the narcissist's outbursts.

Not only is their life force inhibited by such tension, but these people breathe only from the neck up. Their high-pitched voices attest to the restricted flow of oxygen caused by tensed muscles and constricted air passages in the throat area. This condition becomes chronic when a person is constantly under stress.

Image is everything to narcissists. Their vulnerability is hidden from others and from themselves because they are out of touch with their own fears, sadness, and pain. Their carefully crafted persona conveys the image of someone who is a strong, independent, decisive, even powerful person. The truth is that narcissists are often irresponsible, and tend to avoid making personal decisions whenever possible. They are always about to do something, and may be totally convincing in their declarations of intent. Narcissists need and seek power to compensate for their real, but disowned, vulnerability. The persona, without strong feelings to support it, is, after all, only a facade.

Narcissists come to need the approval and admiration of others to keep their ego inflated because they are not nourished by self-love. The ego, not the Self, is fed — as Peter, for example, spends all his energies on creating a successful public persona. This one-sided development of the ego, at the expense of the Self, may produce depression or high anxiety in Peter. It is nature's way of sending strong distress signals to the individual from the unbalanced psyche. In the narcissist, both the Self and the ego are damaged.

IDENTIFYING NARCISSISTIC CHARACTERISTICS

Self-Aggrandizement
The narcissist's deepest fear is to be labelled a failure, not to be in control. Failure can even mean that other people did not notice or pay homage to an accomplishment. Peter's perfectionism causes him to plan and scheme obsessively, so that he has the control and power to do things his way. He must be seen by others to be right, even if this means "borrowing" other people's ideas and neglecting to give them credit where it is due. Such a single-minded pursuit of success leads Peter to become ever more selfish and self-serving. His work has gradually become a form of self-aggrandizement. His image in the business world preoccupies his thoughts every day. Peter would stoutly deny this preoccupation, however. His rationalization is delivered in a pompous tone: "I'm doing all this, of course, strictly for the family."

Specialness
In Peter's family, excellence was expected. His parents made it crystal clear very early on that Peter was special, an "exceptional child." They indulged his every whim, tolerated his wilful determination,

and rarely disciplined him. Peter mirrored their idealization, and built up a carefully crafted persona that broadcast the success, prestige, and power that were expected of him and by him. He felt he deserved only the best and desperately wanted to reach the top. "All this came quite naturally to me," he explained. Since they conflicted with Peter's perfect image, any negative feelings were quickly disowned. Peter *was* his image. In his eyes, he could do no wrong.

Impression Management

As is typical of narcissists, Peter monitored his clothes and appearance closely to project a certain style. He was meticulously well-groomed, and spent much time, effort, and money towards this end. His shoes were always highly polished. He wore expensive suits and the latest in fashionable ties. He often spent Saturday afternoons at his favourite menswear shop. The owner fussed over him and made him feel an important customer, which indeed he was. This "impression management" was designed to provide the visibility, mobility, and aura of success he desired. He joined the right clubs and made sure he was immaculately dressed at all social functions.

As narcissism becomes more chronic, a reversal often takes place. Although Peter still dressed well for work, at home he wore the same old shirts and rumpled pants, until Sally threatened to set fire to them. Unconsciously, Peter wanted people close to him to feel sorry for him. He dropped his club membership because he thought it made him look pretentious. Peter made excuses in order to avoid business functions, preferring to stay at home in a safe shell where he could still exercise control.

Other narcissists may choose a style that is the opposite to Peter's. Some have a studied casual air. Others are labelled eccentric for their unique brand of image-making.

The Centre of Attention

As a child, Peter played a game with his mother. He called himself "Number One Son." She humoured him by playing along, even though Peter was her second son. Later on, Peter loved it when Sally, too, humoured him by sending him cards addressed to "my debonair, sophisticated, charming, witty, and intelligent husband." Unwittingly, others, too, had the opportunity to feed his inflated ego as he performed well at school, and rose up through the ranks of the business world. Peter loved it when waiters or the maître d' recognized him and called him by name. He therefore was loyal to a few good restaurants that fed his ego as well as his stomach. Occasionally, he would get quite irritated and sharp if he felt he was being ignored by the waiter or taken for granted by anyone. Peter needed to be in control, and he didn't like to be kept waiting. No line-ups for him. One bad evening, and that restaurant ceased to exist, at least in his universe.

Selfish Takers

Achieving one's goals, getting from point A to point B, having one's own way, always being right — this is all that really matters. Success does not bring gratitude but a craving for more accolades. Narcissism and gratitude rarely coexist.

Because narcissists are out of touch with their feelings and therefore lack personal involvement or commitment, they are unable to truly give. They almost never say "I love you," and rarely are able to truly love others. They "love" only those they can control. Spouse and children are seen as extensions of their own personality, and therefore are expected to think the same way, and do as they do. Children are rarely accepted for who they are. Sadly, the narcissist's offspring often spend their whole lives trying to get the love and attention that the narcissist is unable to give. One exasperated woman whose father and husband were both narcissistic workaholics exclaimed, "I've spent my whole life trying to get blood out of a stone. When am I ever going to smarten up?" Of late, this phenomenon may be seen in the rash of books written by the children of famous people, such as movie or television stars, depicting their own personal tragic stories of unmet needs and neglect.

Ironically, narcissists see themselves as generous. Yet they depend on the generosity and vicarious warmth offered by others.

They marry warm, caring, nurturing people, and then take, take, take. One wife's lament says it all: "My husband took all my love and gave it away."

Dependency
Narcissists pride themselves on their independence, yet they increasingly depend on others to be responsible for them. Tragically, narcissists often punish those closest to them because they fear this increasing dependency. When narcissists become seriously out of touch with their own feelings, they may be observed watching their spouse for signals that what they have just said or done is appropriate. Their eyes are on the spouse, not on the person with whom they are talking. Yet moments later, they may be heard publicly putting down their spouse over some petty issue.

Duplicity
The contrast between private and public behaviour is often startling and can be very hurtful to the spouse. In public, narcissists can be charming. Outsiders cannot imagine that their wonderful doctor or minister neglects his own partner's need for love and attention. His wife receives glowing reports from outsiders with disbelief, but also with pain.

Narcissists are master manipulators of others' resources, and know how to get what they want from them. Somehow these people manage to get everyone else involved working hard, while themselves remaining aloof and distant. They could teach Tom Sawyer a thing or two!

Arrogance and Ingratitude
Arrogance and taking others for granted seem to go hand-in-hand.

Peter, inflated with a sense of his own importance and specialness, eschewed mundane tasks as beneath him. As Sally phrased it, "Peter seemed to think that all he had to do was show up for family functions. He didn't have to *do* a thing! It was as if we should all be delighted that he made it!" It would never occur to Peter to be involved in menu-planning, shopping, or cleaning up. When guests were there, however, he was the model gracious host, and would even take credit for the success of the party. Sally told me he almost never acknowledged her hard work, and certainly never praised her publicly.

Occasionally, though, when he wished to impress a special guest, Peter would decide to make what he called "The specialty of the house." Much fuss was made by all, since the family wanted to encourage his participation. This rarity was "special" indeed!

Denial

Secrecy and privacy are important to ensure that the perfect persona remains untarnished. Denial is like a psychological wall that protects these people from harsh reality. Narcissists cannot love an imperfect Self, so when things start to go wrong, they don't wish anyone to know.

Narcissists want support, but "help" is a word rarely uttered. Others' words of encouragement carry little weight because words are an expression of feelings. Without feelings, only action is important. Peter often told Sally that it didn't matter what she said; it was what she *did* that was important. Despite the veil of secrecy, Sally knew that Peter's business was in serious trouble. But her probing questions brought only angry responses from him. Peter heard only criticism in Sally's questioning, not the loving concern. His business failures were his business, and none of hers.

Peter was shamed by his failures, but also remained in denial about his part in what went wrong. Because the shame was largely unconscious, it worked away at Peter's gut. Shame manifests itself in self-abuse, or in punishing behaviour towards others. Peter was eating too much, drinking to excess, and had started smoking again. He was excessively picky and argumentative with Sally. Such behaviour typically follows the loss of integrity or professional failure if denial is present. Anything to avoid feeling the pain and remorse that other people would feel in a similar situation.

Inflated egos and the perfect persona usually lead to excesses of power. Narcissists exaggerate their own abilities and remain unaware of their own limitations. They overlook personal flaws and even turn them into virtues. For example, Peter had his own timing, his own schedule, and showed no insight into the chaos this often caused others. Peter would rationalize, "I know I'm always late, but that's all right! The meeting can't start without me anyway!"

Sadly, through all their bravado, narcissists show almost no awareness of what their behaviour does to others. At work, their plans become too expansive or diversified because their capabilities are exaggerated and overestimated. Reality checks are avoided because only positive possibilities are considered. They wish to avoid being seen to depend on anyone, so consultation and delegation are avoided in favour of secrecy, privacy, and closely held power. They therefore typically make unilateral decisions.

Ironically, the more feelings are numbed, the more narcissists need to depend on others. They can't trust their own judgment any more. It is excruciating for them when the independence they pride themselves on dwindles.

The Diabolical Laugh or Sneer

There is a mocking tone of disdain, a chilling quality to a narcissist's laugh. It bursts out when a healthy person would ordinarily express an emotion. As Alexander Lowen explains in *Narcissism: Denial of the True Self,* "A patient appears to be on the verge of tears, but instead of crying, this laugh occurs. An emotional response would show that the person has been affected by the experience. The laughter denies any feeling. 'I won,' it declares. 'I am more powerful than you. I can resist you'" (p. 120). Being one-up makes the narcissist happy!

As one of my clients so eloquently described her response to that laugh, "I can literally feel a dark dread rise up in my stomach as we talk about this. It makes my scalp crawl!" Then she added, "I was always terrified when I heard that diabolical laugh because it usually meant more punishing behaviour was to come!"

Punishing Behaviour

When a narcissist is questioned or confronted, insecurity causes him to react in an overly defensive manner. Unable to tolerate interference in any form, the narcissist lashes out with anger or sarcasm, or withdraws and punishes others through passive-aggressive tactics. The confronter becomes the "enemy," someone to be controlled. If that person makes repeated challenges, the narcissist is quite capable of making sure his "enemy" is punished. He or she may be passed over for advancement, or even demoted. Such people often resign because they feel powerless to confront the boss, and see the "writing on the wall."

A perfect example is described by Anton Kuerti, writing about the pianist Glenn Gould in a *Globe and Mail* article. Quoting from Andrew Kazdin's book *Glenn Gould at Work: Creative Lying,* Kuerti describes how Gould's recording engineer was dismissed suddenly in a telephone conversation on the eve of a planned recording session: "Does this mean our association is over?" Kazdin asked. Gould replied hurriedly, "Yes. Now don't be a stranger ... Maybe I'll see you ˙f I ever get down to New York. Look, I've really got to go. Goodbye." Kazdin continues, "I never heard from him again. This ended our 15-year relationship. No regrets, no emotion, no thank yous."

A family member who challenges the narcissist also may be discarded as no longer useful or necessary. I hear many tragic tales of wives who have been left with few resources after years of living with narcissistic emotional abuse. When they had finally started to stand up for their own rights and values, their narcissistic spouse could not tolerate their angry declarations.

Less severe punishment may be meted out in the form of smaller refusals — to go out somewhere or to go away on a planned holiday. The withdrawal of financial support and initiating a blatant or clandestine affair are more serious ways of punishing rebellious spouses. If a separation or divorce ensues, the confronting spouse is discarded. Many narcissists threaten to cut out their ex-spouse financially, and fight bitter battles to ensure that they get to keep their "hard-earned" money.

Once out of the picture, the spouse ceases to exist for the narcissist. He or she is no longer useful or important to them, even after long years of marriage. It's not hard to let go when emotional involvement is at a minimum. Many narcissists avoid seeing their ex-spouse at all, and too many also do not keep in regular touch with their children. This is especially true if the children have sided with the other parent. Remember, dissociation is a favourite defense mechanism.

Narcissists tend to think that societal rules are for other people. Their arrogance puts them on a plateau above the norm. Robert Fulford in his column "Rediscovering Frank Lloyd Wright" (*Globe and Mail,* January 26, 1994) quotes from Anthony Alofsin's book, *Frank Lloyd Wright: The Lost Years, 1910–1922.* Wright had left his first wife and six children to live with the wife of a neighbour. He held a press conference at which he announced that his genius gave him special rights. "The ordinary man," he declared, "cannot live without rules to guide his conduct … It is infinitely more difficult to live without rules, but that is what the really honest, sincere, thinking man is compelled to do." Fulford comments that "Wright's hypocrisy operated on a colossal scale, like his genius and his ego."

Deceit

Lies, lies, lies! Promises, promises, promises! *Narcissists are always about to do something!* They make unrealistic promises based on what they think others want to hear. Then they do not follow through. In fact, neglecting to tell the truth becomes a chronic habit. Peter had the greatest difficulty acknowledging that his avoidance of telling the truth was lying. When Sally accused Peter of withholding information from her about the very real threat of his company going bankrupt, Peter's twisted, off-the-wall response was, "I'm too diplomatic to call Sally a liar." His projection twisted the truth. Peter told lies with ease. Sally did not.

Lack of Insight

Narcissists are a danger to others because they have so little insight into their effect on other people's lives. *They see others, but don't experience them.* The more narcissistic one is, the less one is able to see another person's point of view. Narcissists have little respect or empathy for other people as distinct, separate, and unique individuals.

Peter shows little appreciation for what his family does for him. Sally has put so much effort into being supportive and helpful to Peter, often at the expense of her own emotional and physical health. It's therefore painful for Sally to hear Peter say, "Well, what do you do for *me*? You've never been there for me either!" Yet he demands their attention, and insists that Sally and the children respect him. Their lives revolve around his needs and his timetable. The children have to come to him. He rarely seeks them out when he comes home.

Although narcissists have little insight into their own failings, they have an uncanny ability to home in on others' vulnerability. Because Sally's friends were extremely important to her, she always took great care to keep in touch and be loyal to them. If she was talking on the phone when Peter came home, he would resent her paying attention to someone else. So when Peter wanted to wound Sally, his favourite retort was, "Well, you have no friends. You're too selfish!" Stunned and hurt, Sally would withdraw. The truth, of course, was that Peter was projecting his Shadow and seeing *his* frailties in Sally. It was Peter who had no friends. He was the selfish one.

Fear of Aging and Death

Surprisingly, narcissists tend to be youthful looking, and their faces often remain remarkably unlined because they tend to avoid personal responsibility. They think of themselves as perpetually young, and refuse to deal with the stress that comes with solving problems and taking action. They remain untouched by others' emotional pain and stress because they stay aloof and uninvolved. The spouse is expected to look after any problems that the children have. Sadly, this is true even when children become seriously involved with drugs or theft, for instance, or act out sexually, trying to find love and attention elsewhere.

Narcissists dread old age and death, and consequently are unable to mourn. Worse still, they lack patience or understanding for those who do suffer. This is especially painful for the spouse who must mourn alone for lost loved ones with no comfort from the emotionally unavailable narcissistic husband or wife.

Narcissists are fatalistic, rather than proactive. They block out sadness and pain lest they become vulnerable and weak. Such denial leaves these individuals wide open to the whims of fate. They typically become increasingly cowardly as fears overwhelm the ego.

Outbursts and Rage

Unfortunately, narcissists may remain without insight yet be remarkably resilient. That is, until too many failures or rejections crack their thin veneer. Self-loathing and -contempt may surface periodically, and at such times, the narcissist will give way to temper tantrums or angry rages. These episodes are usually quickly repressed and totally denied later. Peter was enraged if Sally brought up a situation the next day, attempting to ensure that the problem was solved, so that such outbursts would not occur again. A typical response from Peter would be total denial. "Nothing of the sort happened! You must be losing your mind!" he would bark.

It is important to note that narcissists, as Lowen has noted, have a deep unconscious fear of going crazy. This may explain why severely narcissistic personalities will refuse to go for help. Most of the time, though, their defenses are quickly restored after these psychotic breaks with reality, because narcissists are masters of denial.

Loners

Some narcissists manage to keep up appearances and are able to keep their careers intact. Narcissists who maintain power, often do so through fear and intimidation. They can be cold, callous, and calculating in their control. They hire hard-driving Type A personalities whom they manipulate with perks and promises. Motivational rewards are just enough to keep employees "hungry." Their spouse is there but kept in the background, especially as age takes its toll.

Some surround themselves with attractive, enthusiastic but

naive people who want to please the boss and keep him on a pedestal. These loyal employees make excuses for his intermittent outbursts of anger. Sometimes other people use them. Picture the movie magnate whose office is full of beautiful young assistants. I'm told this is called the "babe factor."

These hard-core power brokers who carve out their own reality become increasingly unwise about, and vulnerable to, the real world. Assessing people solely on their "usefulness," they often become poor judges of character. They also fail to check with others to confirm whether their choices are indeed wise. Subsequently, they themselves eventually may become easy prey for younger, equally manipulative people who use them both emotionally and financially to serve their own career ambitions.

Many less extraverted narcissists lead provisional lives, and become loners as they age and their power erodes. They run out of people to manipulate, and reality comes crashing in with business and professional failures. Nowadays, many are deserted by their long-suffering families, who cannot cope with their erratic and destructive behaviour. Spiritually bankrupt and emotionally empty, narcissists eventually experience depression or psychotic episodes, which may crush their fragile egos. Many escape into alcoholism.

Narcissists of this type want you to feel sorry for them. They often drive older cars, let others pick up the bill in the restaurant, and cry poor, pretending they have no money. Often, they are quite wealthy, but keep this secret from their family. They put off discussing finances. Not surprisingly, though, if they want something, they get it! Narcissists become increasingly conscious of their own instinctual pleasures and creature comforts. It is okay for them to indulge in an expensive meal, but if their spouse wants to go out with a friend, he or she is chastised for spending too much money, or going to a trendy restaurant. Soliciting sympathy may be costly, as this is often the last straw for a long-suffering spouse.

The narcissist's world shrinks, growing ever smaller and narrower. Peter will go to only one restaurant now. If a show isn't on at the local theatre, he refuses to go. His circle of influence also shrinks as colleagues whom he has offended or manipulated avoid contact.

HOW DOES THE NARCISSIST AFFECT OTHERS?

It is one thing to damage oneself and to live out the consequences of narcissism in one's own life. It is quite another tragedy, however, when narcissists wreak havoc in the lives of those closest to them. Their trusting spouses were initially attracted to their charm and youthful good looks, and won over by their habit of telling others what they wanted to hear. Their children may have been inflicted with the narcissistic wound at a time of naivety and innocence when they did not recognize the damaging consequences narcissistic behaviours might have on their own future development and happiness.

In Chapter 6, we will explore the family dynamics in which one parent is, or has become, highly narcissistic.

6
The Narcissist's Family

The Birth of Narcissism and Its Generational Legacy

Narcissism and gratitude, like oil and water, don't mix.

DANGER — NARCISSISM IS CONTAGIOUS

The children of a narcissist copy their parent's self-serving behaviour. In addition, certain personality characteristics are fostered that encourage narcissism to develop in one or more of the children. Often a narcissistic individual will single out one child as a favourite, and that child can do no wrong in his or her eyes.

The Narcissistic Wound

Let's explore how narcissism begins to develop within the family circle. The most severe narcissistic injuries are inflicted in childhood. Surprisingly, there are two seemingly opposite dynamics that wound the child and facilitate the development of narcissism. There are also degrees of injury, depending on the source and the length of time a child is exposed. One dynamic has its history in parental idealization and/or indulgence; the other, in ongoing emotional injury, neglect, or abuse. In Jungian terms, the adult narcissist is referred to as the "eternal child," the *puer aeternus* in males, and the *puer animus* in females. This person's emotional level remains stunted at the adolescent level unless a midlife crisis forces inner growth.

Narcissism is all too prevalent in today's family. Christopher Lasch, in *The Culture of Narcissism,* suggests that because our society lacks a belief in the future, it therefore neglects the needs of the next generation. Today's parents attempt to make children feel loved and wanted, yet there is "an underlying coolness in the remoteness of those who have little to pass on to the next generation and who in any case give priority to their own right to self-fulfillment." Lasch concludes that this emotional detachment coupled with "attempts to convince a child of his favoured position in the family is a good prescription for a narcissistic personality structure" (pp. l0l–2).

THE NARCISSIST AS PARENT

Narcissism affects one's ability to be a good parent. The narcissists' parenting skills are warped by feelings that have been deadened by one of their parents either excessively indulging yet manipulating them, or overtly neglecting or abusing them. They in turn neglect or idealize their children.

The Neglectful Parent
Many parents who neglect their children do so because they themselves have been emotionally crippled. As children, they were psychologically ill-equipped to handle the pain of their own childhood. Often traumatized by ongoing physical or emotional abuse, or witness to the abuse of other family members by a chaotic parent, these children learned to repress unbearable pain and anxiety. No wonder some choose to overprotect or idolize their own children one minute, yet find themselves repeating abusive patterns when stress levels climb and hidden rage erupts out of control. Modelling is a very powerful teacher!

Another common dynamic in these families is the child who

becomes overly responsible because the non-abusive, victimized parent relies too heavily on this child for emotional support. By responding to the frightened parent's need, the child is unwittingly robbed of a carefree childhood. Inappropriate adult roles are thrust upon such a victim prematurely. No child has the emotional maturity to handle the often bizarre power-plays acted out in these disturbed families. The child becomes overly responsible for others, but shut off from his or her own needs and happiness. Personal pleasure often makes these children feel uncomfortable and guilty.

In contrast, the parent who was indulged and overprotected as a child often does not recognize that any emotional damage has been done. These people may have learned to deny negative feelings, attempting to live up to the high expectations of a narcissistic parent. Such parents want their child to make them proud. The implications of this less obvious type of abuse to their own personal development remain largely unrecognized. Therefore, this group will be even less likely to question their own parenting skills. After all, aren't they and their family perfect?

Ongoing Deception in the Next Generation

Anxiety becomes a perpetual state of mind for a child with a narcissistic parent. Expectations are high, and manipulation is a means to control what the child does and thinks.

As in all dysfunctional families, things eventually start to go wrong. One crisis begets another. Denial becomes an unconscious habit that protects family members from feeling disoriented, crazy, or simply less than perfect. It becomes less painful to pretend or lie, to guess what others want to hear. As one client, Bruno, justified his deceptions of his narcissistic parent, "By lying or keeping silent, I covered up all my mistakes. It was the only way I could hide my weaknesses from Dad." He paused, then added thoughtfully, "Little lies helped solve my problem of avoiding the attention, or sometimes rage, I otherwise would have received when he discovered what I had done. Now that I'm on my own, I'm still telling lies. I just can't seem to stop myself. I hate to admit this, but honesty is not one of my best traits." Old habits die hard.

Since chaotic feelings are uncomfortable and even painful, children learn to resort to reason and logic to determine the actions best suited to their own self-preservation. They crave positive attention and will do everything to ensure that they get it. Their "impression management" strategy becomes to "look good at all costs." Demands that children be strong, good, right, and perfect can be powerful.

Tragically, the long-term cost of denial is typically the loss of integrity and respect.

The Shamed Child

A subtle emotional abuse occurs when children are shamed by being repeatedly put down by a parent who has the narcissist's inflated view of self. Children are told they are "stupid," "slow," "no good," "inferior,"and so on. Their self-esteem plummets, yet the humiliation or shame of carrying such a label is often blocked from their awareness. Instead, one sees a heady cockiness, a show-off retaliatory response. Shame is often the source of narcissistic denial in the next generation.

In other cases, the child takes on the shame of a parent. Many workaholics, for instance, seek control of their lives after a parent has been publicly humiliated by business bankruptcy, divorce recriminations, accusations of sexual impropriety, or imprisonment. The seeds of workaholism are often planted at such times because the child is determined to be totally independent and in charge of his or her life, and to be seen as respectable by the community. No one is going to crack this perfectly constructed persona. Control thus becomes essential to emotional survival.

The Idealized Child

A more subtle wound is inflicted when children are spoiled and overprotected rather than disciplined by an anxious parent. This idealized child has a special set of problems.

Certainly, Peter was indulged as a child and made to feel superior. In spite of his parents' good intentions, Peter grew up amidst emotional confusion. He bounced back and forth between his mother's strong, sometimes hysterical reactions, and his father's laid-back, cool detachment. His father took little responsibility for household and children. If anything went wrong at home, he would withdraw into a moody, stony silence or burst into a fiery rage. No one could predict which it would be. Blind to his own faults, Peter's father was all too aware of others' foibles. He got extremely annoyed if there was any trouble at home. The trouble had nothing to do with him. Someone else was always blamed.

Peter, like his father, devalued everyday, simple pleasures and responsibilities. He discovered early on that "home work" received no recognition. So his energies were channelled into his ambitions to be publicly recognized. One goal would always lead to another quest. But nothing was ever enough to fill up his inner sense of emptiness.

Secretly, however, Peter never believed his own myth. Low self-esteem and self-doubt plagued him until harsh reality eventually threatened to dismantle his crowning glory, the business for which he had sacrificed his family life. In one of our sessions, Peter went back to search for the roots of his workaholism. He explored the reasons why he never felt involved in what he was experiencing, and why success had left him still feeling numb and empty inside. As he explained, "It goes way back, really. Even when I first got that Industry Achievement Award, I felt like an impostor. It was as if part of me was watching at a distance as I walked across that stage. That award gave me no pleasure. I just couldn't relate to the whole scene." There was a wide split between Peter's experience and his own detachment from it all. Nothing seemed to give him joy.

"Way back," for Peter, was still recent history. What Peter hadn't realized was that the seeds of his detached feelings were deeply planted in early unfulfilling interactions with his self-absorbed but influential father.

THE THIRD GENERATION — ONE FAMILY'S STRUGGLE WITH NARCISSISM

Unfortunately, a similar, potentially tragic dynamic is being played out in Peter and Sally's family. As we have learned, when one child is singled out for special attention and spoiled by a narcissistic parent, that child in the future is also likely to become a narcissistic personality, and so the cycle continues.

Initially, Peter's narcissistic father idealized his son because he saw in him an extension of his own perfection. He had high expectations for Peter, and Peter knew it. In spite of this idealization, his father was so absorbed in his own inner world that he remained emotionally aloof and was a poor listener. His neglect stemmed from a packed, goal-oriented schedule that left him little time alone with Peter. It would never have occurred to him to take Peter to places a child would appreciate. Instead, he would occasionally surprise Peter by taking him to the office on a Saturday morning. He rationalized that it was part of Peter's grooming, to see his father in action, surrounded by pomp and power. He would leave Peter in an empty office to sit and draw while he busied himself with paperwork or talked on the phone. During lunch afterwards in *his* favourite restaurant, he would ask Peter questions initially, but would soon become distracted and lost in thought.

Peter was now overcompensating for the conditional love that left him with unmet emotional needs by giving his youngest daughter special attention. His motivations were rooted in indulgence. He was not going to be accused of neglect.

As I worked with Peter and Sally, it became clear that their marital problems were only the tip of the iceberg. It was Sally who alerted me to this when she was complaining one day that one of her biggest problems was Peter's refusal to discipline the children. Worse still, he didn't support her discipline. This was especially true with their youngest, teenaged daughter, Penny.

Unwittingly, Penny was drawn into her parents' struggle over how they would share personal and parental responsibilities. Peter was ultra-responsible at work, but shunned responsibility at home.

Because he worked such long hours, Sally found herself, by default, in charge of discipline at home. She didn't relish this role at all; being nurturing and supportive were her best traits. Peter hated it when Sally let off steam and complained about the children's behaviour. He always defended the children and played down her real concerns for them. Occasionally, he would promise to speak to one of them, but would never quite get round to it. Some work-related pressure always kept him too busy. Or, more frustrating still, he would tell Sally that he "just forgot."

Sally was becoming increasingly alarmed for Penny. According to Sally's description of events, Peter sometimes behaved like an adolescent boy with Penny. He flirted with her, fussed over her clothes, and would make admiring comments on her appearance as she left for school each day. Sally was surprised at this because Peter never commented on what Sally wore, even if it was new. He would spend time in Penny's room with her, looking through fashion magazines. Penny's door would be closed. If Sally came in, she was made to feel unwelcome. He would cut into conversations Sally and Penny were having, and turn the conversation around to his own views. He would use a seductive tone with Penny but not with the other children.

In turn, Penny could twist Peter around her little finger. Anything she wanted, she got. Peter would drive Penny wherever she wanted to go, and he seemed to take a vicarious delight in hearing about the intimate details of her sometimes stormy relationships. Penny would say quite outrageous things about her friends. Her mother would suggest in negative tones that Penny was being unkind, and Peter would laugh. He seemed to get a kick out of whatever Penny did, good or bad.

This indulgence, seduction, and refusal to discipline, carried to extremes, can be a form of emotional sexual abuse. Sally had every reason to be fearful. Penny's future development would be greatly affected by Peter's inappropriate attentions. The other children would not go unharmed by this either. Peter's son badly needed his father's attention. His other daughter could not help but be affected as she watched her father's obvious devotion to her sister. Her self-esteem and confidence in her own femininity would suffer. Puberty is an especially critical time for a daughter to be emotionally seduced by a father.

Peter initially saw nothing wrong with his actions. He explained to me that when the children were young, he was overinvolved with his work. His career advancement meant everything to him, and, yes, he was away a great deal. In later sessions, Peter was able to admit that he had been jealous of the closeness Sally had with their children. The family had their own routines and schedules, and Sally was orchestrating it all because she was always there, always dependable.

Peter, who was used to being the centre of attention at the office, felt left out. When his business was well-established and prospering, he resolved to plug back into the family and exert his influence. "By the way," he assured me once again, "everything I did at work, I did for my family."

His re-entry into the family occurred when Penny was twelve, a critical stage for her. He began competing for the children's attention by interrupting and then dominating the children's conversations with their mother. If they asked Sally a question, as they were used to doing, Peter would answer. Soon Sally was getting pushed aside and told not to interrupt. Her opinions were trivialized or discredited. The children, too, started to put her down. This sudden attention from their absent father was welcomed.

At puberty, it is normal and natural for the daughter to become critical of what her mother wears, how she speaks, what she does or does not do. A typical complaint might be, "Why don't you wear your hair short like Trina's mother?" Teenagers, as we all know, can be cruel and sometimes quite vicious in their scathing comments.

Healthy Resolution

In a healthy family, the father would understand his daughter's rebellious need to challenge her female role model. This is the way she defines herself and begins the process called individuation — discovering the essence of her Self. At the same time, he will recognize that his present attraction, from his daughter's point of view, lies in her new fascination with the opposite sex. He needs to be sensitive to this and respectful of these early sexual stirrings.

The father should be sensitive to his daughter's vulnerability but remain firm, as well as affectionate and supportive. His most important task is to support his wife through the criticisms and complaints. If the daughter goes overboard, he must intervene and stand up to the daughter's inappropriate challenges. He might say, "I understand that you are upset, and that is okay. However, what's not okay is for you to talk to your mother like that! Would you please apologize right now." He might then explore with his daughter how she might feel if someone spoke to *her* that way.

Her mother, once supported by her husband, will be able to maintain her composure and position of authority. She is firm, but refrains from lashing back emotionally because she remains objective and does not take the criticisms personally. Resolution comes eventually when the daughter makes the connection that "even though I'm obnoxious and miserable, Mother still loves me — I must be okay!" As she learns to accept herself and her own foibles, she comes to terms with her real mother, not the idealized one she longs for. A more equal, adult relationship and appreciation of their differences emerges as the daughter identifies and resolves her own sense of Self and sensuality, separate from her mother.

Family communication is vitally important at such times. If even one family member is upset, all will suffer. The future relationship between mother and daughter hangs on the individuation process following healthy lines.

Unhealthy Resolution

The narcissistic father cares little for what is in the best interest of the child because his own instinctual needs must be satisfied. Like Peter, he neglects to support the mother but sides with the daughter. He wants to be admired, so he takes the girl's side in arguments, laughs at her when she is cheeky or rude, and refuses to discipline her. Instead, he makes excuses for her. Then he tells his wife, "She doesn't mean anything by that. Stop being so childish!"

Unconsciously or not, this husband is using his daughter to punish and dominate his wife. He may be angry because she no longer keeps him up on a pedestal. Like Sally, this wife may have been complaining about her husband's lack of emotional involvement and his overworking. Once the wife does not mirror a positive image for the narcissist, she ceases to be of value. Only he must be in control. Everyone must pay attention to him.

THE PEDESTAL DAUGHTER

"Pedestal daughters" like Penny have too much power in the family. However, underneath their veneer of self-confidence and arrogance lies a deep insecurity. There is a part of Penny that believes she really is "special." Yet another part strives for perfection and is filled with self-doubt. Penny's anxiety takes the form of her becoming obsessive about her school work. She spends an inordinate amount of time studying late into the night. She bites her nails, worrying about her grades.

Unbeknownst to Penny, her anxiety may cover an unconscious fear of incest, and the threat of humiliation and rejection if she should return her father's overtures. When these girls do respond to their father's flirtations, titillating or ambiguous situations may make both father and daughter feel uneasy and anxious. Over time, the daughter's sexual feelings may be repressed, or even disowned, as a result of these unconscious threats.

A pseudo-sexual relationship with her father makes it difficult for a daughter to relate to other males, especially sexually. Her father is idealized and admired. Awkward, self-conscious, bumbling adolescent boys cannot compete with these charming, youthful-looking narcissistic fathers. Young men may ask her out, but her arrogance and disdain throw them off. Often these girls are admired and attractive to boys, but they do not get asked out because they convey a sharp edge or a brittleness. This superiority masks a critical, and often sarcastic, one-up nature. Relationships tend not to last because these girls lack the warmth and nurturing qualities and empathy necessary for true intimacy. Faced with constant rejection, they lose confidence. Some become "boy crazy," trying to find the elusive male who will make them feel desirable and loved.

Linda Leonard, in *The Wounded Woman: Healing the Father–Daughter Relationship,* suggests that a daughter like this sees the "eternal boy" father as someone her own age, someone she can manipulate through his fascination for her. "The daughters of these eternal boys grow up without an adequate model of self-discipline, limit, and authority, quite often suffering from feelings of insecurity, instability, lack of self-confidence, anxiety, frigidity, and in general, a weak ego," (p. 12).

Power and performance become important to these girls because they have identified with the masculine traits of the idealized father. They are cut off from their own feminine instincts because they have devalued the rival mother. As a consequence, the masculine side of their personality develops; the nurturing, gentle side does not. They may "perform" sexually, but are cut off from their own sexual instincts. Daughters who become rivals of their mother for their father's attention are robbed of the normal resolution of the mother–daughter struggle. Without intervention in Penny's family, she will remain stuck at this adolescent stage of development. Her father will remain her White Knight, and everything her Black Mother does will be wrong. Penny will continue to compete with her mother for her father's attention. She will remain out of touch with her feelings and nurturing qualities. Her hard-edged, critical, caustic side will cause trouble in her relationships.

The roles of masculine and feminine, of husband and wife, are skewed in this family. The mother, by default, assumes the role of disciplinarian. She establishes the values, authority, and traditions of the family. Her weak, indulgent husband abdicates his responsibilities in favour of being Mr. Nice Guy. Absolutely no one wins in this human tragedy. Future relationships for girls such as Penny will be deeply affected by their own budding narcissism. Anxiety and obsessive behaviours will signal their confusion around appropriate role models and values.

Tragically, the narcissist's communications may confuse a

child's reality further. Narcissists can be very charming and convincing. Their certainty about being right and their arrogant pronouncements overwhelm the insecure child who is trying to discover truths in the increasingly crazy world the narcissist creates.

The narcissist's children know instinctively that one does not challenge a narcissist without consequences. Narcissists are not good listeners, although this is not readily apparent. They see things in black-and-white, concrete terms, based on their own experience. Often, conversations are turned to their own particular focus. Different ideas go unacknowledged, or are fiercely argued. Remember that in their world two people of differing views cannot both be right. Worse still, if a child disagrees, the narcissist thinks that "the child thinks that he is wrong!" Such an affront cannot go unchallenged. These intolerable games go on endlessly, unless a healthy solution is sought.

THE ACCEPTANCE OF HELP

Knowing when to ask for help is wisdom! Fortunately, it is not too late for Peter and Sally to turn their family around. Peter's business failures and Sally's depression have forced Peter to take stock of where he is headed. After all, he had agreed to come for help, even if the help was "for Sally." Hard-core narcissists rarely agree to treatment, or stay long enough to break through their incredible denial.

Initially, Peter kept aloof in the sessions. He avoided answering questions or voicing his opinion unless asked directly. He waited for Sally to speak, and then would twist her words around until he looked good and Sally bad. His diabolical laugh at such times was chilling. Sally would cringe, as if struck. No wonder she was afraid of him.

Very slowly, Peter became fascinated with the process of self-discovery, and eventually the sessions became a priority in his week. The fact that he was emotionally crippled had never dawned on him. He challenged himself to take the journey because he still had enough insight to realize that his family was in serious trouble. His perfect persona didn't include a separation or divorce. He did "love" his family, although he really didn't know what real love was.

Even though he did make the commitment to recovery, getting in touch with his feelings was an uphill struggle. For example, one day I asked Peter whether he was interesting and fun to be with at home. He looked annoyed. When I explored the joylessness between the couple, Peter replied that he could certainly relate to a story I told about a wife who had complained that as soon as she and her husband married, he stopped taking her out or even talking to her. Peter's comment was chilling: "As soon as we got married, I no longer had to fight for Sally. I had conquered her, and she was no longer available to anyone else!" Then he added, "I got my mind back to business, and she ceased to be a priority."

Although Sally looked visibly shaken that day, Peter was telling the truth. As yet, he had little awareness of the impact of his words. When I asked him the following week about his reaction to the previous session, he told me that his mind went blank on the way home. He couldn't listen to the radio or talk to Sally. He was numb and couldn't remember anything that had gone on in the session.

When I reminded him of what he had said the week before, Peter looked sheepish and remarked, "That's not very nice, is it?"

Although the dyad in this story is an unhealthy relationship between a father and his daughter that also affects the marital relationship, other triangles can also form when one parent is narcissistic. A narcissistic mother can be overly involved with a son or daughter, and freeze out her husband. Or a narcissistic father can be connected to a son in an exclusive relationship that leaves the mother out of their interaction.

Starting the Journey

By now, you will have some idea about whether depression, anxiety, or narcissism is presently signalling that your feeling side is shut down.

It is now time to begin the three-stage journey that teaches people to Internalize — a process I have developed to help individuals rediscover their feelings and to learn how to problem-solve effectively.

Chapter 7 describes how to become aware of the signals your body is sending to alert you to shifts or changes in your feelings and emotions, how to process and interpret this information (Justification), and how to feel the feeling, stay with it, and experience it fully (Experiencing). Finally, a review of defense mechanisms reveals the different ways people react when feelings escalate to a stressful level.

7
The Journey — Stage 1, Awareness

Learn to Internalize Your Feelings

*Changing attitude is relatively easy;
changing behaviour is not!*

I SEE YOU, I HEAR YOU

Imagine that you are sitting in my office. Your feelings are flat, and you're not too sure just how you feel at this moment.

You may have been the "good kid" in your family. You always fit in, performed well at school, and rarely rebelled, except maybe to skip a few classes or smoke behind the garage. Or perhaps you grew up in the midst of the family's Battle of Waterloo. You're not sure if anyone actually won any of the skirmishes, but you do know that you "run for the hills" and hide if anyone starts up with you.

Or perhaps you were a "seen-but-not-heard," shy child who was left out of a lot of things, like conversations. People around you were too busy to notice what you were feeling or doing, for that matter.

Or perhaps you are a Feeler who grew up in a family of Thinkers who either didn't listen, or if they did, would often distort what you said beyond recognition. "Don't I speak loudly enough?" you wondered.

Whatever the reason your feelings have been squashed, ignored, or discounted, the following techniques can transform your world!

Peter's journey through this process was difficult because he was a strong Thinker. At first, he always had to *think* about how he felt. Later his feeling became more independent, and the translation process became less necessary. Sally, a natural Feeler, quickly restored her Feeling function. Her adventure was to encourage her positive Thinking function so that it became more autonomous and effective.

ANGER, YES, BUT WHAT ARE THESE OTHER FEELINGS CALLED?

Our goal is to know immediately how we feel, at any given moment. We want to be in enough control that we can decide when it is best to act on our feelings, and when it is best to delay action. In either case, it is important to be fully responsible, to act out of wisdom and empathy.

Feeling, as distinct from the complex called emotion or affect, is the way we subjectively decide the value of something or someone to us. It is a way of making decisions and problem-solving. It is rational, unless it becomes coloured by emotion. When an emotion is activated by strong feelings, it tends to distort the other functions. For example, people can't think clearly when they are upset, or their feeling about a situation is coloured by a dark mood.

Emotions vary according to the *intensity* of feeling. Anger may range from mild irritation to violent rage. As intensity increases, the danger is that the emotion, be it positive or negative, may capture us within its grip. Various levels of tension are created that either cause us to act out our emotions or allow us to quietly experience our feelings without the need or desire to take action.

Feelings vary according to *quality* on a continuum from pleasant to unpleasant. The intensity of the feeling will affect its tone and determine how it will be perceived. Fierce rage is distinctly unpleasant for all involved, while the titillating fear of a roller-coaster ride may well feel pleasurable.

We are going to attempt here to get in touch with the major broad feelings: happy–sad; love–hate; warm–cold; admiration–jealousy; joy–grief; pride–shame, and so on. The four negative feelings of anger, anxiety, fear, and pain will be treated separately. Under their influence, we become emotional and tend to lose control more quickly, and often harm ourselves and others.

A high degree of tension is associated with these four primary feelings because the situations that evoke them are intimately involved with goal-striving activity. Although the essential condition for arousing *anger* is the blocking of goal attainment, *fear* can become an emotion of avoidance. We wish to keep power and to be competent when handling a threatening situation, yet we fear "losing it." One can name a fear, as in "I'm afraid of the bear," or "I'm terrified that I'll fail my exam!"

Anxiety, on the other hand, is fed from a number of sources, some of which are conscious, but many of which remain repressed. Anxiety is amorphous, free-floating, and thus more difficult to pinpoint. *Pain* is a complex subject, but at high levels of intensity, we experience acute emotional agitation and muscle spasms. Sometimes pain is referred from other locations. What we call heartburn, for example, is actually an irritant located in the digestive tract. There are also strong differences in how people handle pain, based on age, life experience, psychological and personality factors, social class, ethnic group, and so on.

The sooner we recognize these four feelings, the less intense our reactions will often be. Full control is possible only up to the point where our defense mechanisms come into play. Remember, the role of our defenses is to cover, compensate for, or block negative emotions.

THE PROCESS OF EXTERNALIZING

Before I can teach you to *internalize* your feelings, it is helpful to

understand what you presently do when you process information. Most people I see in my practice have learned to *externalize*
their feelings. When something happens, they go into their thinking mode, and figure out how to react by second-guessing what
the other person wants them to say, think, do, or feel. It's smart
and adaptive in a dysfunctional family to say what others want to
hear and do what others, especially parents, want them to do.
They learn to anticipate, and eventually to manipulate others to
gain some advantage, some power over their own destiny. They are
survivors, or at least they try to be.

Unfortunately, by doing this, they learn to *react,* rather than
to remain independent from what is happening around them. By
reacting, they short-circuit their own feelings. Feelings, when
they remain largely repressed, work slowly, if at all. These people
realize they are angry five minutes later, an hour or two later, or
even the next day. At that point, it is necessary to go backwards in
time to problem-solve.

Retreating typically spells trouble. Here is Vivian explaining
her reactions after-the-fact to her sister Francine: "Francine, remember when you told me about what Aunt Lillian said at that party
the other day? How she never phones you any more, and how
you're writing her off?" (Remember, this version of the story is
Vivian's "*projection*" of Francine's experience.) Vivian recalls all the
feelings this conversation stirred up in her. At first, she felt a mixture of skepticism and criticism towards her sister, then she felt
concern for her aunt. But now, a bubbling anger is surfacing, which
startles Vivian. Her somewhat irrational but invasive response follows: "Well, Francine, I don't know why you expect to hear from
Aunt Lil when you don't even bother to phone your own sister!"

At this point, all hell breaks loose, because Vivian's adaptation of what her sister initially said doesn't jibe with Francine's
recollection at all. Francine proceeds to set her straight about
what she actually said. Tempers flare. Soon the bickering escalates
to a level at which both women are shouting to make themselves
heard. What has made Vivian furious is Francine's distortion of
her own words. (Let's call this projection number 2.)

Sooner or later Vivian learns, usually after many unhappy experiences, that it is best not to try to solve problems with her sister. "Things will only get worse if I say anything," she concludes. So, guess what? For the sake of harmony, she rationalizes, it is best to do nothing! Instead, she becomes passive-aggressive. She blocks her feelings, and blithely lets troublesome conversations flow by her. She ceases to react, at least visibly, and eventually even to listen.

Unfortunately, all those pent-up feelings one day explode like firecrackers on the Fourth of July! She and Francine pitch their flags and have a rumble.

"I've had it up to here with your selfishness!" Vivian bursts out. "You expect everyone to run circles around *you*. Well, I for one am giving you notice! I have no intention of stooping to that level!"

Stress always results when unresolved feelings lurk just below the surface, waiting to explode. Excess adrenalin is produced to fuel any arousal state, but anger is especially lethal. As our bodies prepare for "fight or flight," our blood pressure rises because the heart is forced to work harder to keep on the alert. Our blood cholesterol level also climbs above normal. As well, there is an increase in acid secretion because the body demands extra blood to provide food as well as the extra energy needed to perform when, or if, it becomes necessary. Increased muscle tension in all parts of the body takes its heavy toll. Our head aches, our back becomes stiff, frozen rigid from ongoing fear as this state of arousal becomes too frequent a visitor. Sleep becomes increasingly disturbed and fitful if stress is prolonged.

Problems, unfortunately, don't seem to disappear after "fight or flight" warfare. People who externalize have a lot of "unfinished business." They also tend to be worry-warts, and to fuss endlessly about past or future events. They are like chameleons, reflecting back whatever is going on around them. These *reactors* are affected by the weather, other people's moods, and what people think about them. They have no centre, and are forever shifting, blown by the current wind. Unwittingly, they have given over their power to others.

What to do instead becomes the big question. Learning to do the opposite, to *internalize,* will not be an easy task. Habits die hard. Be patient. Your hard work will help the narrow band of feelings you now live in to expand until you are able to respond with pure joy when it is appropriate, and with sorrow when life's circumstances send grief your way. Instead of walking through life like a zombie, you will *experience* every person and situation fully.

THE PROCESS OF INTERNALIZING — AN ILLUSTRATION

I am now going to explain this process called *internalizing.* But first, let me tell a story. Each part of the story represents a step in the process.

Step 1 — Identification
One Monday morning I woke up feeling "yucky," out of sorts, but not knowing why. Since it was only 6:45 a.m., I couldn't figure out what was wrong.

Normally, I would ask myself three questions: (1) What has just happened? (2) Who said what? and (3) Exactly what am I reacting to in this situation? But since it was close to dawn and my day had not yet begun, I asked a fourth question: What did I dream that still might be affecting me? I remember my dreams well, but there was nothing in my dreams that night that had upset me.

I started to make breakfast for everyone and promptly forgot about my feelings. A half-hour later, alone at the table, I suddenly noticed how I was sitting. I was bent over; I felt very heavy, and I was aware of tears welling up in my eyes. Over the years, I have become aware that this is how I react when I am sad. (By the way, you will have your own unique combination of reactions to sadness.) With this recognition came a flash of insight!

Step 2 — Justification
As soon as I was aware of my own sadness, I recalled a picture from the night before of my daughter's face, looking sad. Then I

remembered. On Sunday night, as I was bustling around the kitchen, getting dinner ready for some guests, one of my daughters entered the kitchen with a long, sad face. She was upset and wanted to talk.

My hurried response was, "Sweetie, would you mind sitting on the stool here so we can talk while I'm finishing this salad?" I was listening, albeit going from cutting board, to fridge, and back several times. The door-bell rang, and I went out to the hall to greet our guests, who had arrived a half-hour early. Somewhat frazzled, I forgot completely about my daughter back in the kitchen.

Not my version of being a good mother! The choice between getting dinner ready on time or listening to someone who is upset is usually not a hard one. The guests' early arrival apparently jumbled my priorities, and this present disappointment with myself was a delayed reaction.

My sadness had another source, however. A close friend was dying of cancer, and three years before she had asked me to go through her death with her. Time was ebbing away for her, and death was imminent. This present experience was a further reminder that it was time to begin the process of grieving.

Step 3 — Experiencing

Now that I had justified two valid reasons for being sad, I gave myself "permission" to be thoroughly sad.

I needed time to work through my present feelings and anticipate the future loss of my friend. On days that I went to work, I'd try to make sure that my clients left on time, that I had a few minutes between sessions. Also, at lunch break, I'd decide whether I felt like going for a walk or wished to be pampered with a large pot of tea and comfortable service. I'd choose a quiet restaurant and just relax. I'd let my thoughts run through the mixture of feelings I was experiencing as a result of these insights.

If I was not feeling better by evening, I might decide to stay home and have a "peace-and-quiet" evening. Accordingly, plans to go to a meeting or movie had to be changed. Instead, I'd relax, take a long bath, and go to bed early. Emotions can be draining and fatiguing. It's taxing to remain effective at work when personal issues demand your attention.

On days when I wrote and didn't go in to the office, I would lower my expectations about what I hoped to achieve. I would take time to feel my sadness. In the background, I might play quiet classical music to fit my mood.

After I had worked through these feelings and made some decisions about what I intended to do as a result of my insights, I didn't have to stay there any more. I was now ready to *let go* of my sadness.

Step 4 — Problem-Solving

Only at this point could I take action to resolve my problems. There was no use trying to rectify the situation while I was self-absorbed, felt empty, and had nothing to give.

When I'd worked through my feelings, and my energy had returned, I sought out my daughter and apologized for my thoughtlessness. I asked her if we could talk some more now that we were both free from interruptions. I also phoned my friend at the hospital and asked her what was going on there today. I was now more able to be supportive and sensitive to others.

This whole process forms a Gestalt, a finished package. However, even though I'd let go of my sadness and tried to make up for my shortcomings, there was still some unfinished business. I wanted to learn from my mistakes.

Step 5 — Seeking Wisdom

Sometimes we learn from others, and sometimes others learn from us. When a number of things are making me anxious, I imagine each one as a building block, similar to the ones we played with as children. In my mind, I pile each stressor on top of another and ask this question: "Of all these problems, which can be resolved *only by me*? And which absolutely *has* to be done *today*?

Then I do the one or two things that are best done immediately. Taking action, however small, usually eases distress. Problem-solving brings a sense of accomplishment and raises self-esteem.

I know from experience that other tasks are better left until another day when I'm feeling more "up." With added energy and clear thinking, I will be much more effective. When drained of all energy, people tend to feel defeated and helpless. And hopelessness, by the way, feeds depressive feelings.

Remember, doing things poorly, in a rush, or under excess pressure, is rarely wise or efficient!

HOW DOES THE PROCESS OF INTERNALIZING WORK?

Within this story lies the process you will follow to begin to *Internalize.*

Step 1 — Identification
What you feel depends on what is happening in your body. To cue into your feelings, you must *first* become aware of all the nerve endings and muscles in your body that react automatically to your mental and physical environment. Information from the nerves and muscles is relayed to the brain. If you are fully aware and connected to your body, you will be alert and able to respond with sensitivity, or to experience anger, whatever is appropriate to the situation. You may choose to take corrective action at the time of awareness or to delay resolution until a more appropriate occasion.

1–1. Awareness
You'll notice from the story that I suddenly became aware of my feelings of sadness at the kitchen table, some time after discovering that something was not right with me. Insight came only when I recognized that I was bent over, feeling heavy, and slightly teary.

Three distinct channels brought sadness into my awareness: a change in physiology (teariness), a change in energy level (heaviness), and a change in body position (bent over). Let's explore each channel in more depth.

1–2. Physiological Change

Physiological changes are complex and varied. They are not only unique to each individual; they may also be specific to each person's experience of that time or place. External influences — such as unusual situations, others' reactions or moods, or even the weather — may affect these changes.

Clients often tell me that their first warning of anxiety is a tightness of the muscles in their stomach. For others, it is an acidic taste from bile secretions. Some people notice their shoulder muscles tensing, hunching up towards the neck. Others reveal anxiety by fidgeting, or talking with their hands, or biting their nails, and so on. What are your signs? Do you jiggle your foot? Are your ankles or upper thighs tense? If so, are your legs tightly crossed? Do you feel tension in your arms? Are you, by any chance, folding your arms across your chest, restricting your breathing as well? Is your forehead creased in a frown, or is there pressure behind the eyebrows, or at the sides of your temple? Do you have a permanent frown line etched between your brows?

The jaw and chest areas are especially important because breathing becomes restricted here. How does this happen? A tensed muscle is short and fattish. A relaxed muscle lies flat and is more elongated. As anxiety escalates, tense muscles create a constriction in the air passageway. Listen to your voice. Like a pitch pipe, its tone will rise as you grow more upset. Constricted breathing means that much-needed oxygen is cut off from the brain. One cannot think. When people say they are confused, what is often happening is that their brain is cut off from oxygen, its life source.

Is your jaw tight, or are your lips pursed? If you experience any pressure in the chest area, chances are that the muscles surrounding the trachea and oesophagus are also tight. Can you feel any constriction in your throat? Is your voice higher than normal? Or has "normal" for you become a high, squeaky tone?

I've noticed combinations in my own reactions to stress. When I'm fatigued towards the end of a busy workday, even ordinary background noise suddenly becomes annoying. At the same time, I'm aware that my right ankle is bent upwards, signalling excess tension in my right leg. Typically, I've discovered that this means that my shoulders also are hunched up. These insights make it possible to rotate my ankles, and at the same time, do relaxation exercises for the tension in my shoulders. I can also turn off the radio playing background music in the waiting room. Usually, I don't even hear it.

If you recognize ankle and/or neck stress, take a moment to try this: Hang your arms at the sides of your chair, and let your head fall forward towards your chin. Imagine there is a great weight attached to your wrists that is pulling down, making your arms feel heavier and heavier. Continue until you experience a tingling in your fingers. Feel the muscles across your back and shoulders now. Are they stretching out and elongating? If so, keep your arms hanging at your side, but raise your head, and let the relaxation continue to spread. To release ankle tension, rotate your ankle at the same time. This way, you are reducing the damage done to both areas simultaneously.

Incidentally, any time you are aware of fatigue, slow down! While you are working, take a long, deep breath, then extend your exhale slightly longer than usual. The next breath will be slightly deeper. Only through awareness of your physiological reactions is an immediate remedy possible.

For each of the major emotions, try to zero in on *where* you feel muscle tension, and which nerves are signalling distress.

1–3. Energy Level
This one is relatively simple.

Heaviness describes a decrease in adrenalin that occurs during sadness or depression. At such times, there is a change in the chemical reaction in the synapse, the space between the body cells. Here the dendrites, the receptor membrane of a neuron, receive stimulation, and the axons conduct nervous impulses away to produce activity in the distant parts of the organism, where it may stimulate other nerves, muscles, or glands. The electrical charge flowing through the body cells is slowed down as it hits the changed chemical reaction in the synapse, so we feel sluggish. When people are depressed, they move their eyes more slowly, speak with more hesitation. Their reflexes are slow, and their co-ordination is affected. Their digestive system churns, and they often become constipated. *Everything* moves more slowly.

Lightness describes an increase in adrenalin. When "fight or flight" responses are appropriate, the adrenal glands work over-time, digestion is speeded up, and other hormones are released into the bloodstream. The heart adjusts to an "emergency" by changes in rate, force, and contractions. As A. Hart points out in *Adrenalin and Stress,* the heart has "no direct connection to the ner-vous system to receive signals from the brain, but it is designed to respond to signals from the complex chemical messengers circu-lating in the blood — including the adrenalin hormones." Unfor-tunately, over time the same messengers, when out of balance, can literally destroy the heart (p. 16).

Remember that stress can be hidden. We adapt to situations that are harmful to us. What's more, good things are also stressful. We may feel excited by our work, and be happiest when chal-lenged. Or we may become excited when faced with a crisis or emergency in our latest project. Yet despite this gratification, we may still experience panic reactions, irregular heartbeat, ulcers, or high blood pressure. The heart does not acknowledge the differ-ence between "good" and "bad" stress; it responds only to the excess of adrenalin.

When you experience a strong emotion, ask yourself if your adrenalin is up or down. Do you feel heavy or light?

1–4. Body Position

Body language is complex. When you feel assertive or angry, do you lean or move forward? When on the defensive, do you sit back or withdraw physically from the situation? When anxious or agi-tated, do you tend to become restless, get up and down frequently, or move around in your chair? Do you tap your feet, or drum your hands on the desk? Do you go to the washroom more frequently? Do you look down and slump forward when you are sad or discouraged? Do you cross your arms and legs to protect yourself?

One day one of my workaholic clients, an ambitious executive, was sitting slumped in his chair. His head was resting on his chest, and he was staring at the floor. I asked him to freeze, and then imitated him. After a few moments, I commented, "I can hardly breath now, can you? I have a suspicion that part of you doesn't want to be here!" Gordon laughed and told me he had no idea he was sitting like that. This gave us a chance to discuss whether he was here for himself or to please his wife. He was used to being in charge, and being in a "learning" position was not easy for him, he admitted.

When I was writing my book on workaholics, I wrote only on Mondays. Each week I found it hard to get back to where I was the week before. I could tell I was anxious because I would start to write, and then suddenly remember that I hadn't checked in with my answering service. I would start to write again, and then remember that I needed to put the wash in the drier.

At this point, I would toss my pencil above my head and then make a wide sweeping circle with my arms. This motion served to open up my chest area so that I could breathe properly once again.

Circles plug us into the nurturing, feeling side of ourselves. Thinking, which is goal-oriented and goes from A to B, is represented by straight lines! Pretending you are conducting a symphony when you are upset isn't such a bad idea.

Make notes to record the information you are gradually discovering about yourself. It's like detective work! Try to become aware of your body position when you are aware of a shift in emotion. Note physiological changes and your energy level for each feeling. Later on, this information will jump to your attention and be recorded in your mind automatically.

1–5. Labelling

By labelling, I mean identifying feelings. Sometimes we recognize our body's reactions, but we don't know the name of the feeling. At other times, we know the label, but have to work backwards from there to become aware of our typical reactions.

Jenny, a social worker, told me that she knew when she was angry. "This is ridiculous. No one has to tell me I'm angry!" When I asked her what was happening inside physiologically when she was angry, she admitted, "Well, I don't know that!" I suggested that the next time she found herself angry, she pay attention to see if she could figure it out.

The following week, she burst into my office and said with glee, "Guess what I found out about myself this week? The other day, I was *really* angry. I found myself turning purple. My fingers dug into the palm of my hand, and I locked my jaw. I could even hear my teeth click!" Then she looked surprised. "I never knew I did that." Later, we'll find out what was happening in Jenny's life when she gained this insight.

1–6. Achilles' Heels

Watch for situations that typically trigger certain feelings. In other words, learn which situations tap into your weaknesses or sore points. If you start to problem-solve right away, this will help reduce your stress. Quick action will make the situation easier to handle.

Let's say your father was a perfectionist, and he criticized you unmercifully when you were growing up. Your stress level around criticism is apt to be sky-high, and you may need to react sooner than others when you face *any* criticism. Say, for example, that someone has just reprimanded you, and is about to continue. You need to intervene. "I don't handle criticism that well." (You don't need to burden the listener with the Family Saga.) You might add, "I'll think about what you just said, and get back to you. We can discuss it further then."

If the other person respects your vulnerability, he or she will stop. If not, you may have to take a stronger stand. "I don't think you understand my position. I'm leaving now, but I would like to continue this discussion when I feel calm and able to listen."

1–7. Homework

"How can I get in touch with my physiological changes, my energy level, and my body position, all at the same time?" you might ask.

Try this exercise daily until it becomes a natural process. At least six or eight times a day, stop and ask yourself these questions: How do I feel *right now*? What do I call this feeling? Where is my body reacting? What muscles or nerves are sending messages letting me know about this feeling? Has my body position just changed? Am I sitting, standing, or moving?

You will tend to remember to do this when there has just been a shift or change in emotion. Our minds process information in a steady stream. Unless there is a shift of topic or stimulus, there is little reason for awareness to shift.

Step 2 — Justification

As soon as you can identify and name the feeling, it is time for some reality-testing. Ask yourself, "Is this emotion a valid one, considering what is going on? If not, where did it come from? And is it a healthy response considering the situation?

It is important to explore what is going on at a conscious level, and further, what may be arousing the emotion from a deeper, unconscious level.

2–1. Conscious Data

Reflect on what is happening in your immediate experience that might have triggered the identified feeling?

Ask yourself:

1. What just happened?
2. Who said what?
3. What exactly am I reacting to in this situation?
4. What did I dream last night that still might be affecting me?
5. Am I overreacting or acting impulsively because of a layering of old feelings over present ones?

Remember to search for information from your day, as well as "unfinished business" from the past few days or weeks — or sometimes even years, right back to childhood if necessary. Stories often have long histories! In my story, there were two justifications for my feelings of sadness. One was the incident from the night before involving my daughter. The other was the impending death of a close friend.

Let me relate another personal example. This time the experience occurred on the same day as my recognition of it. One day, about eight years ago, I was returning from a dental appointment, and was stopped at a traffic light near a McDonald's outlet. A little old lady dressed in layers of beige-coloured clothing was going through the garbage bin. Her threadbare coat with its frayed hem covered bulky sweaters and a woollen dirndl skirt. A tired green scarf was wound round her neck. Her wizened face was framed by a lopsided bonnet tied around her chin, and she wore wire-framed spectacles. I can still feel the pathos as I watched her fumbling deep inside the waste bin for what seemed like forever. Her grocery bags were propped up against the bin. Was she looking for discarded hamburger, cigarette butts, or half-eaten buns?

I had observed street people in New York, but this was the first I had seen in our neighbourhood. I was naturally upset by what I saw. As I drove back to my office, I wondered where she slept, where her family was, and how circumstances had led her to this.

Back at the office, I got involved with clients and forgot all about her. That is, until my five o'clock client was late. For no apparent reason, I suddenly felt overwhelmed. What in the world was troubling me? The sessions had gone well, and there had been no telephone interruptions. All at once I "saw" her, and through association, figured out that my feelings of pathos needed to be dealt with further. I needed to learn a lot more about people like her, and what was being done for them in our community.

Awareness after-the-fact occurs because immediate problems take first priority on our energy. The mind has a way of determining priority and ordering our experiences, temporarily submerging troublesome information until it finally resurfaces during a lull in activity.

2–2. How the Mind Stores Information
The next step, which involves getting in touch with information

about feelings from the unconscious, is not an easy one. At this point, let's digress a moment.

The mind stores information in bits and pieces. The corner of the desk in my office, for example, has a number attributes — it is triangular-shaped, grey-coloured, made from Formica, one-inch thick, and it is called a desk top. The mind gathers all this information and stores it separately, and as a whole. To retrieve a person's face from memory, a number of facial features must be recalled. Often, we remember that someone's name starts with an S, but we must wait until further information clicks into place. Then we might recall that the person's name is Shelley. A poet, a writer, or the name Percy may have been the association needed to provide us with the clue, the missing piece.

W. Kintsch, in *Learning, Memory, and Conceptual Processes,* reports that D. O. Hebb, a researcher interested in learning and behaviour, postulated two kinds of memory. Long-term memory is "based upon a structural trace and is permanent except for interference from other long-term traces; and short-term memory, based upon an activity trace" (p. 146). Information that is rehearsed out loud for more than sixty seconds goes into long-term memory, and its capacity is essentially unlimited. Forgetting is relatively slow and, according to Kintsch, takes two forms: "actual loss of information and inability to retrieve information which is nevertheless still in storage" (p. 142).

Short-term or trace memory, Kintsch further explains, is the information we remember, like a seven-digit telephone number, that fades within fifteen to twenty seconds. This memory has a limited capacity, "although it may be retained in primary memory for more extended periods through rehearsal." Obviously, the more easily one learns to repress information, the more difficult it becomes to retrieve this unconscious memory.

Much of our memory does lie within the unconscious, and our psychological growth often depends on uncovering such repressed information, both from early childhood and from the recent past. Only then may we gain the insights necessary to transform unhealthy thoughts and actions into mature and positive behaviour.

In the 1950s, Wilder Penfield, a brain surgeon in Montreal, stimulated the brains of his patients during surgery in order to determine what functions the various parts of the brain perform. He was able to map correspondences between areas on the surface of the cortex and subjective experiences. A. Lazerson, in *Psychology Today: An Introduction,* describes one finding. By "applying a tiny electric current to points on the temporal lobe of the cerebral cortex: One woman heard a familiar song so clearly that she thought a record was played in the operating room" (p. 315).

I remember hearing about an investigation in which one lobe of the brain was triggered during surgery. The patient had a memory of a picnic many years before. This person apparently could smell the food at the picnic, feel the sun, hear the birds, and remember conversations he had had with classmates whom he had not seen for years.

This type of research led to the "computer" theory of memory. Up until then, researchers had no idea of the scope of information stored in the unconscious. As a student, I remember being delighted to learn that all I had to do was figure out how to retrieve that information through the processes of association and/or recall. In association, an object or person is linked to another through mental connections or bonds between ideas, memories, or sensations. In recall, stored information that we have learned or experienced in the past is retrieved or remembered at will.

2–3. Unconscious Memories

In order to understand our feelings, we need to sort out what we are bringing in from the past, as distinct from what is actually happening in the present. It is important to look for layering of old feelings over present ones. When a couple fight over money, for example, it is likely that residual emotions from past quarrels will flood up and colour their present feelings.

Imagine you have just met someone who makes you feel anxious, although you're only mildly aware of this. Your conversation is going well, but suddenly this fellow says something sarcastic, and you find yourself overreacting like crazy. An overreaction to a situation or to a person is often a signal that the unconscious is working overtime. At this moment, you realize that this man looks like a kid in your Grade 6 class who used to hammer you with sarcastic, stinging comments. He is not that person, however, and you have reacted out of all proportion to what is actually going on.

If you are able to recognize this association immediately, you can take responsibility for your inappropriate response. You might explain to the man that he just happens to resemble an old school chum, who, by coincidence, also used sarcasm to your discomfort. "I guess you triggered some ghosts there. I apologize," you might add.

Jenny, a client mentioned earlier, whom I'd asked to monitor her responses when she became angry, gave me a wonderful example of the unconscious at work. After completing high school, she had gone across the country to attend university. During her second year, she fell in love with her university professor. They married after her graduation, and things went well until she decided to return to university to get a master's degree. This training helped Jenny develop her own thinking and professional expertise, and she became more vocal about her own opinions and creative ideas. Concurrently, she also became more assertive about the need for her husband, Simon, to help her around the house.

The marriage eventually did not survive the tensions that Simon's scathing criticisms and punishing behaviour created between them. Jenny returned to her parents' home to rest and recharge; her self-esteem was badly shaken by the experience. She told me she had written to Simon requesting that he send on her belongings. What arrived one day on a truck, c.o.d., was all her books; the long, heavy boards from her bookcase; and the bricks that propped up the shelves. Nothing else — no records, clothes, make-up, knickknacks. A very angry statement from Simon, it appeared. She was absolutely furious!

Jenny recalled that she didn't sleep very well that night, so she got up about five a.m. and went downstairs to her parents' den. "I walked through the door, and all of a sudden, I felt extreme anger. At the time, I had no idea *why* I was angry. Then I remembered you suggesting that the next time I felt angry, I take some time to learn about myself."

Jenny continued, "I sat myself down. As I did this, a book on the couch caught my eye. It must have been from the pile of books that arrived the day before. Maybe Mom or Dad had been reading it." When she entered the room a few minutes earlier, Jenny had not "seen" the book because she was lost in her own thoughts. However, her brain "saw" it, and through association, registered the rage left over from her experience the previous day with the van delivery.

It was only after Jenny actually "saw" the book that she was able to locate the source of her present anger. Her response made perfect sense now. As Jenny put it, "It's frustrating that it takes me so long to understand my reactions! But hopefully, if I figure out this Internalizing, I just might clue in earlier."

The sooner after the event that the association or recall takes place, the quicker the recognition. There may then be time to find solutions while the other person is still present, or the event is still taking place.

2–4. Establishing the Level of Feeling

When exploring whether your feelings are appropriate, it helps to imagine the feeling (for instance, sadness) on a perpendicular line. To the left of this line, there is a stress curve running on a 45-degree angle to the top. The top is the point at which your defenses take over.

You can handle moderate levels of sadness with little obvious discomfort. However, both ends of the stress curve cause equal discomfort. The lower end — not being able to express sadness — is stressful. (Have you ever attended a funeral and worried that you might sob uncontrollably if you let yourself go? Instead, you force yourself to tune out of the service, to think about something else, just to get through it. You may manage to block your sadness, but this effort will take its toll on your energy.)

Near the upper range of the curve, your sadness level is elevated

ESTABLISHING THE LEVEL OF FEELING

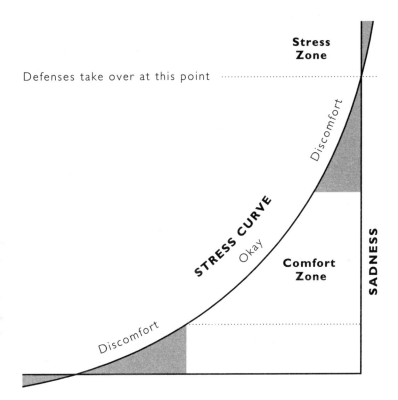

to the point that you are obviously experiencing discomfort, and even pain. Your eyes may be filling up with tears, or you may be experiencing a choking sensation.

2–5. Sounding the Alarm

The crucial question to ask at this point in the internalizing process is, am I still comfortable with what is going on, or am I becoming overstressed?

I know when I'm not okay because I get a "jiggly" or agitated feeling, and I can't sit still. I call this sensation "uncomfortable," and it is a signal that I must problem-solve right away. Otherwise, my defenses will mobilize and complicate or block my ability to seek solutions. Words such as irritated, perturbed, antsy, or "hyper" may best describe your distress signal.

Before you are able to problem-solve, however, there is one more step. You have to *feel* your emotion.

Step 3 — Experiencing

When we fail to do our best, or we lose something of value, or things don't go our way, we suffer mini-losses. Our response to these losses I call "mini-grieving." Such a response is usually of relatively short duration.

Major losses may result from the death of someone close to us, the break-up of a relationship, an illness or accident, or the loss of a job. Whatever the reason, time and energy must be devoted to working through and grieving that loss, however long it takes.

We must *feel the feeling* once we identify what it is, *stay with it,* and allow ourselves to experience the emotion. And we must take the time to work through what we are experiencing. Remember, from the original story, how once I recognized that I was feeling sad, I plugged into that sadness and fully experienced it. Those fearful of "going down" will bang pots and pans instead, or distract themselves by jumping on their personal "Gerbil Wheel," and running themselves ragged. Or they will sit comatose in front of the TV and give in to their despair. They can't think, they don't feel, so no solutions surface in their consciousness.

One of my clients, Dino, told me that one day he found himself going downstairs when it suddenly hit him how anxious he was. "I sat down on the middle stair, then and there. For the next few minutes, I stayed put and pondered all the reasons I had for being anxious." Then he grinned. "I felt like a kid discovering what was in Pandora's box! And surprisingly, at least to me," he added, "the stuff I came up with wasn't all that bad!"

People who are prone to severe depression are often terrified of letting themselves go down into painful feelings. Who is going to pull them back up if they sink? Ironically, when I accompany a client by listening to his or her painful story, offering empathy along the way, and agreeing that things are pretty bad, something remarkable happens. The person starts to tell me why *everything* isn't terrible. Some story about a positive event typically emerges in their consciousness. Once this has happened enough times, people realize that they can pull themselves back from the brink of despair. Suddenly, these awful moments don't last quite as long. And they don't happen so often!

This sorting-out process takes time and energy, and therefore drains your resources temporarily. Often the solution is to *simplify, simplify, simplify.* Lower your expectations about what you hope to achieve that day. Make sure you get extra rest and relaxation time to sustain your strength.

3–1. Nurture Yourself

Stay alert, and let your favourite sense, be it sight, sound, touch, or smell, fill you up. If you like music, play your favourite tape. If you love colour, leaf through one of your treasured art books. Or step outside and watch the clouds drift by, and observe the interaction between sky and earth. Take time to smell the flowers and the freshness of the air.

At this point I often use humour to improve my disposition. One morning last fall I was stopped at a red light on my way to work. Two cute twin girls, about eight years old, with pig-tails hanging down their backs, were crossing the street in front of my car. I noticed that around each twin's waist was a bright red skipping rope, which effectively tied them together. The twin in front looked to be in charge of these antics. I watched as they waited to cross at the light to head for school, and wondered if the same little imp would take the "lead." Sure enough, she did, and away they marched.

As I continued my journey, I entertained myself wondering if being twins motivated these girls to play this amusing game. My mind wandered to a radio program my sister and I listened to as children. "Happy Hank" told us when to put on our panties, undershirts, skirts, blouses, socks, and shoes, every morning! I laughed as

I contemplated whether Happy Hank would survive our modern-day censorship. The poor guy would probably get arrested!

As I neared the office, I thought I saw what looked like two workmen playing patty-cake! Drawing closer, I realized the men were installing fence posts. Each was pushing back against the drill handle as it came round to his side. By the time I got to the office, my "mood" had dissolved into amusement.

If you share this muse, you can go out onto the streets at any time of the day or night, and play with what is happening before your eyes. It's a wonderful gift to help you lighten up.

3–2. Exceptions to Staying with Your Feelings

It was mentioned earlier that there are four negative feelings that will be dealt with separately. Don't stay in the Big Four — Anger, Anxiety, Fear, and Pain. These feelings quickly escalate, and before you know it, you will exceed your stress limit, and lose control. Try this exercise: Divide a piece of paper into four squares, and at each quadrant's upper left-hand corner, write l. Anger, 2. Anxiety, 3. Fear, and 4. Pain, respectively. Then, as you monitor your feelings throughout each day, record your reactions.

You may discover, for instance, that your physiological responses to anger are among the following:

- I bite my nails.
- My stomach tightens and feels cramped.
- My forehead creases as I frown, and so on.

Your energy level will be up, activated by a surge of adrenalin preparing you to take action.

Your body positions may reveal a defensive stance:

- I fold my arms across my chest.
- I straighten up, and get rigid and stiff.
- I lean far forward as I speak, and so on.

After working on this list for six to eight weeks, ask yourself this important question: Which one of these responses happens *first*? In the future, your *first response* will be the one you pay special attention to. Then you have the opportunity to reduce the symptoms of stress before muscle spasms, chest pains, or headaches do further damage to your system. Your well-being depends on prevention. Don't wait until more extreme reactions signal your distress. By then, it's usually too late to maintain control. Defenses have a way of "taking charge" of your life.

3–3. Defense Mechanisms

It is important to *act* as soon as you are aware of being overstressed. Otherwise, you will lose control of your feelings and your defenses will take over. You may find yourself locked in the grip of a mood, or flooded with overwhelming rage.

We all use defense mechanisms every day, and to a degree, they help thwart pain and protect us from feelings of insecurity, threat, or low self-esteem. In other words, the individual is fooled, regardless of whether others see through his or her vulnerability. Defenses curtail our Thinking and Feeling functions, but the conscious ego remains unaware of this dynamic.

These same adaptive defense mechanisms become unhealthy when their use serves to block or distort our reality over time. Denial leads us towards neurotic, even psychotic, behaviours. If defenses remain unconscious, they tend to work against us. We become crippled by their distortions, and great damage may be done to others when we are caught in their strong grip.

Some defenses are adaptive at one point in our lives, but haunt us when associations break through the layer of denial. A child whose ego strength is inadequate to handle abuse may block a painful memory from consciousness altogether. That is, until years later some incident triggers a terrifying childhood recollection or distraught feeling. The mind has an incredible capacity to block incidents we cannot handle, for whatever reason.

The following brief descriptions of the key defense mechanisms are adapted from R. Campbell's *Psychiatric Dictionary* and A. Lazerson's *Psychology Today: An Introduction*.

PROJECTION. One's own attitudes, feelings, or thoughts are ascribed to others, especially if they are considered undesirable. Instead of feeling our distress, we lash out and blame others for our mistakes.

Innocent people are scapegoated, while we free ourselves of the pain by denying responsibility.

OBSESSION. In order to avoid experiencing anxiety when an idea, emotion, or impulse persists in forcing itself into our consciousness, our Thinking becomes obsessive. We distract ourselves by focusing our thoughts on one particular idea or the pursuit of a goal. At pathological levels, the sufferer loses conscious control of his thoughts. Any attempts to manoeuvre or block repetitive thoughts typically fail to divert attention, and anxiety increases.

Compulsions are obsessive behaviours that come from a strong impulse to act contrary to one's will. A person leaving for work may have to return to the kitchen four or five times to check to see if he turned off the stove. Only then can he lock the door and leave. Such rituals can become extremely complicated as a number of routine actions are added. Failure to perform the trivial or stereotypical act generates anxiety. Only temporary relief, however, is gained from each repetition.

Eventually, obsessions and compulsions develop a life of their own and dictate behaviour. The person gradually loses self-control and power, and becomes neurotic. Psychotic episodes reflect a complete loss of reality. The obsession or compulsion becomes totally irrational or bizarre. The individual is relentlessly driven to perform the compulsive act, or thoughts of going crazy will surface. Such thoughts become torturous as fear grips the psyche and will not let go.

RATIONALIZATION. An act or idea is justified or made to appear reasonable when, in fact, it is irrational and illogical. "I decided not to go to her party because she is so immature," was one excuse used by an insecure client who was terrified of group interaction. Rationalizing is a cognitive cover-up, an explanation of behaviour or feelings that preserves a person's self-esteem, and helps him or her avoid anxiety when there is a threat of conflict. False but plausible reasons are given to justify the person's conduct. Rationalization usually involves a web of explanations, and if one fact is challenged, several more are held in reserve to support the claim. Deluded self-justifications eventually become so convoluted and complex that the person fails to problem-solve altogether, and becomes caught in a tangled web of stories.

Since excessive intellectualizing protects the person from the emotional aspects of a problem, the effect of some action on other people is totally disregarded. Empathy and compassion take a back seat to thinking here.

DISSOCIATION. This is the act of separating or disconnecting oneself from conflicting attitudes, impulses, or even parts of the personality. One part of consciousness splits off. Troublesome people and things are ignored or dissociated. In a more pathological form, they cease to exist, removed from consciousness. One chronic workaholic who had become very abusive with his family never saw them again after his wife left with the children following a physical attack on her son. He quickly moved to a different city, soon remarried, and refused to answer any calls or mail from his children. The most extreme form of dissociation occurs in cases of amnesia or multiple personality, where two or more distinct, but not autonomous, personalities are present in one individual.

ISOLATION. Isolation or compartmentalization is the fragmentation of the psyche. One part of the personality is kept separate from the whole. A man who declares emphatically that he is a good husband and father, yet neglects to mention that he is having an affair with his secretary, and rarely comes home for supper before the children are ready for bed, is compartmentalizing his life. Each compartment is kept separate and distinct.

REPRESSION. The repressed person remains oblivious to anxiety or guilt-producing impulses, or fails to remember deep emotional or traumatic past events. One woman I know takes pride in always having a smile on her face. Negative situations rarely touch her, and she refuses to watch the news or read the newspaper. "There's too much going on in the world," she protests. Repression is not deliberate; it is not forgetting. Intensive psychotherapy, hypnosis, or drugs are often necessary to recover the lost memories or painful conflicts that triggered the original response.

REACTION FORMATION. In this mechanism, conscious traits and behaviour patterns are developed in the ego that are opposite to the disowned unconscious feelings. Extreme empathy may cover sadistic impulses; exaggerated manners may conceal disdain. The intensity of the exaggeration is a clue to whether another person's motivation is truly well-intentioned and genuine. A university student lavished praise on his competitor and told him how much he admired him. When out of earshot, however, he let slip a sarcastic and caustic remark about his hero. Later, he denied anything but admiration.

There are other defense mechanisms, such as *regression,* which may involve a temporary return to an earlier stage of adaptation when the person is threatened or under stress, and *sublimation,* where instincts or impulses are redirected or modified to meet the conventional standards of society.

We all need to be aware of our own defense mechanisms. Unfortunately, denial makes this difficult. It's best to remember that these mechanisms are adaptive only to a point. After that, *beware!*

Pitfalls on the Journey

The next step in our journey towards joy is, oddly enough, learning when *not* to problem-solve! I cannot promise that Internalizing will teach you always to be in control. All of us get upset. My hope is that you will learn to identify when you are starting to "lose it," thus giving yourself enough time to avoid costly mistakes.

Chapter 8 is about establishing inner control. To be effective and wise as well, each of us must ensure that we are in charge of our Feelings. Be patient. It takes time and energy to seek workable solutions and reach consensus.

Not an easy task certainly, but let's begin.

8
The Journey — Stage 2, Rescheduling

Problem-Solving. Now or Later, That Is the Question!

Slow and steady wins the race.

INTERVENTION — TIMING IS EVERYTHING!

Like Sally and Peter, you are beginning to be superaware of your body. When something happens, you monitor your reactions. You tune in to exactly *where* you are experiencing the signals for that emotion. You label the emotion by naming it, and then try to figure out *all* the places in your body where nerves and muscles are on the alert.

You then use your Thinking to ask yourself these five key questions: (1) What just happened? (2) Who said what? (3) What exactly am I reacting to in this situation? (4) Is one of my dreams still upsetting me? and (5) What is flooding up from past experiences that adds to my present distress?

You may realize you are suddenly getting *quite* upset. Now is the time to act. Without intervention, you're liable to start projecting blame, or becoming obsessive, or otherwise going off the deep end and using one of your other defenses.

Now is the time to take action, to make things better. But how? An inner voice warns, "Your stress level is getting too high!" And then you realize, "I don't feel all that confident that I'm in charge of my emotions right now."

The basic dilemma becomes the question "Do I problem-solve now — that is, communicate my response to someone else's troublesome action — or make a decision to reschedule my intervention to a later time." It is important to make a wise choice, to handle each situation well and at the appropriate time for both parties.

If you decide that you are still in control of your feelings and you are thinking clearly, there are two further considerations before you continue. One concerns timing, and the other concerns the appropriate action.

Timing

Your escalating stress level may shout *hurry up*, you'd better problem-solve *now*, before you lose control. At this point, an important question becomes, "But what is going on with the person I need to speak with?" Sensitivity is essential when other people are involved in *your* solutions.

1. IS THE OTHER PERSON ABLE TO LISTEN? Sally has been aware all day that her anxiety is sky-high. She and Peter had a tremendous blow-up on Monday morning. Sally had been worrying about Peter's health for some time. During much of the weekend, Peter was irritable and short with Sally. She watched him pacing up and down in agitation. His face looked flushed and puffy.

Sally, the proverbial "fixer," decided to "help" by saying, "Peter, how about sitting down and having some breakfast with me this morning? You need to relax and start out your day with a full stomach. You were like a caged lion all weekend." Sally's invitation was well-intentioned, but it sparked a flame in Peter. He heard only criticism. Peter no longer wanted *anyone* to tell him what to do, even if it was good advice.

Peter lashed out at Sally, sneering, "I'm sick and tired of your nagging, whiny voice! You've got time to sit around all day, drink coffee, and read your newspaper. It must be nice!" Then he added an all too familiar dig: "Why don't you get yourself a decent job, and I'll be glad to retire!"

Sally was devastated. Peter's cruel jab hurt deeply because Sally had tried to get herself back into the workforce. Two years earlier, she had taken several small business courses, and had begun a commercial venture with a friend. At first, Peter was amused, but this gave way to stubborn resistance. Sally was frustrated at every turn because Peter continued to put demands on her time. He refused to baby-sit when Sally needed to work late. He still expected Sally to entertain his clients, and to accompany him to business conventions. Peter belittled her efforts, in truth, because it took attention away from him.

Any time the kids complained about the extra work they had to take on, Peter would use the opportunity to nitpick, usually about some mundane matter. To add fuel to the fire, he would accuse her, in front of the children, of not being there for any of them! Sally finally caved in, and resigned herself to staying home to keep the peace.

This particular day, rather than spend all day fretting, Sally made a decision to remain calm. She resolved to speak to Peter when he came home that evening. Then, she let go. At six o'clock, Peter walked in the door and announced to one and all that he had the flu. "I'm going straight to bed."

If Sally had decided to go ahead anyway with her prepared speech, she would have been fighting a losing battle. Both parties must be fully present if lasting solutions are to be found. As we will soon learn, Sally's best course was to let Peter know she did wish to talk to him, but was willing to postpone what she had to say until Peter was feeling better.

2. TIME OF DAY. Some people are best in the morning. Others don't truly wake up until noon. They shine at night. Staying up late is no problem for this group. Keep in mind your own and others' biological clocks when you next decide to speak to someone else about an unresolved issue.

We all suffer periods of low energy. For some, about an hour after lunch is deadly. Chuck told me he realized that the quarrels between him and his wife, Shirley, occurred most often between the time he got home from work and supper time. I suggested that he might have a bit of hypoglycemia and be irritable because of a drop in his blood sugars. Chuck agreed to have something to eat and go for a walk before dinner. Then he added, "I think I won't speak to Shirley about what it is I'm upset about till after supper."

About a month later, I asked Chuck how his new approach was working. He looked somewhat sheepish as he explained, "I've been waiting until after supper, as I said I would." Then he confessed, "The problem is, though, quite frankly, by then I can't remember what it was I was going to talk to Shirley about!"

I was not surprised by this, because in the meantime, Chuck and I had been working on the Myers-Briggs typology, and discovered that Chuck was a Feeler. It's somewhat unusual for a Feeler to go into engineering, unless it involves human engineering. Chuck admitted he had gone into engineering to please his father. He hated his job and did not feel at ease with his co-workers because his way of communicating and his different values left him feeling like the odd man out. Unfortunately, Shirley found herself on the receiving end of Chuck's frustrations when he walked in the door at night. "Miraculously," Chuck assured me, "things seem to be getting better between us."

3. COMPLICATIONS. Sometimes alcohol or drugs complicate an already difficult situation. One couple I worked with kept going out for "romantic evenings," as they called them. Inevitably, they would end up quarrelling, and their relationship remained rocky. I asked them whether they were drinking too much, and both flatly denied any such thing.

I still suspected alcohol might be a problem, however. One day, after another distressing tale, I asked the couple if they would be willing to try something. "If one of you is angry, would you promise me that you won't drink any alcohol that night? The other person is free to do whatever he wishes." This was reluctantly agreed to, and over the next month, they did have some good times together.

Then one day I got a frantic phone call from the wife. "There's no way I'm staying with that man! Last night was the last straw." She proceeded to launch into an angry litany of her husband's faults, until I finally stopped her.

"By the way, Shirley, did you have anything to drink at the restaurant last night?" There was a long pause, and then a high, squeaky voice drifted over the phone. "Well, as a matter of fact I did," she reluctantly admitted.

I laughed. "Sounds to me like you blew our agreement!" Shirley hesitated, and then she laughed, too. "I did, didn't I?"

"Well, try again," I encouraged. Then I added, "I think we'd better have a serious chat about whether you two just might have an alcohol problem." Many months later, Shirley and Chuck enrolled in an Alcoholics Anonymous program and agreed to quit drinking altogether. Shirley told me that the day she phoned me was a turning point for her, an "ah-ha" experience.

As she put it, "Never before had it really dawned on me that alcohol leaves me with no self-control. I can't communicate the way you taught me when I have even one drink." In Chapter 9, we will find out how Shirley learned to communicate so that Chuck was able to truly listen to her.

Appropriateness

As well as the timing of any intervention to problem-solve, the appropriateness of the situation must also be considered. If you become upset, consider the following *before* you proceed to act.

1. DO YOU LIVE OR WORK WITH THIS PERSON? Problem-solving takes a great deal of energy. It is important not to waste our resources fussing over situations or things that, in the long run, do not really matter. Otherwise, the question becomes, "If I problem-solve now, will I be spending my energy wisely?"

Now, ask yourself these three questions. First, can the other person handle my intervention? Second, will it do any good? (For example, is the person I'm angry with unwell? Is he too young to understand the significance of my upset? Is she too old, not very bright, or too confused in her thinking?) Last, is this someone I have to interact with again?

If you live or work with the person, then it is important to invest your energies in improving communication or rectifying misunderstandings or injustice. If not, let them go. When a store clerk or gas station attendant is rude, it's easy to get mad. But instead of verbalizing your annoyance, just mutter something like "What a jerk!" Then, *let go*. Few such situations truly merit pumping unnecessary adrenalin into your already overloaded system.

2. WHAT TO DO IN A GROUP SITUATION WHEN YOU BECOME UPSET. If your spouse, partner, or friend says something upsetting in public, an important question to ask yourself *before* you start to problem-solve is whether *now* is the time to respond. No one else need be embarrassed or, for that matter, involved in your upset.

Let's say you and your spouse are at a friend's dinner party. Your spouse tells a story about an embarrassing episode from a recent trip. You find yourself becoming very upset. Rather than speaking to your spouse while you are both surrounded by party guests, let him or her know right then that you are not at all pleased. You might make eye contact and frown, or cough. Then, when you leave the party, say, "Honey, do you remember earlier in the evening when I frowned at you? I was very upset that you even mentioned that trip to my colleagues." Knowing why you are upset, your spouse can explain why he or she chose to reveal this information.

Otherwise, you will find yourself on the defensive, trying to recreate the whole scenario to pinpoint what was said, and when it was said. Your inflammatory version of the conversation might go something like this: "Remember when you were telling that story to the Adamses about our trip to Texas? Why did you have to *go on and on* about it? I can't believe you *had the gall* to tell them I was thinking about moving to the States because our health system is deteriorating here?" You then launch into a long explanation of all the reasons this was supposed to be kept secret. After all, you haven't decided to make the move yet. "I can't believe that you would *jeopardize my career* here. You just *don't think* sometimes!"

What happens while this conversation is going on? Your spouse, feeling very criticized and threatened by your attack on his or her judgment, is preparing to justify his or her actions. Your spouse proceeds to disagree with you about what he or she indeed did say. And soon, the two of you are off to the races, arguing about who said what, what is secret or not secret, etc. Sound familiar?

Another scene finds you in a business meeting. One of the board members says something you think reveals unethical practices on his part. You have to work with that person on a committee, and it is important that you share your concerns and differing views. However, the board meeting may not be an appropriate time to do this.

As soon as you are aware of your own dissonance, let the other person know by quietly stating that you would like to speak with him after the meeting. There is no point in confronting or embarrassing someone when all the facts and explanations are not in. When you leave the meeting together, you might say, "I spoke to you about getting together now because you and I are both on that rules and regulations committee. I have an ethical problem with Rule 1." There is no attack here on the other person's ethical position. The two of you can take the time to share your divergent views, and strive to come up with some kind of resolution. This respectful approach avoids misunderstandings caused when one person criticizes or comments on his *own* interpretation of someone else's position or values.

Reconstructions of conversations are rarely accurate, and generally resisted. Arguing about who said what is seldom productive.

Now that we have considered the timing and appropriateness of our intervention, it is essential that we know how to *not* problem-solve but remain responsible. Your initial reaction to this suggestion may be: "What's this? How can I be a responsible person if I don't solve problems when things happen?"

Rescheduling

Our true responsibility is to keep our own integrity intact and to treat others with respect, empathy, and dignity. Pride is a foolish emotion that compels us to worry about how things appear to others. Dignity, on the other hand, is very important to our self-esteem. If one remains ignorant of the dark, Shadow side of the personality, it is apt to erupt in temper tantrums, or cause us to withdraw into a poisonous, stony silence. Each time this happens, our personal integrity is eroded further.

1. THE BOILING POINT. Our task is to know when our stress level becomes problematic, to know when our defenses begin to rule our behaviour. The process of Internalizing alerts us to our degree of discomfort. If you recognize when your face turns pink, long before rage changes it to a purplish hue, then you have plenty of time to problem-solve while you are still in charge of your emotions and your actions. In Chapter 9, you will learn how to problem-solve in a healthy way, but first you must be in control.

Rescheduling is appropriate when your anger, anxiety, fear, or pain gets the better of you. None of us is capable of being in control all of the time. When you feel confused, chaotic, or caught in the grip of a mood (for example, you feel bitchy, sulky, stubborn, morose, etc.), cancel all thoughts of immediate conflict resolution. Knowing when to call *time-out* is important. Let's say a teenager has just confided to her parents that she takes drugs. Dad's anxiety soars, and Mom's imagination goes wild. At this point, neither is capable of listening.

If Mom and Dad have the presence of mind to know they are temporarily out of control, they may tell Janet that they are too upset right now to talk coherently about this. "Your mother and I better take a walk to get ourselves calmed down. This is distressing news." Then Mother may add, "But when we get back, we'll sit down and try to figure something out!"

Janet sees her parents depart for their walk. Instead of feeling abandoned, somewhere deep inside she feels a sense of relief. She knows, from past experience, that when her parents are really upset,

Mom usually cries and Dad typically shouts. There is some hope in the air, instead of despair, as Janet awaits their return.

2. LEAVING A SITUATION. "I'm great at this part," boasts Henri as I teach him how to reschedule. My response to this is, "I know. That's why you're here!" We both laugh since Henri now understands that leaving a situation is a passive-aggressive way of showing anger. This form of anger creates unfinished business, as nothing gets solved when people withdraw and avoid responsibility.

If you have to leave a situation because you are overstressed, *always say why you are leaving, and when you are coming back.* Fear of abandonment is a basic emotion inherent in us all. When someone walks out on us, slams a door, or otherwise deserts us, an instinctual fear rises from the depth of our being. Our response may be an outburst of anger, a sinking feeling in the stomach, tension in the neck, or just plain angst.

Say why you are leaving. If you say you are too upset to be rational, you are being honest and responsible. By withdrawing from the situation to think about what the other person said, or to figure out what is really going on, you are not abandoning that person. On the contrary, that person will feel flattered because you care enough about them to devote your time and energy to the relationship.

Don't forget to say when you are coming back. Try to arrange a time far enough ahead that you will have time to collect your thoughts. Mull through the reasons you are feeling so upset about what has happened. Take time to consider some possible solutions. You might say, as you leave, "Let's sit down after dinner tomorrow night when the kids are in bed. I'll let you know then what I come up with. Okay?"

Or if tempers are flaring on both sides, "Maybe the two of us need some time-out right now. Let's both think this through, and see if we can figure out what in the heck this is all about." Underlying key problems are rarely seen without objectivity and distance.

Non-verbal communication, such as leaving a scene, is ambiguous at best. At worst, this passive-aggressive behaviour leads to misunderstandings and confusion. The ego-centred part of us is quick to feel that the world revolves around us. "Your behaviour must be a response to something I've done!" is the assumption. Some martyrs go even further. "It must be *my* fault that you left."

The Triangular Pattern

If I admit to being out of control because my defenses have rushed into action, how do I get back my "cool"?

Think of a right-angled triangle.

THE TRIANGULAR PATTERN

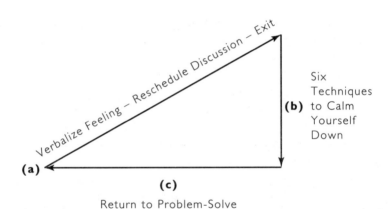

a) You make a conscious decision to *exit* because you are over-reacting. You *verbalize* your distress, and *reschedule* — arrange another time when both parties are free to discuss the situation.

b) You attempt to regain your control by performing one or several of the techniques that follow in order to calm yourself down.

c) You follow through on the promise to return to problem-solve. Be sure you really are able to think and feel clearly so that wisdom guides your solutions.

Regaining Control

Action-Oriented Ideas

If you are free to move about, plug into some activity that helps reduce your stress to a comfortable level. No pumping of adrenalin, please!

- Go for a walk or a slow jog. Watch the scenery. Look for interesting distractions.
- Do stretching exercises to help tense muscles elongate and ease out stored tension.
- Take a long warm but not hot bath. Set a candle on the side of the tub, and watch the colours in the flame.
- Sit in a rocking chair, and slowly rock until you feel some release.
- Build a fire in your fireplace. Watch the flames, and enjoy the warmth.
- Play your favourite music, and sit in an easy chair by a window. If you feel energetic, dance, or just move around, until you feel like laughing!
- Phone a friend and let off steam. Choose only friends who *don't* problem-solve for you. Empathy alone is just fine!
- Use your imagination to develop new ways to calm down. Continue this list, adding ideas as they come to you.

Passive-Oriented Ideas

If you must stay where you are, if it is awkward to leave, or to escape the upsetting situation, the following six techniques may be helpful in calming yourself down.

1. SLOW DOWN AND DEEPEN YOUR BREATHING. Because you are experiencing stress, chances are you are cutting off your breathing. Try this: Breathe in for one count. Hold for one count. Then breathe out slowly for two counts. On the next breath, breathe in for two counts, hold for two counts. Now exhale for an extended time. Continue slowly. You don't want to suffer hyperventilation and end up feeling faint. Make sure your shoulders are back and you are sitting tall. Try to relax.

After about five minutes, your breathing will become slow and deep. By now, more oxygen should be reaching your brain. Test this by determining whether your thoughts have more clarity. Are you feeling calmer and more in charge? Keep practising through-out the day. And remember, it's wise to do this any time you start to feel tense.

2. MEDITATION. The point of meditation is to achieve the state of "no-thingness," the absence of thought. Robert Campbell, in his *Psychiatric Dictionary,* explains transcendental meditation: "It appears to be a natural process, perhaps a fourth physiologically and biochemically definable state of consciousness (the others being sleeping, dreaming, and waking), that does not require any mental or physical control, any change in life-style or belief-system, nor does it involve hypnosis or suggestion" (pp. 660–61). The end result of meditation is reduced activity in the autonomic nervous system, which can lead to a lowering of tension and anx-iety, and an increase in contentment and tolerance for frustration.

I cannot teach you to meditate here, but I can help you deter-mine which type of meditation might work best for you. Dr. Richard Bandler and John Grinder, two researchers who studied communication in the seventies, developed a system called Neuro-Linguistic Programming. In *Frogs into Princes,* they relate that they observed effective communicators, such as therapists Virginia Satir and Fritz Perls, in order to discover what techniques, cues, and responses worked or didn't work in communication.

Bandler and Grinder noticed while watching the interactions between therapist and client that some people looked up a lot, others looked to the side, and others looked down. Three channels were named: Visual, Auditory, and Kinesthetic. We each have a dominant channel. Visuals, when they are trying to remember an image, will look up to the right. When they want to create an image, such as "What would I look like with purple hair?" they will look up to the left. Auditory types look to the right side or down to the right when they are remembering sounds or words. They look to the left side when constructing sounds or words. When experiencing feelings, and also smells and tastes, Kinesthetic people look down to the right. There is some variation, depending on whether a person is right-handed or left-handed, but there seems to be a consistent pattern within each individual.

To explain further, suppose a Visual person attends a ballet. On returning home, she tells her husband about the beauty of the ballet. Her eyes often dart up to the right as she speaks. Her Kinesthetic spouse listens, but his wife notices that he looks down and starts to read his newspaper. She gets increasingly angry, and finally shouts, "You haven't heard a word I said!" He looks up startled, and assures her he has heard every word. Halfway through her description, he wished he had gone with her. He slipped into his feelings of regret and lost eye contact.

Not only can this theory help relationships, it can also suggest which type of meditation will work best for you. Some time ago, I was trying to decide whether my visual or auditory channel was stronger. One day my son and aunt were having a discussion about whether they would rather be blind or deaf as a result of some injury. Both agreed that they would rather be blind. I shot back, "Heavens, I'd rather be deaf!" Their choice made perfect sense, as both are singers. My choice helps explain why, if I do attend an opera, I spend a great deal of time with my eyes shut. My visual impressions overpower my hearing. Similarly, on a guided tour of an art gallery, I get frustrated when I look at a painting and try to listen to the guide at the same time. My dominant visual function drowns out the auditory information. There is too much competing stimulation, so I prefer to look at pictures on my own.

Visual Meditation. To achieve a meditative state, if your dominant function is visual, focus on a single object, such as a vase. It is best if the object is off by itself, rather than surrounded with other distracting things. A lovely thing to meditate on is a candle, but the flame must be steady, not exposed to drafts. Place a candle on the edge of your bath tub. Let the warmth of the water calm you at the same time that your meditation creates a peaceful space. If a competing thought interrupts your gaze, refocus.

Practise until your mind is cleared of all distractions, and you are able to rest.

Auditory Meditation. People with a dominant auditory function find the repetition of a word or phrase, called a mantra, the easiest way to meditate. The word *mantra* may be used. Or, words like *still, peace, warm.* Repeat the word over and over until you feel a calming effect. If interrupting thoughts intervene, simply refocus.

People who are obsessive often have problems with the mantra. They can't seem to empty their minds to free themselves of unwanted thoughts. To rectify this, when you find yourself becoming obsessive, make a loud, preferably low, buzzing sound. This jars your thoughts and interrupts the obsession. Then try the mantra again. If others are present, put all your thoughts into an imaginary salad crisper, and spin the handle to make a word salad. Now resume the mantra exercise.

Kinesthetic Meditation. If emotions are dominating your thoughts, try stomach breathing. To learn this, lie flat with your hands folded on your stomach. Now breathe in, but instead of breathing out, try to push the air down into your stomach. Your stomach should stretch up like a balloon, pushing your hands up. Hold as long as you can, and then exhale. Keep doing this until it becomes easy. Now, visualize your breath going into your mouth and arcing down to your stomach, ending up somewhere near your belly button. Reverse this arc, and exhale through your mouth.

When you first practise stomach breathing, do so in a horizontal position. Your system is not used to the extra oxygen that is inhaled, and you may feel light-headed. Before you stand up, sit for a few moments until your heart rate stabilizes. As well as benefiting you by introducing more oxygen into your system, visualizing your breath following the arc can be somewhat hypnotic. This meditation is excellent if you wake up in the middle of the night and find yourself brooding obsessively over some troubling thoughts. Your body gets more oxygen, and your thoughts are occupied visualizing the journey of your breath, back and forth in a rocking motion. You will begin to relax, and will be able to get back to sleep.

3. VISUALIZATION. Another excellent technique to calm yourself down quickly, anywhere, anytime, uses memory and imagination. Imagine a scene, somewhere you have actually been, where you felt totally relaxed and peaceful. Now place yourself in that picture. What are you doing? What are you wearing? What time of day is it? Is there a wind? Is the sun shining? Are there any sounds? Are you alone, or is somebody else in the picture? Any details that add to the senses, and make the picture more complete, are helpful. Keep rehearsing that same scene until you can recapture the peaceful feelings you originally experienced.

The memory I use is of a day when my sister and I were rock collecting on the shores of one of the Great Lakes. It was twelve noon, and I had sat down on the edge of the lake with my feet in the water. Beside me in a small puddle were tiny pebbles like jewels of many hues. I was fascinated by the intensity of the colours, and could feel the water lapping gently at my ankles as the waves lapped at the shore. My sister was off in the distance, busy at her task.

I have only to think of that scene for a few seconds and I feel my shoulders relaxing. It feels as though the water is taking away all my tension as it recedes. It's like pulling the plug in the bath tub and watching the water swirl down the drain. Practise your picture until you can recapture the wonderful release and celebrate the beauty of the experience.

4. HUMOUR. What a wonderful gift it is to be able to laugh, especially at ourselves. My Ph.D. dissertation was the first empirical study on humour in psychotherapy. Presenting this work in a paper titled "A Shift to a New Perspective," I introduced what I called "verbal picture painting." The following story will illustrate how this technique can introduce objectivity and distance when feelings overwhelm us. A very agitated client, Matthew, was telling me about a new boss who was driving him crazy. This man was a neatness freak and totally obsessive when it came to having *his* office look well-organized and "perfect." On that day Matthew had come back from lunch to find everything on the surface of his desk jammed into his top desk drawer. As he described his fury to me he became red in the face and talked faster and faster. I stopped him. "While you've been talking, I've got your boss, Harry, all dressed up! You guys have just gone out for lunch, and Harry goes into the closet. He brings out an old khaki army uniform, with brass buttons, epaulets, breeches, jodhpurs, and spurs. To top it all off he has an old army hat with a long feather set at a rakish angle. He's an old army man, and in his glory." I continued the saga. "He snaps to attention, and starts to strut around your office looking very important. He comes to your desk, and it is a total mess. 'Ah-ha!' says Harry, with a big smile on his face. He lurches forward and shovels everything in one fell swoop into your desk drawer. He straightens up, puts his hands on his suspenders, puffs out his chest, and utters a grand sigh!"

Matthew laughed. I explained, "You're never going to be able to think about Harry doing his number without thinking about that silly story. It's like a film screen overlaying that memory."

Humour, used this way, gives you a new perspective. A word of caution, though. The kind of humour used here is exaggeration. No sarcasm, or black or sadistic humour, please. Take some ludicrous aspect of the situation, focus on it, and use your imagination to play with it. You can dress people up, have them doing ridiculous things, or whatever, to distort the reality of the situation. It's as if you are a fly on the wall, looking at yourself with new eyes. This objectivity provides the distance needed to gain a fresh perspective on a troublesome incident.

Humour can be developed. It needs only time, energy, and lots of imagination! It can take many forms. Sometimes I suggest to clients that they draw cartoons of painful situations and place words in the "clouds" above the characters' heads. The cartoon titles are often quite revealing. One young student who was suffering high test anxiety was asked to draw a picture of someone who might help him. Sam drew a picture of himself on a throne with a crown on his head, and a sceptre in his right hand. He titled his drawing

King "Wish-All." Then he commented, "This king looks happy, he's enjoying his false realism! If he can take away exams, he can take away the worry." Sam laughed. The insights that emerge when humour surfaces are sometimes incredible and always creative.

5. TOUCH. Touch is a powerful force for healing. In fact, the Therapeutic Touch movement is entering new territory each year. There is no direct touching; the technique uses the energy field that surrounds each person and object. Daniel Worth, in "Non-Contact Therapeutic Touch and the Healing of Wounds," in the *Journal of Subtle Energies,* describes a controlled study that examined the effect of therapeutic touch on the healing rate of wounds in human subjects. By the eighth day, this group had an average wound size ten times smaller than the untreated group. By the sixteenth day, thirteen of the twenty-three subjects were completely healed, while none of the controlled group had healed.

Energy fields appear to be very powerful. Try this. Hold your hands about an inch apart in a praying position for some minutes until you feel a slight heat build up. Then move your hands very slowly apart, until you feel a cooling. Then again very slowly, move your hands together. A resistance or energy force will seem to have developed in the space between the hands.

Self-touching is healing. Watch people who are very upset. Often, they rub their hands across their skirts or pant legs. Or they cross their arms and hug themselves. When I worked at the hospital, the schizophrenic patients would sit outside my office and rock to and fro. Try sitting in a rocking chair when you're agitated. Rock yourself until you feel calm. It really works. Your energy is focused within the body, and soon your mind is distracted by the motion.

Next time you find yourself in pain, cup your hands under your chin, as if you were comforting a small child. It helps make *you* feel cared for. Remember, if you do hug yourself for comfort, be careful that you release your arms so that you are breathing between hugs.

Purposeful self-touching in order to comfort oneself is very calming. The pads of our fingers are ultra-sensitive. Done gently and with great care, it can be therapeutically healing. We must all learn to nurture and care for ourselves, especially when we are undergoing stress.

6. SPIRITUALITY. If you are in touch with your spirituality, *letting go unto God* is a powerful tool to restore inner peace. You may pray to ask God to carry the burden you find too painful to bear. Or you may ask God to surround you with His white light, to protect you from harm. Be still, and try to imagine yourself circled by a warm, soft glow. Those with a strong spirituality will understand the power of such a request.

For those of you who resist or do not believe, I have a joke to tell. There is an atheist hanging by his fingertips from the branch of a tall tree. He just can't hold on any more. Sounding quite frantic, he looks up to the skies and calls out, "Is there anybody up there?"

There is a long pause, and then the booming voice of God calls out, "I am here, my son!"

"I'll do anything, I'll do anything!" the poor man shouts.

"Then *let go*," God orders the man. There is a pained, frightened look on the man's face. Then he looks up beseechingly in the opposite direction.

"Is there anybody else up there?" he asks in desperation.

It is very difficult to let go when you do not have enough faith to believe that you won't fall into an abyss. Workaholics, for instance, must keep control at all costs. I warn my clients that their journey back to health will likely lead them to a search for the Self. Since the centre of the Self is the soul, recovery often leads the workaholic to find, or in some cases rediscover, his or her spirituality — the inner connection between humanity and God's higher power. It is a journey many of us are always on, consciously or unconsciously. M. Scott Peck's book *The Road Less Travelled* has sold millions of copies for this very reason. It is the story of his own odyssey, and people relate to his inner search.

These six techniques to calm yourself are useful tools to help you re-establish control. Some of the techniques are better than others in specific situations. Obviously, it is hard to meditate if you cannot take the time to do so. Fantasy pictures, on the other hand, may be evoked at any time and in any place. Practise until you feel comfortable with each.

When you are back in charge of your emotions, then return to the situation, as promised. You should now be ready to communicate what you think and what you feel in a calm voice.

About Listening and Respect

In Chapter 9, we will learn how to say what we need to in a way that others will be able to hear and to understand. The way to go about this I call *non-controlling communication*. We will also find out about how our ego boundaries, if ill-defined, get us into a pile of trouble. Controlling and manipulative behaviour and language are the result of blurred ego boundaries, and create a confusion that leads to dysfunctional communication. The two parties become hopelessly entangled because each invades the other's space and privacy. We will also learn why second-guessing what another person feels or thinks is fraught with error.

9
The Journey — Stage 3, Non-Controlling Communication

Unplugging Our Ears, and Staying on Our Own Side of the Fence

"I know you better than you know yourself!"
AN INFAMOUS QUOTE

Our journey so far has shown us how to recognize our feelings through the signals our body sends us. We can now acknowledge what we think or feel at the time an incident occurs, and are starting to consider whether we are overreacting because of the influence of some past incident on the present situation.

The next step is to communicate this information to others. If we are to do this in a responsible manner, we will *not* withdraw. Nor will we lash out when someone invades our space. We are now Internalizing, in control, and ready to problem-solve.

Effective problem-solving involves taking some action that, it is hoped, will transform a negative situation into a positive resolution for us and for the others involved. It comes about for two reasons: because we choose to be responsible, and because we have the wherewithall — the knowledge, skills, and personality — to carry it off. Statements such as "John is such an effective communicator" or "Sheila solves her problems with such tact and wisdom" quite often reflect the maturity of the people being admired.

As we have learned, we are sometimes able to problem-solve as soon as the situation presents itself. On other occasions, when we are not in full control of our emotions, we must reschedule our response and take action at a later time.

ASSUMPTIONS

Let's start the process of problem-solving with two assumptions that are based on the premises that we must be fully responsible for our own behaviour and feelings, and that we must be careful not to second-guess what is going on for someone else. Neither premise takes the arrogant view of one insecure man who insisted on being one-up on his wife. In smug tones he declared, "I know you better than you know yourself!"

The *first assumption* is that people find it difficult to hear you if they are being controlled. If I want to communicate so that other people can hear me, I must be clear, honest, and non-threatening. I must tell the other person what I *feel*, what I *think*, and what my *needs* are. However, I must also leave that person free to respond to me *if* he can, *when* he is able, and *in the way* he chooses.

After all, other people need the freedom to approach others in a way that fits their personality. My version of how things should go may not be theirs. The truth of the matter is that the odds are less than even that you are right about how someone else thinks or feels. But more about that later.

The *second assumption* is that, as an adult, I am responsible for communicating information to others. People should not need to "fish" in order to discover what is wrong. In other words, if I don't give other people enough information about what is happening to me — how I am feeling, what I am thinking, and what my needs are — I am being irresponsible. It's like a child who goes around pouting, hoping her mother will notice that she is out-of-sorts. "What's the matter, dear?" is the hoped-for response to such passive-aggressive behaviour. Co-dependents, people who are in a caretaker role with others and are afraid to "rock the boat," are good at this covert controlling tactic. Such manipulation need not be part of healthy communication.

Imagine that there is a line between you and another person. I call it the *fence*, but it is really your ego boundary.

FENCE – EGO BOUNDARY

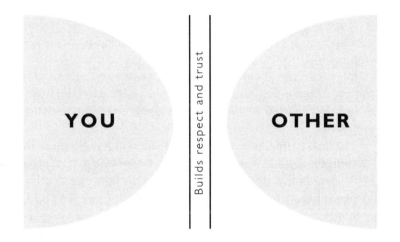

The clearer you are about where you stop, and others begin, the healthier you will be. Unhealthy families, in contrast, are enmeshed, like two hands with the fingers crossed through each other. The family members regularly problem-solve for each other, and often are invasive. There is no clear line around each family member that defines that person's ego boundary, as there is in healthy families. There, people respect one another, and trust that other members will not invade their space. Only when invited to do so will one member offer his thoughts to another. As we will soon learn, problem-solving for others, or "crossing the fence,"

shows lack of respect for the other person as a unique and separate individual.

We are now going to learn how to communicate without crossing this imaginary fence.

THE "I" MESSAGE

Something upsetting has just happened. Someone has just been rude to you. To be responsible, you need to let that person know how you experience this behaviour. However, your responsibility stops at *what* you say, and the *way* you communicate this information. You cannot be responsible for how someone responds to you.

Remember that your response must leave the other person free to express his views, *if* he can, *when* he is able, and *in the way* he chooses.

If I want someone to listen to me, I need to tell her *how I feel*. This sort of statement is called an *"I" message*. It will be easier for her to listen to what I have to say if I begin by telling her what I feel.

Here's an example. Imagine that you have just said something to me that I consider rude. If I tell you what I *think* first, I might say, "That's a rotten thing you just said!" At the same time I'll lean forward in my chair, and my voice will be raised. I may even point my finger at you. Notice that I used the evaluative term "rotten."

Your response may be either to "run for the hills," psychologically speaking, or to lash back at me.

Now, let me tell you what I *feel*: "I feel that what you've just said is rude. Politeness has been a strong value in my life. It's one of the characteristics I admire so much in others. I would really appreciate it if you would take care to respect the importance of this to me." Notice that there are no evaluative terms like "rotten" involved. It is simply a description of how I feel at the moment. However, I do have to let you know exactly what I am reacting to. In this particular case, it is rudeness.

When giving "I" messages, it is important for me to let others know what my *needs* are. In the previous example, I explained my need for politeness. However, it is also important to resist the temptation to tell the other person how to fulfil that need.

To illustrate, imagine that you feel lonely and isolated from your partner. You might say, "I really miss having some romance in our relationship right now!" The temptation now is to suggest just what the other person should do about this. "I wish you would send me some flowers or something" might be the broad hint, but your partner is not going to have much fun simply following your request. It is better to compliment your spouse on something he or she has already done.

For example, "Remember at that party at the Smiths' a month ago? We were standing talking to Pat and Eric, and you put your arm around me." The important part follows: "I felt so special when you did that!"

The spouse is left to be creative, yet is affirmed and complimented on something he or she has already done.

"I" Messages Must Be Brief

Try to be brief and to the point. *You do not need to defend how you feel!* This is where people so often go wrong. They send an excellent "I" message, and then they blow it!

Back to the example in which you were rude to me. I start to tell you how I feel. However, instead of stopping there, I go on. Here are some ways I might defend how I feel:

- "You're *always* rude" or "You're *never* polite" are ways to raise your ire. What's more, "always" or "never" statements are rarely true.
- "You were rude to George last week at that cocktail party" is a good "elephant memory" message. Try to stay in the present.
- "The kids think you are really rude, too," enlists the troops to your side. Ganging up on someone is a bullying tactic.
- And the clincher, "Your mom told me you were a really rude teenager!" That last one usually elicits an explosion, and no wonder. We like to hang on to the idea, or the myth, that our mom, at least, thought we were great!

All the above are examples of dirty fighting. I call them the soldiers. And I really do deserve to be "shot down" for using every one of them.

"I" messages are very effective, even with difficult people. Alice, one of my clients, told me that she had gone home to talk to her mother about something that had always upset her. She decided to use an "I" message, and then stop. Her mother had been very critical of her as a child, and their relationship was quite tense.

Alice described what happened. "I told my mother what was upsetting me, and I didn't defend what I had to say. My mother waited for me to go on, because I always did," admitted Alice. Then she added, "When my mother realized I wasn't going to continue, she looked surprised, sat back, cocked her head to one side, and looked me in the eye. 'Well, dear, I never knew you felt that way!' is all she said."

Alice was quite pleased. "You know," she laughed, "I think it is the first time we ever really heard each other. That "I" message thing really works!"

Stay in Your Own Territory

On your own side of the *fence*, within your own ego boundary, you have a great deal of power. You can stand up for yourself and be assertive! The briefer your "I" message, the clearer and more concise your communication will be. You won't be messing up what you have to say with confusing, extraneous information. Communication overload usually makes it impossible to follow, let alone to really listen.

Unfortunately, we have no power to change others. If you forget to use the "I" message and, instead, challenge someone else to do something, he or she may withdraw into silence and refuse to answer, or walk out. Most people resent being told what to do.

Many people who cross the fence do so to keep power by telling others what they want to hear, instead of the truth. These passive-aggressive types promise to follow through and then choose to do nothing. Procrastination is a wonderful way of looking good and getting away with murder! Pleasers, people who can't say no, also use this tactic to avoid responsibility. Keeping harmony at all costs is their justification for avoiding telling the truth.

A Safe Atmosphere

"I" messages create a safe atmosphere and make listening possible. There is no blaming, judging, or interfering in others' business. Since there is no talk about who is right or wrong, there is no need to become defensive or to prepare a counterattack.

People are simply trying to tell, in purely descriptive language, their experience of what has been said or done by others. The "I" message will leave you feeling confident that you are being responsible and, at the same time, are standing up for your own rights and freedom of speech.

CROSSING THE BOUNDARY — USING "YOU" MESSAGES

Recognizing how you control and manipulate others is a crucial but difficult task. Most of us do not realize the subtle or blatant ways we do this.

Unfortunately, *"you" messages*, unlike "I" messages, do not always begin with "you." Covert "you" messages include someone raising his eyes in disbelief, or saying something like "Nonsense!" or "You've got to be kidding!" or "Oh come on!" In overt "you" messages, someone is telling another person what he should *do, say, think*, and *feel*. Quite often, the person is pointing a finger as he or she tells the other what to do.

Ironically, finger-pointing may help you identify when you are controlling others. For example, Kelly discovered she was a finger-pointer *par excellence*. Every time she did this in our sessions, I would articulate my "I" message. "I can't hear you right now. I'm quite distracted because I find myself watching your finger instead of listening."

Kelly got quite good at "I" messages. However, one day she was so upset about something her husband, Ken, had done, that she started in on him early in the session. Wagging her finger, she warned Ken, "You shouldn't have said that to the kids. You were being totally irresponsible! There's no excuse for ever doing that."

As she spoke, Kelly became aware of her outstretched finger. She reached out, grabbed it, and drew it towards her body. We watched as she struggled with her thoughts. Finally, she came out with a perfect "I" message, and we all laughed in relief. She had caught herself, once again, in her old behaviour of controlling her husband.

Kelly went on to explain to me that she had been to her family home twice since she had started to use the "I" message. "You won't believe this, but my mother still wags her finger at me all the time!" I laughed, and assured Kelly that I could very well believe it. If we come from a family where there is a lot of controlling going on, guess what we learn to do?

When we get nasty or vicious because we are angry, hurt, frightened, or enraged, we often resort to name-calling, insulting, putting others down, or being sarcastic. "You" messages flow up from our unconscious when our Shadow side is activated by negative emotions. As you yourself will soon discover, one must be in control in order to use "I" messages.

Typically, such controlling behaviour leads the other person to launch a counterattack or make a hasty exit. Soon the problem has escalated into a power struggle that no one will win.

The Teeter-Totter Power Struggle

One of the major ways to create a power struggle in any relationship is to use the "you" message.

When you interfere in another person's business, you take on responsibility for what happens from then on. If someone else tells you about a personal problem, and you tell them what to do, or suggest some possible solutions, you will rob that person of his or her own experiencing. Ultimately, both parties will resent each other.

"What's wrong with helping people?" you may ask. Or, "Why shouldn't I protect my kids from making mistakes?" Then you might add, "I don't want them to suffer as I did!" Oddly enough, "helping" and "protecting" are rationalizations for manipulating and controlling. But let me explain.

Imagine that I'm holding up a pencil in the horizontal position. On the right side is the person who has a personal problem. We'll call her Helen. Helen is telling her husband, Mario, who is on the left side, about some difficulty she is having at the office with a co-worker. As soon as Mario jumps in to tell Helen what she should do about the situation, the pencil tilts down to the right. Mario, by intervening in Helen's problem, has tipped the balance of power in his favour. If Helen follows Mario's advice, she may no longer "own" her own solutions. It's like helping your kids with their homework the night before a test. If the child does well, he can't take credit for his marks. He certainly can't take you to university with him! If he fails the test, he can project blame outwards and neglect to learn from his errors. Finding out what we are *not* good at is an important lesson in life.

The implicit message here is that the other person cannot handle his or her own problems. As soon as we offer solutions, the message is one of dependency — *you need me!*

The irony in Helen and Mario's interchange is that Helen is a Feeler who needs to talk through her own solutions. When Mario problem-solves for Helen instead of simply listening, he unwittingly takes away her independence. Often, as a result, she loses her initiative and self-confidence. Helen is left feeling like a child who needs to be told what to do. No wonder she doesn't feel good about herself.

The power struggle between Helen and Mario resumes when Helen attempts to regain her own power. She resents Mario's interference, yet in a way she wonders if she set him up by telling him about the office problem. But, she ponders, "Surely I can talk to my own husband about things that bother me!"

Mario isn't happy either. Although it temporarily feels great to have broad shoulders, and know that others depend on you, this situation eventually gets tiresome. When you have too many problems of your own, the last thing you need is to be responsible for the happiness of another person. Mario ends up resenting Helen as well.

The teeter-totter balance of power tips again. Helen gets back at Mario for problem-solving for her by using the silent treatment. She withdraws and quietly steams at his suggestions. Or she retaliates and decides that the next time Mario has a problem, she'll be sure to tell *him* what he should do. "After all, fair is fair," fumes Helen.

Nobody wins in this or any other such power struggle. In fact, both parties typically end up resenting each other. Now, instead of just the original problem, there are many added problems. Mario's suggestions feed into Helen's vulnerabilities and insecurities. Her talents don't lend themselves to his solutions. Instead, negative inferences leave her confused about how to proceed. Mario, instead of feeling good about his involvement, now feels the heightened tension hanging in the air. He stays on the alert for a backlash and, in turn, grows defensive. His own trigger-happy anger sits ready to pounce.

If you wish to be in a peer relationship with someone, neither person should be in a power position. Mario simply needs to listen to Helen. He might offer empathy and support for her predicament. No problem-solving allowed! The *magic question* for Mario to ask Helen, if he wants to relate to her on a peer level, is, "What do you think you can do about this?"

Helen is left with her own dignity, and the implication is that she is quite capable of handling her own affairs. If I problem-solve for somebody else, the message is the reverse. "You can't handle your own problems." I put you down by inferring that you are not capable of doing your own problem-solving. The inference is, "You need me, or others like me, to help you." Nobody feels good about these messages.

By the way, parents who problem-solve for their children, instead of asking them what their own solutions might be, are robbing these children of the chance to develop self-confidence, make their own mistakes, and learn from their errors.

Be patient. It's not easy to switch to a whole new approach. We usually have to go through some pain before we are willing to change and to grow.

GOOD LISTENING

Good listeners usually have many friends. People love being able to discuss problems with a friend who offers empathy and support only.

Remember that good listeners *do not give advice* unless their opinion is requested. To this, I would add a warning proviso. I believe that this should read: "unless their opinion is requested about an *impersonal* problem only." If somebody asks me what I think the stock market is going to do tomorrow, I might hazard a guess. However, if I want a peer relation with that person, then I will also return the question, and ask that person what her own opinion is about the market. This is conversation on a peer level.

Now, if someone asks me a question about what she should do about a personal matter, I am best *not* to answer that question. Instead, I need to serve as a sounding board and allow the person to bounce her own ideas off me.

I believe it shows arrogance when we try to problem-solve for someone else. Our history, our sources of knowledge, our sexual orientation, our morality and ethics, and our opinions are unique to each of us. It is presumptuous to think that what would work best for us would be suitable for another person.

Here's an example of this process of good listening that involves young people. Let's say my eighteen-year-old daughter asks me, "What do you think I should do this summer, Mom?" My best response would be something like this. "Gee, sweetie, I don't know! What are you thinking about?"

She tells me about three possible summer jobs. The first one she appears to know a great deal about. She has talked to many people, and found out important details about the company itself. This job option is obviously an important one to consider. She sets priorities as she describes her feelings about it. She stresses some things and leaves out others. She mentions statements of other people she has spoken with. In fact, she is doing her *own* problem-solving as she speaks.

The second job she is considering happens to be at a lodge I'm familiar with. While she is telling me about this place, I become somewhat uncomfortable because I'm thinking about the tipping system they use for employees. I also wonder if she knows about the bus schedules changing at the end of August. However, I remain quiet while she tells me about her third choice.

This particular job I know nothing about, and the company is new to me. She also seems pretty vague about what it is the company sells and what would be expected of her.

She finishes, and then asks again, "Well, what do you think?" At this point, I have to be very careful *not* to go over onto her side of the fence. Instead, I might comment on the process of her thinking. "You seemed to know a lot about that first job. You sound excited about it." You'll notice that I used the word *seemed,* as it is best not to presume you know for sure how someone else feels. Then I might add, "I know very little about that company, so I don't have any thoughts to contribute, one way or the other."

I do have some information about her second idea. However, I must respect her space in the way I deliver that information. *I must be invited over, before I offer any suggestions.* To let her know about my thoughts, I might say, "As I was listening to you talk about that lodge, I remembered feeling upset about the tipping system they use there. It really is not fair." Then, the important question: "Would you like me to tell you about it?"

She agrees, and I now have the invitation I need to share my thoughts. I also mention the change in bus schedules at the end of August, but she already knows about that. I don't need to be invited over because she already has that information. The bus schedule is important because the staff are expected to work the September weekends, and also Thanksgiving. Otherwise, they don't get their summer tips. My daughter is attending university quite a distance from the lake district. Getting back to school for Monday-morning classes might be a problem next fall.

Her third job idea was so vague that I would simply say that I had a hard time following it. I may ask, "Do you think you might want to find out more about that job before you make your final decision?"

The conversation may end on this note. "But sweetie, which one of these jobs would be fun for you? Which experience might be good to have on your curriculum vitae?" She will "own" her own decision, and will be totally responsible for whether it works or not. At no time did I take that responsibility away from her. Her self-confidence will develop as she explores her strengths and her weaknesses. She will find out a great deal about herself, whichever job she takes.

When I am doing family psychotherapy, I see so many children who have not been allowed to make their own decisions. Then, when they are twelve or thirteen, their parents suddenly decide that these children should be responsible. One typical complaint is that the children are not doing their chores around the house. I may ask the parents what jobs they wish the children to do, and then ask them to stay out of the following conversation.

"Now that you guys know what Mom and Dad want done, would you please negotiate with each other, and see if you can divide up the jobs? Feel free to be creative in the way you do this." Eventually, the chores are allotted among the three children, and I make notes for future reference.

When this family returns two weeks later, I enquire about how things are going. Mom or Dad usually tells me that George isn't doing what he said he would. At which point, I may turn to George and ask him, "How come?"

George's response: "I want to do what Michael is doing!" I say, okay, and then suggest that this is a problem that the two of them can work out here. I proceed to tell them a bit about mediating, about "getting to yes," and then I, too, stay out of the conversation. When the boys have reached agreement, I ask, "Are you two both okay about this now?"

George rarely has been treated in this peer fashion. I didn't bawl him out when he changed his mind. By leaving the two boys to solve this problem, I respected their space. The solution will be theirs, and it is up to them to succeed or fail at it. Usually, there is little trouble from George from then on. He feels important. Someone finally is listening to him, without commenting on whether his ideas are good, bad, or indifferent. He is left free to be responsible or not.

Good listening is respectful and leaves the other person with his or her dignity intact. One more point, however, needs to be made about good listening. It has to do with second-guessing what others feel and think.

Why Second-Guessing Is Unwise

Be careful not to second-guess what is going on inside another person's psyche. Instead, make it a rule to *always ask, instead of tell!* If the situation does not allow for this, then plan to check out your perceptions later with that person.

A story best illustrates this. Years ago, a fifty-year-old woman was referred to me by her general practitioner. Valerie was barely functioning, and had taken a three-month leave-of-absence from her job. We worked together on her journey towards Internalizing her feelings. She was starting to feel much better.

Valerie decided to ask her Aunt Mildred over for tea. It was the first company she had had in months. As she told it, "We were sitting at the dining-room table, laughing and talking. I felt like my old self again. It was wonderful!"

In the middle of this, her husband, Bert, came in from the backyard. As Valerie described it, Bert glared and looked disapproving. "My heart sank, and I started to cry," she reported.

"What did you do?" I asked.

Valerie explained that at this point she and Bert had to withdraw to another room. Valerie was furious and let loose a torrent of feelings. All thoughts of "I" messages went out the window. "I told him he always looked that way, that he had spoiled every good time in my life!" Apparently, this attack was the last straw for Bert. Inside, he was boiling mad, because for months he had been pussy-footing around Valerie, respecting how fragile she'd become. But now that he had seen signs that she was starting to recover, he decided to let her have it.

Valerie recalled the terrible things they had said to each other. Their arguing apparently had grown increasingly destructive. I asked

Valerie, "How did you know just *how* your husband was feeling when he came in from the backyard?"

Valerie, quite incensed, shot back at me, "Don't tell me I don't know how that man feels! I've been married to him for twenty-eight years, and I know him like a book!"

I laughed and replied, "I have some trouble believing that." And then I explained to Valerie why this was so. During the 1960s and early 1970s, efforts were made to train people to rate certain aspects of psychological experiments — to guess what other people were feeling, for example. They tried all sorts of techniques. Researchers used pictures, actors, and real people in the studies. The researchers could not get even close to reliability (Krech et al., *Elements of Psychology,* p. 468).

Understanding the many permutations and combinations of physiological response, energy level, and body positions in different people experiencing the same emotion, this is not surprising. Bert's facial expression looked to Valerie like someone glaring with anger. I told her that if a wife in one of my sessions tells her husband what he is thinking or feeling, I typically ask the wife to rephrase what was said and put it in the form of a question. When the husband then replies, it often becomes clear that the projection was not accurate at all. In fact, it usually says more about the speaker than about the person who is being described.

I then suggested to Valerie that we replay that scene again. "Your husband has just walked in the back door, and you get upset at the look on his face. Would you allow me to role-play a bit here?" Valerie agreed.

"This time, you might say to Bert something like, I looked at your face when you came in the door, and I thought you looked angry." The important peer-relationship question follows: "What was going on with you?"

As we soon learned from Bert, he had developed ulcers during this stressful time in their lives. While the ladies were having tea, he was in the backyard raking leaves. Suddenly, he began to suffer terrible stomach cramps. When Valerie saw him, he was tiptoeing through the dining room, trying not to disturb them. He was on the way to the medicine cabinet in the bathroom where his medication was kept.

The whole thing had been a disaster. They could never take back the awful things that were said. Yet, in the long run, it was the best thing that had happened for the couple. They began to see how they projected all sorts of misinformation onto each other when they were angry. They also agreed to test out the accuracy of their projections to prove to themselves that, more often than not, they would be wrong. Valerie and Bert soon became experts at *asking, instead of telling.*

Why "You" Messages Are Dangerous

People have to be in control to use "I" messages. If you can feel your cheeks flush pink long before you turn a purplish hue, then you have lots of time to problem-solve. When you eventually are able to Internalize, you will be strongly aware of your feelings and the signals your body is sending you. You will be able to communicate at the time, or close to the time, that something has started to make you anxious or upset.

Unfortunately, when feelings escalate and flood up unbidden from the unconscious, "you" messages tend to pop out unannounced. This happens because you are no longer fully in control of your emotions. The Shadow, as we learned earlier, dwells in the unconscious. Its dark aspects are responsible for much of our negativity and our destructive and vindictive behaviour.

Because so much of the Shadow is hidden from our awareness, we often fail to take responsibility for what has been said. We "forget," dissociating anything negative we do not wish to own. Or we compartmentalize and keep certain information quite separate and removed from the rest of our reality. Either way, the dark side of the Shadow spells trouble for us. For those we affect, it is especially problematic. In this case, "What you don't know can't hurt you!" is a dangerous denial of reality.

Remember, "I" messages are healthy and responsible communication. "You" messages are manipulative and controlling.

THE JOURNEY MOVES ON

The three stages of the journey — (1) Awareness: Learn to Internalize your feelings; (2) Rescheduling; and (3) Non-controlling communication — involve a long, slow process of change. You may encounter inner resistance because you have been Externalizing most of your life. So be patient. It won't happen overnight.

Remember to keep stopping yourself, get in touch with your feelings through your body awareness, and then ask those five questions. Persevere until you know the answers, as close as possible to the time of the event.

The encouraging news is that once you use the "I" message more naturally, people respond positively. You, in turn, become an excellent listener. And you'll be surprised how much you learn from other people. Let's face it, being right and having your own way all the time are pretty boring.

And, the best news yet, friendships are formed through peer relationship interaction. The "new you" will not be a Dr. Jekyll one day and Mr. Hyde the next. You will learn to be respectful of others. They, in turn, will respond with new attitudes and behaviour towards you.

Seeing the Results of Your Efforts

In Chapter 10, we will explore the differences between Feeling and Thinking language. You will discover that Feeling behaviour is quite distinguishable from Thinking behaviour. You will learn how to rephrase things in Feeling language. As well, you will recognize when you are on the negative and positive side of both functions.

Don't worry! You are not going to give up your best function. If you are a Thinker, you are going to *add* the Feeling function to your repertoire. You will discover many new facets of your personality, and these will give you a greater maturity and offer wonderful new challenges. Feelers will affirm their best function and make sure it is working well. They will need to concentrate on developing the best aspects of Thinking to counteract their own negative Inferior Thinking, which takes over when they are upset.

Once you go through the hypothetical door to open up your opposite function, there is a whole new world to explore. That is where the excitement, the freshness, the joy are stored. Push the door open, and see where it goes!

10
Feeling and Thinking
Language and Behaviour

"I Thought We Spoke the Same Language!"

You can't grow if you don't know you are stuck.

A young medical doctor and his wife came up to me after my lecture on understanding the addiction of workaholism and its devastating effects on the family. "After reading your book," the husband said, "we realized that we were pretty good at rewarding our two children for their accomplishments." This, apparently, was quite easy for them to do. They both complimented and rewarded the children on a regular basis.

Then the wife joined in: "We talked it over, and decided to make a conscious effort to reward our kids for their 'being and feeling' side. Unfortunately, what we soon discovered, to our great discomfort, was that we don't really have a language to do this!"

I've thought often of this couple's eagerness to do the best for their children. It is quite amazing, when you think about it, that two bright, well-educated, and articulate people can suddenly realize that their language is inadequate. This young couple identified an imbalance in their Thinking and Feeling vocabulary that was inhibiting their communication skills.

DISCOVERING A DIFFERENT LANGUAGE

Feeling language is scarce when one's feelings are numb! Feelings often get blocked to avoid the pain and negativity of a chaotic childhood. This imbalance of functions leaves a person vulnerable to dysfunction in adulthood.

Such a person, Jon, a forty-year-old accountant, became trapped in workaholism and emotionally crippled as a result. Jon was increasingly aware that he now functioned at two speeds. As he put it, "I either felt low as a submarine, and zombied my way through each day, or I felt supercharged. I would pump adrenalin as if it was going out of style." Increasingly, Jon lived in a state of emotional greyness, and he was suffering frequent bouts of rage. If there was any disorder in the home when Jon returned from work, he would simply go berserk. His erratic behaviour and verbal abuse had reached crisis proportions. His wife, Tania, was unable to overcome her depression because of the ongoing trauma, and the children were chronically anxious. Stefan, their six-year-old, showed signs of regressing. He was wetting his bed frequently, and his father's outrage at this only made the situation worse. In contrast, Alec, the older child, stood up to his father. His aggressive outbursts added to the family's turmoil. Tania was at a breaking point.

Tania gave Jon an ultimatum. Either he get his act together, or she was initiating separation proceedings. At this point, I suggested to the couple that Jon withdraw to their cottage for a week. Barely functioning and feeling totally numb, Jon needed to remove himself from the situation for everyone's sake. His stress system was overloaded. Any aggravation, however slight, set him off.

On his return from the cottage, I saw Jon alone. "What were some of your thoughts while you were away?" I asked.

"Well, I feel much better," he began. "I went for a walk every day, and I worked on the steps at the cottage."

"Yes, but what were your thoughts about how you have been treating your family?" I prompted.

"Well, I didn't think too much about that!" was his reply.

My heart sank. It was apparent that Jon was still totally out of touch with his Feelings. His Feeling language was minimal, except when his anger forced negative feelings to the surface. He couldn't afford to let in any more pain for fear his fragile Self would be totally destroyed. He was stuck. In retrospect, though, this week did prove to be a watershed. Jon began an earnest plunge into the therapeutic process. It was as though his life depended on it.

Some weeks later, the couple were sitting in my office together. There had been no outbursts at home. On the contrary, Jon was able to stand back and objectively rationalize, for example, why the fort the children had built in the middle of the living room was really okay.

Jon and I were discussing the overwhelming amount of anger that had surged up to the surface in our sessions in the previous few weeks. As he spoke, Jon's arms were stretched in a circle in front, his hands clenched, not quite touching. Every muscle stood out on his arms, and his shoulders were hunched over and tightly locked. He was busily analysing past injustices. "No one was allowed to be angry in my family. It never would have occurred to us to even think of building a fort in our living room. Children were to be seen and not heard. That much was crystal clear!" Jon was intellectualizing his insights.

"Would you please stop for a moment?" I asked. I imitated Jon's tense arms and their circular position. I asked him to assume that stance again.

"What does that position make you think of, Jon?" I asked.

Jon hesitated. "It looks like a dam. I feel like I'm holding in this torrent of rage. If it ever gets through that hole between my hands, then all hell will break through!"

I pointed out that up until now, Jon had been intellectualizing. I wanted him to just *feel* how much stress he created in his body when he was expressing the historical reasons for this rage. "Just hold that position for a few moments. Try not to think. Just *feel*. Now, exaggerate your tension!" I instructed. We both held that pose. My shoulders ached as they arched forward. The muscles in my arms hurt as the tension across my back spread through to my fingertips.

After a few minutes, I said, "Now, Jon, try shaking out your arms. Just let go, like this." I watched as he intently followed these instructions. "Just imagine all that negative energy flowing out in concentric waves, washing away from your body."

Finally, Jon sat quietly. "This is the first time I've been aware of the difference," he said thoughtfully. When I asked what he meant, he explained, "I know that I intellectualize all the time. I've been aware of that for a long while. But," and then he looked pleased, "until this moment, I didn't know what the alternative would be!"

Jon, Tania, and I laughed together, partly in relief. Jon had finally got out of his head and into his body. Nothing disastrous happened, as he had feared. His feelings didn't overwhelm him. His anger didn't explode. At the end of the session, Jon summed up the experience: "I really did feel those waves take my anger away! Thanks for stopping me. I think I'm finally on to something."

THE RISK OF OPENING UP PANDORA'S BOX

Changing is scary! As Jon had put it at the end of our first meeting together, "Promise me, Dr. Killinger, that at the end of this journey you've been describing, I won't end up hating myself!"

"On the contrary," I replied, "I think you'll be quite proud. When your Feeling and Thinking functions are better balanced, the decisions you make will be wiser and better-informed. And, you'll likely be more effective and compassionate in the way you seek solutions to problems."

I believe that people like Jon act out their repressed Feelings because they are unable, or sometimes unwilling, to free up deeply entrenched, painful memories. The challenge becomes one of exploration, then transformation. Often, lasting change is accomplished through revisiting stressful childhood experiences, and viewing them from the adult's perspective. Remember that the child sees things from a uniquely ego-centred focus in which everything centres around his or her experience. Past fears and trauma were often too difficult to handle at the time each incident occurred because of the child's age and stage of development. Often unacknowledged hurts cripple future growth.

Knowledge is the key to unravelling the mysteries contained within Pandora's box. As adults, we have the advantage of objectivity and life experience to review the past. We must factor in the personalities and histories of our parents. They are real people, not the ones we had idealized. They had needs and deficiencies and those determined their behaviour. Previous generations and times had also shaped *their* behaviour.

Sociological factors such as the war, the Depression, unemployment, addictive behaviours such as alcohol, gambling, smoking, and so on — all must be considered. Children remain largely ignorant of the complexity of such influences.

Through confronting our conflicts and searching for meaning, we progress towards balance and maturity. The paradox is that growth does not come without journeying through our pain.

RECOGNIZING PATTERNS OF DESTRUCTIVE BEHAVIOUR

A first step towards self-knowledge is to recognize signs in your behaviour that signal that the dark, Shadow side is becoming powerful in your personality. Watch for changes in the language you use. Do you find yourself talking down to people, or saying things that humiliate or punish others? Do you hear yourself swearing or using abusive language? Do you act out self-destructive behaviour, such as overeating, excessive drinking, or smoking, and then belittle yourself for it? Do you ignore signs of body distress and remain numb rather than seek help? Do you experience a sense of alienation, isolation, or depression, and feel your self-esteem plummet further? Do you have an obsessive need to be in control, and insist on telling others what to do? It is important to recognize that *fear* underlies these manifestations of anger and abuse.

When you are able to master the process of Internalizing, a broader range of feelings will break through to the surface and be available to you. Listen to their intensity. What shades of meaning do these layers of feelings convey? Is this anger I'm experiencing mild or extreme? Am I overreacting, or do I really care that much about this particular issue? Both positive and negative feelings must be acknowledged before healthy behaviour is possible. Recognition allows you to nurture yourself, instead of continuing to punish yourself and others, albeit unconsciously. Welcome the recognition of your Shadow side. This knowledge shows you where you need to grow.

As new shadows surface into consciousness, set each fresh "insight" on the top ledge of an imaginary fence to remind you of the things you want to work on. You'll experience a flash of recognition each time you slip up and repeat that same negative behaviour. For example, you may catch yourself arrogantly projecting criticism onto someone else. "For Pete's sake, I just did it again!" may be your impatient response to this insight.

Change is never easy. Old habits die hard. Keep trying, and don't be discouraged. Resistance and laziness will pull you back to old ways if you don't remain vigilant.

The couple we are calling Sally and Peter opened up Pandora's box. Through self-exploration and learning new skills, they transformed the negative behaviour and language they found within their family. We will now return to their story.

New Behaviour and a New Language

Sally

As you may recall, Sally scored as a Feeler on the Myers-Briggs Test Indicator. When I first met Sally, though, she was depressed and largely unaware of how deeply angry she had become. She didn't hear the snap in her voice, nor did she realize how much she lectured her family.

Sally progressed quickly through the process of Internalizing because she was restoring the Feeling side that came naturally to her. Also, she became superaware of the times when negative thinking was distorting her normal language and behaviour. She would grimace every time she became aware of her sharp, short delivery and her acid tongue. "Surely this wasn't me!" she protested.

Keeping harmony had cost Sally a great deal. Her naivety and depression blocked out reality and kept her from growing. She hadn't recognized that her own personality was changing. Fear of confrontation, along with Peter's threatening disapproval and rages, kept Sally trapped in her own trauma. Her feelings remained flat so that she could avoid dealing with her painful reality.

Sally's energy was renewed as her depression lifted. She was now ready to develop the positive side of her less-developed Thinking function. She purposefully read her newspaper for a half-hour each morning. She became much better informed about the thoughts and ideas of others. She learned to be more critical of what she read, and tried to analyse why certain things were happening. She attended lectures on current affairs and panel discussions on contentious subjects. Entering this fresh world of ideas and thoughts was very exciting. Understanding took on added meaning.

Eventually, Sally made a decision to go back to school. Through re-establishing her Feeling side and encouraging her positive Thinking, Sally developed new confidence. Her thoughts were well-informed and articulate, yet delivered with grace and assurance.

Sally grew from the trauma of what she called "The Terrible Years." Peter's bankruptcy was the catalyst for this family. Bankruptcy is about as concrete as things can get. Denial and naivety have difficulty surviving that cruel reality. "It was the worst of times. It was the best of times," as the saying goes.

Sally soon realized, with some awe, just how much there was to learn about her rational, logical, analytical, pragmatic side.

Peter

For Peter, a natural Thinker, the journey towards Feeling was most difficult. For a long time, he would have to translate his thoughts into feelings. "I had to *think* about how I felt all the time" was how he described this struggle.

Eventually Peter was able to acknowledge that he had indeed become emotionally crippled. Sadly, his distress was compounded by the shame of lost integrity. As he put it, "I recognize now the real reason I came to see you. Something in me was crying out. I can see that my Shadow was pulling me further down into disaster. I couldn't stop myself." Shady business practices, secrecy, deceit, and greed had led him away from his former idealism. Bankruptcy woke Peter up. His pride, however, took an awful tumble.

The jolt of pain he suffered when his business failed suddenly made the need for psychotherapy more relevant to Peter. Survival was something Peter *did* believe in. He battled through his airtight denial and his strong defenses of dissociating and compartmentalizing. Peter had forgotten how to tell the truth.

As new insights broke through to consciousness, Peter became more open to revelations about his childhood, and these shed light on his present situation, and the drastic change in his personality. Surprisingly, instead of the pain that he dreaded, relief flooded in. "No wonder I did that!" became a frequent exclamation.

I knew that Peter was ready to take a further step because he was showing real concern for the damage he had done to his family. Tears spilled whenever he realized a new aspect of the turmoil he had caused in Sally's life. Nowadays, his face appeared softer and gentler. This was a sign that Peter's feelings were working.

"I never used to cry," Peter explained. "It always hurt me physically because there was such a block in my throat. I could only choke." Then he added, "I was watching a movie the other night, and I could feel tears spill down my cheeks. I reached over to Sally, and we just held hands for a while. It was just a great moment!" He laughed in relief.

Some time later, Peter hesitantly asked me if I could write a "cookbook" or something like that to help him. He needed more insight into how he could change his surly, brusque behaviour. He was still offending people, but didn't know how. Would I help him learn some different ways of saying things? Peter's request indicated a need for more concrete direction. Peter had feeling now, but no language to express it.

Peter's Cookbook
Changing an attitude is one thing. Transforming behaviour is quite another challenge. It certainly isn't easy. Thinkers and Feelers

phrase similar thoughts in very different ways. Peter and I worked together on some of the key changes he wished to make.

It is important to remember that Thinking and Feeling are ways of making decisions. Thinking has a *focused awareness* that concentrates on getting from A to B. In the extreme, Thinking becomes narrow and one-tracked. It deals with things one at a time, and follows a logical process aimed at an impersonal finding. Ideas and goals are formed through the Thinking process. This function also checks for flaws or errors in decisions based on emotion and intuition.

Feeling, on the other hand, uses a *diffuse awareness* that is directed outwards. In fact, it is often too other-directed! Feelers may disregard what matters to them simply because they wish others to be happy. Even their own body signals may be ignored when the early signs of illness should be alerting them to health problems.

Feelers can concentrate on a number of things at once. Feeling considers the person's own thoughts, but also is open and receptive to cues and feedback from other people, and from the surrounding environment. Feeling bestows a personal, subjective value on things. Feeling decisions, therefore, evolve from one's personal value system, and are influenced by what one appreciates.

Feeling opens us up to *wait, watch, and wonder.* The key concepts of Feeling are openness, receptivity, and reaching out to others. It is our thoughtful, sensitive, empathic, tactful, gracious, loyal side. It values harmony above all. Sharing, intimacy, and devotion are its goals. People and relationships are its interest.

The following tasks may help you to nurture and develop your own Feeling side. Expect to feel awkward and self-conscious when you first exercise your Feeling "muscles," especially if you are a Thinker. Eventually, as Feelings work independently, expressions will seem more natural and genuine. You will not have to translate, to *think* about how you Feel.

A. Better Listening and Healthy Communication

"How can I be a better listener?" Peter asked. In time, Peter learned to recognize the moment when he turned himself off and switched to his own inner dialogue. "I'd hear myself rehearsing what I was going to say next," he observed. "I realize now that there was no way I could do two things at once. I'd have no idea what the other person was saying." It took discipline for Peter to refocus. He often had to ask a question, or request that the other person repeat what he or she had said.

Peter also learned to listen in retrospect to his own communication. After saying something, he would ponder whether he had been clear. He remembered some of the reasons Thinkers are often poor communicators: Thinkers tend to clutter up their communications with adjuncts, qualifications, retractions, saving clauses, doubts; or they don't give enough information and sound blunt, sharp, abrupt; or they talk for too long and are too intense about their idea, and neglect to focus on the listener; or they bore the listener by lecturing or preaching and not exchanging views; or they fail to personalize and own what they are saying, talking instead in generalities, and using theoretical logic; or they get "historical," bringing up incidents from weeks, months, or years before to support their point of view. Peter gradually understood that this type of communication was offputting and often impossible to interpret.

HOW TO IMPROVE YOUR COMMUNICATION

1. Go beyond your own subjective viewpoint. In order to be *other-directed,* you need to develop diffuse awareness. Practise by watching for feedback when you state an idea. Observe others' reactions and facial expressions, especially the eyes. Talking and watching at the same time is not an easy task for the Thinker. Focused awareness, in contrast, centres on the speaker's own thoughts and delivery.

2. Observe and question without judging. As you are speaking, watch to see if the listener shows loss of interest, restlessness, boredom, confusion, a blank expression, no understanding, or loss of eye contact. Try to curb your naturally critical temperament. Remember, the negative side of Thinking tends to be judgmental, critical, skeptical, and pessimistic. Ask yourself, How might I be turning that person off? Am I lecturing, or going round in circles? Am I arguing, or is my logic difficult to follow?

3. *Comment on your own communication.* At first, when Peter realized he had somehow lost contact with the other person, he would blurt out, "You're not listening to me!" Not surprisingly, this "you" message was perceived as a criticism. "It's your fault!" is the underlying message. Peter then tried a humorous approach, as he termed it. "Are you guys wearing earmuffs today?" No one laughed.

Impulsive, opinionated thoughts are best "censored through sensitivity." Since Peter wishes to be better understood, Feeling language that uses the "I" message is easier to listen to. "I may not be describing this very well!" indicates that Peter is taking responsibility for his own miscommunication. Or, "Sometimes I get carried away with my ideas and get verbal diarrhea!" shows the listener that Peter is at least conscious of his shortcomings.

4. *Solicit feedback from the listener.* Following your explanation or comment, ask whether the listener understood. "Is this making any sense to you at all?" or "I'm not sure whether this subject is something you're even interested in?" ensures that listeners realize you are sensitive to their reactions. Slowly, Peter is learning that not everyone cares about his interests!

The listener must be important to the speaker. The black-and-white, concrete Thinker who is driven to find pragmatic answers to questions concerning ideas and goals tends to be most interested in getting from A to B. However, Peter is very aware of Sally's keen interest in the people involved in such pursuits. As his feelings surface, Peter, too, expresses genuine curiosity about the lives of the people he works with every day. Before, these people had a job to do in the scheme of *his* world. Now he understands that they have a life outside his sphere of influence.

5. *After listening to the feedback on your ideas, invite the other to share his/her own views.* Exchanging views is true communication.

Conversations ought to be a two-way process. Peter, himself now growing increasingly impatient with people who monopolize conversations, learned to suggest, "I've had the floor long enough. I would really like to hear your views on this whole thing." His fresh curiosity about how different people saw the same situation led Peter to criticize his former indifference. "Before, I didn't give a damn what anybody else thought! People were just getting to be a grand nuisance." When he had asked his managers what they thought, as Peter tells it, "I was just being Mr. Nice Guy. I couldn't tell you two minutes after what the hell they said."

Although discussions typically involve an exchange of views, arguments attempt to convince the other that "I am *right*. You are *wrong!*" Narcissists, who have to be "right" and have their own way, introduce a strange twist. According to their reasoning, "If you disagree with me, that means *you* think that I am wrong." Peter's paranoia turned innocent conversations into defensive counter-attacks. He would conclude, "If everyone thinks I am wrong, then nobody respects me." Two people cannot possibly both be right in the world he has created!

To encourage discussion and preserve harmony, listen carefully to the views of each person involved in your conversations. Agreeing to disagree is possible only when people truly respect the rights of individuals to hold their own unique views.

6. *Don't use closure statements.* Unwittingly, people with controlling natures often add closure statements at the end of their thoughts. Peter would end his remarks with a conclusive phrase such as "This makes sense to me" or "That's what I think!" It's like putting a strong "period" at the end of your sentence. Such finality suggests that the speaker's conclusion is sacrosanct.

Avoid using closure statements. Instead, leave the subject open-ended, or solicit the opinions of others. Peter, realizing he needs time to digest new or conflicting information, has learned to buy time. In Feeling language, he reveals new sensitivity: "Let me think about that! It's an interesting idea, but new to me. I'd like to talk about this again when I've had time to absorb it."

7. Avoid being short, blunt, or obtuse. Clear communication results in shared knowledge. Remember, Thinkers tend to formulate their ideas, and package them *before* they speak. Feelers often *talk through* their thoughts before reaching a conclusion.

Short, blunt, sharp remarks tend to jar the listener. Key information is often left out when people forget to tell you what the subject is. Who or what is this person talking about? Obtuse thinking confuses rather than informs.

The intensity of your communication may convey an emphasis you do not intend. It's like *underlining* as you speak. Is the weight or the formality of my words appropriate to the subject matter? Am I raising my voice without realizing it? Again, watch your listener for clues. You may be shouting and not know it.

8. Express your thoughts within a context. When you state an idea, try to lead into it with a preamble or introduction. Dropping thoughts without a context is like discharging a bomb without targeting it! Listeners cannot share your perspective or see the setting of your experience. Peter understands that his "left field" delivery alienates others. Learning to set the scene, Peter introduces his views on a local political issue: "Yesterday I was watching a panel of experts on the six o'clock news discuss the new legislation about waste disposal sites. My opinion is totally different from those guys'!" Peter may then clarify his thoughts and offer solutions to this particular problem.

9. Convey your enthusiasm or keen interest. Because Thinkers tend to intellectualize, they often fail to reveal how strongly they care about something. Others may be misled by the flat tone of their delivery, which contrasts with the intensity of their voice and the strength of their body language. The listener is left with the question, "Which signals should I follow?"

Peter is learning to add a feeling component to his delivery. He wants others to understand how emotionally involved he is in his concern for the environment. This subject is an important one for Peter. His listeners may well attend more closely out of respect for this commitment. "I'm quite excited about this new program," conveys Peter's true experience.

Enthusiasm and excitement communicated through superlatives come from his Feeling side. Peter would not have used words like *excited* before. In the past, his strong Thinking, rational, logical, pragmatic side dominated his personality and his language. "That's an interesting idea" would be as close as Peter would come to revealing the emotion behind his thoughts.

10. Be honest and keep your integrity. Focus on honesty by being totally responsible for the integrity of your own thoughts and behaviour. A word of caution here. The feelings expressed in your words must be real and truly experienced. *Do not say what others want to hear, unless it is the truth.* Manipulative behaviour comes easily to people who grew up in dysfunctional families, since as children they did not want to make waves. When Peter was polite and accommodating in the past, he had an ulterior motive. When he wanted something, he knew exactly what to say. He knew how to please, and how to convince. Much of the time, though, Peter was not even aware of his own manipulation. He acted as he always had in the past.

The dishonest used-car salesman who knows exactly how to disarm a reluctant buyer is a prototype of a manipulative person. Something deep inside often sings out to warn the clever buyer. Other, more naive clients, however, often fall for a convincing sales pitch.

B. Openness

Feeling behaviour and language foster sensitivity, empathy, thoughtfulness, grace, diplomacy, and harmony. Together, they encourage discussion rather than argument. An open sharing of ideas and experience brings people together, and encourages good listening *and* communication skills.

Openness leads one to be *other-directed*, considerate of the welfare of others. Controlling leads to manipulation, the loss of respect for the rights of others. To counteract his controlling nature, Peter worked on his openness and sensitivity.

1. BE AWARE OF YOUR PROJECTIONS. Openness will be achieved only when controlling stops and the power struggle ends. People like Peter control from clues gained by interpreting others' messages. They project and guess what others want them to say, think, do, or feel. Only when Peter stopped Externalizing and learned to Internalize was he able to curb his second-guessing tactics.

Peter learned to go inside himself to listen to his own reactions and formulate his own truth. Then he conveyed his ideas, using "I" messages. He also learned to communicate his views only when he was in full control of himself. If he was not, he delayed problem-solving by rescheduling, or he left the scene to regain personal control. His tendency to scriptwrite, to rehearse a dialogue between himself and another person before the conversation even began, gradually stopped, and he became more spontaneous. He had a new respect for others.

Not only is scriptwriting disrespectful and patronizing, it is a waste of energy and time. Remember that more than half the time you will be wrong in your perceptions.

2. STOP CONTROLLING. Risk being more open, flexible, and spontaneous. Try not to rehearse what you are going to say or do next. Instead, concentrate on your own "side of the fence." Be clear about your own thoughts and feelings, and verbalize them with care and concern for the listener. Communication should be free of judgment. Put simply, you are trying to convey a description of your experience of the situation. This is your reality. The other individual's dignity and respect are honoured and left intact.

Do not second-guess how the other person will respond to your words or actions. A good rule of thumb to guide you is *always ask, instead of tell.* Remember, interpreting what others are likely to do is controlling behaviour. Peter used to take great pleasure in telling others what was going on in their lives, even though he got incensed if others did that to him. Peter now tries to phrase questions that leave the initiative with the other person. For example, Peter asked Sally one day, "I'm having trouble understanding why you said that to Penny! Would you help me understand your reasoning. I'd appreciate it." Sally, in turn, truly valued his curiosity. She sensed that Peter no longer felt he knew her better than she knew herself, as in the old days.

Avoid making assumptions about the motivations of others. Reach out instead by asking questions, such as "Could you tell me why … ?"; "Were you upset by … ?"; "Do you think … ?"; "How do you feel about … ?"; "I wonder if … ?"; "That sounds pretty disturbing. Was it?"; "I'd have some trouble handling that. Did you?"

3. OPEN BODY LANGUAGE. If you are genuinely concerned about another person, this positive attitude will show in your body stance. Ask yourself what message your body is conveying. Are you making eye contact as you speak? Resistance to openness is revealed if your arms are crossed over your chest, or your legs are crossed, or your thighs are held tightly together. Are you fidgeting, unable to focus, and impatient to have the floor once again?

Occasionally, my clients rehearse for me what they wish to say in a job interview. When I point out their defensive postures or uptight body language, they are often surprised. Typically, when bodies are tense, breathing is constricted as well. No wonder people often cannot think clearly during an interview.

4. MOODS AND PROJECTIONS. One cannot remain open and sensitive to others when caught in the clutches of a fully developed mood. Put simply, if you are caught in a mood, do not project your negative feelings onto others. Recognize the earliest signs of a mood beginning, and intervene. For techniques to help you control your moods, see "The Road to Recovery" chapter in my book *Workaholics: The Respectable Addicts.*

Try to respect other people's moods, but do not take responsibility for them. The initial tendency is to project onto that person your version of why he or she is caught up in a bad mood. This often happens because the ego-centred part of us tends to make assumptions that the reason for the other person's mood lies with us.

The safe thing to do is to *offer empathy only.* Respect their right to feel their feelings. Try not to talk people out of their mood. Refrain from suggesting going somewhere or doing something to pull them out of it. When Sally withdrew and cut herself off from Peter, he would suggest that they go to a show, or out for dinner. Sitting in stony silence in a restaurant, or becoming more agitated by the loaded emotions presented in a movie, is no solution for someone caught in a mood. Overstimulation only increases feelings of helplessness or anxiety.

Simply acknowledge the other person's feelings, and ask if there is anything you might do. "You seem a little down today. Would you like me to make you some tea?" is Feeling language. Give support by showing concern. Each of us is responsible for getting out of our own mood. So relax and be patient.

Above all, do not try to problem-solve for them. Avoid criticism or judgments. Someone caught in a mood is unable to Think or Feel, let alone seek solutions to problems. Projecting your version of the problem onto someone else only compounds the problem. Resentment results when unsolicited advice is given. It is likely that the moody person will lash back, and an endless discussion will ensue that goes nowhere. Sound familiar?

Give space and allow time for the other person to work through unhappy feelings. Go and do your own thing. No one in a mood needs to be burdened further by your upset reactions.

If you wish to follow it up later, you might ask, "I would really like to know what was the matter the other day." Chances are, the other person will then be in a better position to answer that question. However, some people resent this invasion of privacy. They have let go, so why bring up old stuff? As Peter, who hates redundancy, says, "Why beat it to death?"

C. Generosity and Appreciation

Genuine caring and appreciation, especially in Extraverts, need to be shared to be fully conveyed. Introverts, however, because they keep feelings locked safely inside, often neglect to verbalize appreciation. Introverts conserve energy, whereas Extraverts expend energy, and coincidentally, beget more by doing so!

For Thinkers, it often isn't logical and rational to care so deeply. So appreciation from them is often scarce. Ideas and goals are safer targets for their energy. People who demand and expect certain behaviour from Thinkers may be experienced as troublesome or tiresome.

1. GRATITUDE. I believe that one of the secrets of happiness is to be truly grateful. It is relatively easy to appreciate the good things that life sends our way. The more difficult task is to be open when negative situations knock on our door. It takes courage to open that door and be receptive to whatever lesson life sends our way. It helps to lighten things up with humour: "I hope I grow an inch with this one!"

2. SHOW ENTHUSIASM. Appreciation is conveyed by expressing enthusiasm for other people's ideas, thoughts, and deeds. Praise, encouragement, and support come from the Feeling side. Whereas Peter would say, "Good work!" if a job was well done, he had difficulty saying to his wife, "That was a wonderful thing you did for your sister." In fact, underneath, he envied the ease with which Sally performed thoughtful acts. Thinkers, because they are naturally competitive, also place things on a hierarchical basis, and rate themselves in relation to others on that ladder. Words like "wonderful," "terrific," "great," and "super" sound phony to them. They are reluctant to elevate others above their level.

Thinkers need to counterbalance their naturally critical and skeptical reserve. "My ball team would laugh themselves silly if I used the language you're teaching me!" challenged another determined Thinker. I laughed, and encouraged him to try out some new language that evening at the office game. "What a great hit!" was the most Jake could imagine himself saying, as he left the office muttering. Jake, like Peter, soon discovered that when he showed enthusiasm or said supportive things, people beamed back. It didn't stop him feeling silly for a while though.

Another Thinker, working on developing her Feeling, burst into my office one afternoon. "I've just made friends with my archenemy!" Patricia enthused. This man got the promotion she had aspired to. "You know, this guy isn't half bad. When I told him about this journey I'm going through in here, he started to tell me about the problems he is having at home." Patricia empathized: "No wonder he was such a pain in the butt." By articulating her feelings at the office, Patricia found that others, who secretly had been afraid of her, now responded with smiles and, as she quipped, "relief." No one could accuse Patricia of being humourless now.

When another client, Joseph, was thanked by his wife, Clare, for the dinner the two had just shared in a new restaurant, he replied curtly, "Don't thank me. It's your money, too!" When Clare protested about her husband's lack of manners, we discussed together how this situation could have been handled with more grace. When I asked Joseph for suggestions, his blank stare revealed his puzzlement. Often, the person is learning a new set of adjectives and verbs that sound like a foreign language. He may not understand yet what is wrong with what he used to say.

3. BE SUPPORTIVE. Generosity can be shown by support for others' independent actions. A very controlling mother once told me, "I wanted the kids to get their act together before I *let* them go on and do their own thing!" After a discussion about how she could say that in Feeling language, Geraldine, who was obviously trying to be supportive, offered, "I hope they're going to be okay. I hope things go well for them." Her sincere wishes for the best for her children were in stark contrast to her endless advice and control.

4. COMPLIMENTARY COMMENTS. Don't hesitate to compliment someone about how well she looks, or what a good conversationalist he is. Many times, people do notice such things, but nothing gets said or done to acknowledge the person's particular talent. "You look really great today!" is Feeling language. "Smart suit!" conveys the compliment, but it lacks enthusiasm. It takes energy to reach out, and so many people refuse to grow because they are psychologically lazy. They restrict their responses to what comes naturally, and miss out on the smiles and joy that compliments elicit from others.

5. BE GENUINE. If what you have to say is not honestly felt, don't say it. People feel manipulated, patronized, or put down when others deliver insincere messages. When a message is negative, take special care to be diplomatic, gracious, and thoughtful in how you phrase your thoughts.

D. Warmth and Sensitivity

Warmth and sensitivity describe two specially appreciated attributes of the Feeling side.

1. WARMTH. Warmth is often conveyed through body language, smiles, and gestures that enhance the gift of words or tokens of appreciation. Reaching out to touch or leaning forward towards someone as you speak can add a deeper meaning to your message. Gently touching someone's arm or shoulder is easier and more natural for Extraverts and for Feelers. Others will feel awkward at first performing such gestures. However, next time you wish to show appreciation in a social situation, try introducing warmth and see what happens.

2. SENSITIVITY. It helps to be sensitive to the "why" behind people's behaviour. The focus needs to be on understanding the thoughts and feelings that motivates people's actions. Feelers, whose values centre around people and relationships, often have an easier time of being gracious in awkward situations.

Sensitivity is especially necessary when gifts are offered and received. Accepting gifts of any kind is difficult for someone who needs to be in control. Whether it be a compliment or an actual gift, the receiver may neglect to affirm the gift-giver. Thinkers, because they tend to be skeptical, often question the giver's motivation. This discomfort may produce a defensive acceptance, such as an ungracious "You shouldn't have done that!"

However, if this same person is open to sharing, he may learn to comment on the feeling *behind* the gift. Whether a person likes the gift or not should not affect appreciation. For example, Peter learned to respond, "What a nice idea!" or "That's very thoughtful of you. Thanks so much."

Peter confided that he was often unhappy about the gifts he received. As he explained, "I have very definite tastes!" Many Thinkers do not even realize it, but they often say nothing at all at the time the gift is given. Or they look very uncomfortable. The rationalization offered is that they don't want to "hurt" others' feelings by saying anything.

Feelers' gifts are often simply an expression of their warmth or sensitivity. There need be no ulterior motivation, other than the wish to show appreciation. Successful gift-giving is not an easy art.

E. Diplomacy and Criticism
The other side of the coin to gift-giving is offering constructive criticism. Here, generosity of spirit needs to be the focus, not power-plays.

1. FAIRNESS. A balanced presentation in which the speaker offers support along with the criticism is best. No one "*always* does something" or "*never* does something."

When criticism is appropriate, soften your delivery by confirming a positive aspect first. Peter, with his tendency to blurt out negative statements, might say something like, "That was a rotten thing you said to so-and-so!" Instead, a more gracious tone is achieved when he says, "You're usually polite. In this particular situation, your words come as quite a surprise!"

2. OBJECTIVE EMPATHY. If someone else is telling you about a goof she made, or a time when he showed poor judgment, further critical judgments are rarely helpful. In fact, the person's shame is compounded. The individual now has a "double whammy" to contend with. Because Sally was so naive, she did not realize the impact on her daughter when she became overly involved in the painful situations Penny experienced. Years before, Penny had come home from school one Valentine's Day. She was devastated because she hadn't received one card. The look on her mother's face, unfortunately, doubled her grief. In Penny's eyes, she had failed her mother, too.

Sally's objective thinking was not working in this situation. Her ego boundaries blurred across into Penny's territory, and she took on her daughter's pain. If she had been able to be more objective, her reply might have been, "Gee, honey, I can't imagine how that happened. Are you disappointed?" Penny could then have vented any feelings she was experiencing.

When someone tells a painful story, it is important not to jump in and sympathize with the victim. Parents' criticisms, especially, have a powerful impact on children. Soon, that child will "neglect to tell the truth." Why tell somebody something if you will be further devastated by doing so.

3. SHARING SHADOWS. At times, however, it may be supportive to share your own foibles or weaknesses with others. Be careful, though, not to pre-empt the storyteller. One day, Peter wanted to know what was wrong with telling one of the kids what *he* would have done, or how he would have handled a similar situation when he was young. I answered by describing a theatrical stage, with a father and son standing in the spotlight, centre stage. The son is telling his dad a sad tale about something that happened the day before. The father responds by going off on a tangent. He makes an "end run," so to speak. He walks across the stage while telling his son how he would have handled that situation.

I asked Peter to imagine that he was the lighting manager for that theatre. "Where would you direct the spotlight during this scene?" Peter's response followed as insight crossed his face. "On the father, of course. He's the guy whose going on and on!" The son, standing in the middle of the stage, alone, would likely feel unheard and misunderstood. The focus of the conversation, and the spotlight, had shifted to his father's ideas and experience.

Keep the spotlight on the speaker is good advice. Remember to *listen fully* to what the other person has to say. Ask questions that solicit more information. By doing so, the feelings relating to the speaker's experience will be brought to the surface as well. Brevity on your part is important when you do decide to share. For example, after his son has talked through his problem, Peter might show empathy by saying, "Something like that happened to me when I was a kid, too!" If the son wants to ask questions about what did happen to his father, then his dad has been invited over into the son's territory. This is a far cry from unsolicited advice.

F. Harmony

If people always have to be right and have their own way, apologizing will not be part of their repertoire. Narcissists, for instance, feel that what they are doing is just fine. After all, they are different and special. What applies to others does not necessarily apply to them.

1. APOLOGIZING. It's the old story. People would rather be right than happy. Value systems enter into this dilemma. If ideas and goals mean more to you than people and relationships, then it makes sense that backing down from a position, or defusing a contentious issue, is not an option for you. Ludicrous examples occur when people threaten to leave a relationship in a heated moment. "I can't possibly apologize. Once I've said I'll do something, I do it," one husband told me.

An apology does not necessarily suggest that you are "wrong." Two people may both be right, but not to the narcissist. He interprets other people's differing views as an indication that they think *he* is wrong! Swallowing pride and demonstrating humility do not come easily to people who have become arrogant. Other people's need for harmony and conflict resolution will be frustrated. There can be no resolution when narcissists remain convinced they are right.

2. DIGNITY. Acknowledging and affirming another person's reality, while at the same time holding on to your own beliefs, is possible. Pride is often a foolish emotion. But a person's dignity does need to be honoured. Acknowledge that you have heard the other person's point of view even if you do not agree with it. To ensure that you have understood, rephrase what the other person has said.

Peter learned to say, "Let me make sure I understand exactly what you are saying." He would then paraphrase, as best he could, and then ask if his interpretation fit.

3. LIGHTEN UP. Because Thinkers have such highly focused awareness, they often come across as very intense. Sometimes, a reason to apologize stems simply from the heated delivery of an argument. Intensity drives home a thought, and this strong focus may convey more than you intend. Derogatory or tough language, such as swearing, attacking someone personally, or exaggerating to make a point, often heighten the impact of your statements on others.

Peter began to realize how he overpowered people. He wanted to learn to state his opinions without overwhelming his listeners. Probably the best way for him to do this, if he catches himself forcing an issue, is to comment on his own delivery. A statement such as "You'll have to excuse me. I really get carried away with my ideas sometimes!" may soften his message. Laughing at your own foibles often serves to break the ice. It isn't helpful if others get defensive and shut off.

4. BRIGHTEN UP. Peter, without realizing it, had developed a permanent frown, two lines deeply furrowed in his brow. His rigidity and stubborn nature had left a permanent reminder. When my clients are getting in touch with their feelings, I often notice a change in the shape of their faces. As the rigidity of the psyche lessens, their features soften. Their cheeks take on a more rounded shape, and muscles around the mouth relax.

Peter, aware of his facial tension, began to do exercises to relax his muscles. He opened up his jaw and purposefully yawned when he became tense over some issue. He even practised smiling in front of the mirror in the morning, to start his day.

His newfound inner harmony and openness to others and their ideas brought a more relaxed state. He no longer kept his arms and legs cramped up as he had when he was caught defending himself against an increasingly chaotic and negative world.

5. SMILE, AND OTHERS SMILE BACK. We may deliver negative vibes to those we encounter each day. Or our positive energy may be a precious gift to others. Your choice!

F. Humility

The balanced individual shows humility because he has learned how much there is to learn. Such people know intuitively that "a little knowledge is a dangerous thing!" They are open and receptive to new ideas. They do not force a decision. They remain conscious of the big picture. "What I don't know today, I can learn tomorrow" might well be their motto.

The mature person is well aware of both his weaknesses and his strengths. Bravely facing the whole complexity of humanity, she always considers both the positive and the negative aspects of each individual and each situation. Naivety, or remaining credulous and unworldly, is fought at every opportunity. There is an acceptance that life is difficult. Life's lessons are opportunities for growth.

Mature people have learned not to problem-solve for others, but to listen. They strive for peer relationships with others. They share power by compromising. They take turns, and mediate by talking through difficult issues. They recognize that they are special in the eyes of God, but recognize and treat others as equals. They acknowledge their own humanity. They have developed a comfortable humility, and do not need to prove themselves to others.

Such people have a good balance between their Thinking and Feeling functions. Both functions work, and support one another. Wise decisions are made with care and consideration for others, and for the truth.

Creative Problem-Solving

In Chapter 11, the end of this journey we have travelled together, a method of problem-solving will be offered that has been adapted from ideas presented in Matthew Fox's book *Creation Spirituality: Liberating Gifts for the Peoples of the Earth*. The title of a popular song by Tina Turner, "What's Love Got to Do with It?" will serve to introduce the themes of maturity, spirituality, creativity, and joy. A journey that takes us towards any or all of these destinations will serve us well.

11
Problem-Solving
Through Creativity
The Logical Circle

*You're only young once, but you can be
immature forever.*

"How will I know when I'm better?" is a question often asked by
impatient clients who want recovery to happen *now*! My standard
answer, after many years of searching, is this: "When the power of
love in you is stronger than the power of greed." This will signal
that feelings really work, and that values have shifted accordingly.
As one client put it, "My wife and my kids are on the front burner
now, and I intend to keep it that way!"

In reality, however, all of us experience continual internal
struggles between Thinking's goal-oriented focus and Feeling's concern for people and relationships. On a recent ski trip to St. Anton
in Austria, an older member of the group followed a different trail
and became separated from the group. It was about 10:30 in the
morning. We waited for some time, to no avail, then continued
skiing. At the top run the group gathered, and I listened as someone suggested going to Stuben, a nearby village, for lunch. Several
people chimed in with their support, thinking this was a great idea.

"What about Kevin?" was the cry from the Feelers in the group.
They assumed that our lost skier would likely wait for us at the inn
in St. Christoph where we had planned to have lunch. "We've got
to stick to our plan."

A chorus of protest rose: "Let's go to Stuben! None of us has been there." This time, the Feelers grew visibly upset and put down their collective feet! "No way! We're not going to abandon Kevin!" After much disgruntled banter, the decision was made: "On to St. Christoph!"

My comment to the man beside me was, "Well, the Feelers won this time!" He replied, "I was sort of on the fence on that one!" Later in the week, a sigh passed through the group as we passed Stuben en route to Zurich airport. "Well, maybe next year!" was heard from the back of the bus. The Thinking side of us hates to lose.

No one was wrong here. Both groups valued different things. However, my experience observing life situations shows that Feeling types often have to shout to get their thoughts acknowledged. The truth is that all of us sit on the fence at times and go against our natural disposition. The difference is that Feelers, who have difficulty telling a lie and make decisions based on their value system, are more likely to suffer guilt and remorse when they act in a way that goes against the grain. Thinkers, because they are more focused and goal-oriented, became absorbed in getting from A to B. Their pragmatic nature permits them to rationalize and justify any of their decisions that go against society's rules and regulations. "I'm rushing, Officer, because I've just got a call that my wife is ill!" The real reason is that he is late for an important meeting. Safety factors and even truth pale beside exciting goals.

In the balanced personality, the person has choice. A conscious decision may be made to use our Thinking function when ideas and goals are the focus, and people's welfare is not directly affected. When people and relationships do matter, it is appropriate to let our Feeling function dominate and influence our decisions. Take care, though, lest the naturally more aggressive Thinking side run roughshod over the Feeling side!

As a model for mature problem-solving that uses both Feeling and Thinking functions, let me offer the circle. In his book, *Creation Spirituality*, Matthew Fox speaks of four paths along the spiritual journey that tell us "what matters" (pp. 18–26). Path one, the Via

Positiva, represents awe, wonder, delight, mystery. Path two, the Via Negativa, represents suffering, darkness, nothingness, emptying, letting go, letting be. Path three, the Via Creativa, embodies creativity, imagination, giving birth to new ideas. And Path four, the Via Transformativa, stands for justice, celebration, compromise.

These paths, as envisioned by Fox, represent a sacred hoop in the form of a cross, describing the journey towards spirituality and wisdom.

THE LOGICAL CIRCLE

The title for my model for problem-solving popped into my head one day, a gift from the Intuitive side! *Logical* represents the Thinking side, the hierarchical ladder — straight, linear processing. One goes through logical and progressive steps to get from A to B, in search of the truth. Rational, pragmatic, practical, analytical reasoning best fits this "straight-line" Thinking.

Feeling is represented by the circle image. A circle lies in harmony with the round earth and universe. It has no jarring or sharp edges. Harmony dictates a mediatory process by which both sides in the issue are considered, and the welfare of both participants is paramount. Discussion rather than argument, reaching agreement by consensus, and protecting the dignity and integrity of all are its guidelines.

Concentric circles, I believe, best describe our growth patterns. In the centre of the circle, the ego is present at the child's birth and first days of life. New persons and life experiences offer opportunities to break through to ever-increasing circles of growth. Throughout our life, we go through cycles in which we suffer growing pains and conflict, regress temporarily to gather strength, and then experience fresh insights. Whether it be a positive or negative experience, we have an opportunity to advance. Failure can be a wonderful teacher, if we learn our lessons with humility.

As we pass through these circles of discovery and grow psychologically, the Self is slowly defined. Individuation is the process by which you evolve to establish yourself as a person — unique and separate from others. Maturity brings involvement in the wider world around us. Transformational growth offers the privilege and responsibility of touching and influencing others' lives. We hear ourselves called to give our gifts away to others still on the inner circles of burgeoning life. Creativity and joy sustain us, helping us through struggle, and even chaos.

The Logical Circle model for problem-solving has five steps. The following diagram illustrates the first four steps that lie within the circle. It is a journey inwards to discover the Self and to transform what needs changing. Self-affirmation and gratitude for what we do have provide the enthusiasm and renewed energy needed to face the outside world. Step five lies outside the sphere. Our newly discovered strengths can be used to help others.

THE LOGICAL CIRCLE

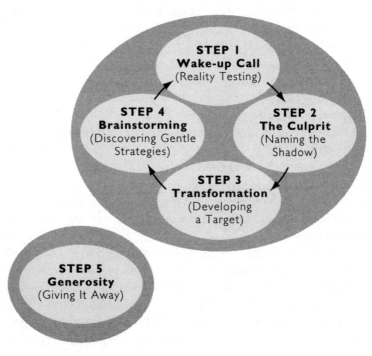

Step 1. Wake-Up Call

Reality-testing can be painful. Life experiences often knock us on the head, and thereafter we are no longer the same. We fail an exam, and our career plans or choices are limited. Someone stops seeing us and doesn't call. We don't understand why. A wife decides to separate from her husband, who is shocked. "I thought we got along pretty well!" he protests. Your boss calls you into the office first thing in the morning, and gives you the bad news. By noon, your personal belongings are packed up, and you are out of there. No warning! No awareness? Life is so difficult, you say.

Sometimes we receive critical feedback from our Significant Other. "Do you know how incredibly controlling you are?" yells a henpecked husband to his bossy wife. A distraught wife, torn between loyalties to husband and child, warns, "That was a really mean thing you said to Johnny!"

Authority figures often daunt us. "Your performance this term is just not acceptable. The staff are afraid of you. Morale in this office is at an all-time low," announces a supervisor. Your career takes an unexpected dive.

Quite often, you know instinctively something has to change. Since everything in your life is going wrong, you begin to question your own judgment. A black cloud seems to be following you around. People who, a year before, seemed to enjoy your company, are now avoiding you. At work your secretary sometimes looks stunned and fights back tears. "What did I say wrong?" you ask yourself. At home your wife is cool and aloof. "Well, there's a long story there!" It becomes clear that your behaviour is upsetting others.

The "Wake-up Call" tells you it is time to ask yourself some confrontational questions. Remember to challenge your honesty as you answer. This is your chance "to tell it like it is." Start your reality-testing by zeroing in on one or more recent examples of your own behaviour that have proved troublesome to others. Use your Thinking to analyse when and how each incident happened. What you are doing here is generating your own feedback.

Reality-Testing Questions
   a) What was I actually saying or doing at the time?
   b) When did it happen? What time of day or night?
   c) What was I so upset about? Was I in a bad mood at the time?
   d) Was the other person tired or tense when it happened?
   e) Who else was present who might give me some feedback?
   f) Was this unusual behaviour, or do I do this often?
   g) Who do I tend to do this with? Who do I say such things to?
   h) Is this a new insight, or old news?

This is just a sampling of the questions you need to ask. Remember, growth stems from honesty, not denial.

Step 2. The Culprit
Now that you have zeroed in on some examples of times when your actions offended others, it is time to "Name the Shadow." What is the *essence* of what is wrong here? Give a name to the negative Shadow you wish to work on. Is it impatience, rudeness, insensitivity, guilt, lateness? Now, free-associate with the word you have chosen. Try to find at least five associations, and list them one under the other. For example, guilt brings to mind:

   regret
   sorrow
   bad
   punish
   prison

It is now time to set goals for yourself.

Step 3. Transformation Goal
Motivation is needed when you are trying to change some aspect of your behaviour or your personality. Make a true commitment, for the next few weeks, to concentrate on changing this one flaw in your character, or the behaviour that is causing you and others problems. Set realistic and concrete goals so that you will be able to measure progress along the way. Name the goal words that best express the *opposite* meaning to the words on your Step 2 list. For example, the opposite to guilt may be pride:

guilt	pride
regret	pleased
sorrow	celebrate
bad	good
punish	reward
prison	freedom

Draw a square around each list. The list on the right serves as a guidepost to signify how you wish to be, or what you want to do.

Step 4. Brainstorming

Brainstorming, a term coined in *Applied Imagination* by A. Osborn, an advertising executive, describes a problem-solving technique. A group attempts to find a solution to a specific problem through the spontaneous generation and amassing of ideas, with a moratorium placed on all criticism to the ideas presented by its members. Individuals can also brainstorm on their own.

Brainstorming taps into our Intuition, as well as the Thinking and Feeling functions. Brainstorming makes use of people's creativity and the ideas that come easily and naturally to them. If it is to be effective, it must consider and recognize difficult issues created by people's weaknesses and shortcomings. Innovative solutions often cause great discomfort because people are challenged to use facets of their personality that presently seem foreign or awkward to their natural way of being and of doing things. Patience, persistence, and compassion are essential to sustain the haltingly slow transformational process. Enthusiasm and support are great, but not everybody naturally possesses these attributes. For many, becoming more enthusiastic is in itself a goal.

In our therapy sessions, the client and I spin ideas off each other in order to become more effective at brainstorming. My part in this usually consists of asking questions, or making comments that relate to what the client is saying. You may wish to ask a close friend, someone who is also interested in personal growth, to brainstorm with you. Remember that brainstorming taps into your

Intuition, and one suggestion generates another as answers pop up unexpectedly, as if by magic.

Sally

Let's retrace the first three steps Sally took leading up to the brainstorming process.

Sally's Wake-up Call came from her own internal confrontations. She had been noticing the following behavioural patterns:

a) "People take advantage of me. It happened last week when Belinda expected me to look after her daughter when she went to the dentist."

b) "I can't say no. I was furious, but I didn't say anything. No one else was there to give me feedback on how I handled myself."

c) "I block when I get so upset. Something in me just shuts down."

d) "I lie. I tell people what they want to hear. I didn't say a word to Belinda, but I was steaming inside."

The Culprit, the Shadow Sally decided to work on, was her *naivety*. "That's what causes me to lie. I can't stand the part of me that tells others what they want to hear. I'm such a coward. Worse still, I do this with almost everyone. Even my husband and my mother! I've been vaguely aware of this for a while, but our session last week really brought it home. Boy, is this sick or what!" She laughs.

Her free associations with the word *naivety* are listed here, along with her opposite goals (Step 3).

naivety	truth
denial	honesty
dizzy blonde	smart
amateur	professional
irresponsible	responsible
childish	adult

Sally's Transformation Goal, the target that she chose as opposite to her naivety was to "always seek the truth." Any time Sally felt "stupid" about something, she resolved to ask herself, "What might be a more intelligent, rational, or logical way to handle this situation?" Her thinking cap would go on, ready to brainstorm.

Brainstorming, for Sally, was a natural process. Now that her Feelings were working well once again, her Intuition clicked in easily. Ideas popped up, one after another, and she needed little assistance. These are the notes I made as Sally worked through how she was going to be less naive in the future:

– *"I've got to open up more. Extravert. Say what I really think!"*
– *"Use the I message to describe my half — what I think, what I feel, and what my gut tells me is right."*
– *"Risk the other person not hearing or being hostile. I've got to be more brave if this is ever going to happen."*
– *"I need to be more independent. When my husband talks for me, I need to ask him to let me figure this out."*
– *"Then I need to go away and figure out how I feel. I need to thoroughly feel."*
– *"I've got to ask myself what is rational and logical here? Be skeptical!"*
– *"Am I looking at the facts, or only seeing what I want to see?"*
– *"Look at the big picture. Stand back. Gain some objectivity."*
– *"It's lonely being naive. Not part of the world. I need to read and expose myself to new situations."*
– *"Ask myself if I'm being consistent with my value system? Is this keeping my integrity?"*

Sally continued to work on this list at home. Any time she heard herself tell people what they wanted to hear instead of the truth, she would correct herself as graciously as she could. Other times, when a new idea popped up, she would add that solution to her list. When she found herself going blank, she would run through some of her brainstorming ideas to see if one of them would work for this particular occasion.

Rereading her list after some frustrating situation, Sally often discovered that associations pulled up more gifts of wisdom. Sally grew very fond of her "Clever List," as she called it.

Peter

Peter's Logical Circle, as described here, shows how he battled with one of his most troublesome Shadows, his *impatience*.

The Wake-up Call for Peter arose from his awareness that the Gerbil Wheel existence he led left him rushing through *all* aspects of his life. People and their needs were a nuisance that he barely tolerated. Nowadays, Peter honestly did want to spend time being fully there, especially for Sally and the children.

Reflecting on his own behaviour of the week before, Peter observed:

a) "I'm still trigger-happy. The other night I jumped at Sally out of the blue. She was just minding her own business, doing her own thing. There's still part of me that wants all her attention."

b) "I didn't get an immediate response from one of the kids, and I started yelling. I'm a bit better, but *my* expectations still run me."

c) "At work, someone was hesitating in the middle of trying to explain something that was painful for him. I wanted him to hurry up and stop wasting my time. There's that selfishness again. I guess that's behind a lot of my impatience."

The Culprit, in all three examples, Peter decided, was his strong impatience. "It's behind so much of what goes wrong for me. I steamroll over people because of it, and I can't delegate properly because people have to fit into my agenda and my timetable."

Peter realized that he had been like that even as a teenager. It was worse when he was moody. "But I have to admit, I never saw half of this before." He laughed. "I was like that road-runner cartoon. You couldn't see me for the dust I kicked up chasing after those hare-brained schemes I cooked up. I didn't want too much time to think!"

Peter's free associations with the word *impatient* are listed on page 211, along with his opposite goals (Step 3).

Peter's Transformation Goal required a radical departure from

impatient	patient
intolerant	tolerant
March Hare	tortoise
insensitive	sensitive
bulldozer	gentle
poor listener	good listener

the way he had lived his life until recently. "How do you use a bulldozer gently?" was his $64 question. "It will be a red-letter day for me when I'm content to be a tortoise." His laughter had a wistful quality, I thought. Hard edges were falling off Peter at an alarming rate.

"Brainstorming is something I do at the office," Peter kidded. His humour was peppered through our conversations of late, and the sarcasm and black humour of our early sessions was scarce. The notes below follow Peter's brainstorming, with my comments in brackets. Peter needed more support because his Intuition, like his Feelings, was slow to return to its former level of functioning.

- *"I've got to relax more. Believe it or not, I keep trying those six calming techniques you taught me. Got to watch my breathing though — I can feel the tension choke up in my throat."*

- *"I'm so intense, it isn't funny. Instead of being so damned goal-oriented, I've got to trust the process more. It reminds me of the day you told me about knitting that yellow sweater!"* (My analogy had been that if I'm knitting a sweater, I may worry throughout about whether it will fit Johnny. In my anxiety, I won't hear the clicking of the needles, the feel of the wool, the subtle smell of lanolin, nor will I notice the sunflower yellow of the garment. The joy of knitting will be totally lost in anxious fits of measuring and stretching, or worrying that the arms will be too short, or the bodice too wide.)

- *"If people are going to mean more to me than getting from A to B, I need to be more curious about what makes people tick."* (It may mean asking people enough questions to know their stories. Also, it might be helpful to educate yourself about developmental capacities related to the ages of your children. Do you think you expect too much?

- *"Since I was overly responsible and never had a real childhood, I'm probably unrealistic in what I expect."*
- *"Even at work, I'm unrealistic. I fail to understand other people's strengths."* (You might challenge your judgment here. Ask yourself whether this person is good at what you expect him to do.)
- *"The part of me that has to have my own way, wants to be right —* the words single-minded, rigidity, *and* distancing *come to mind. Take a couple of steps back. Ask myself: Is it really* vital *that I be right?"* (Do you think being right has anything to do with the inability to get vicarious pleasure from others' situations that we spoke about last week?)
- *"If I can't get vicarious pleasure or pain out of someone else's happiness or discomfort, then I'm cut off, removed. That's when I get judgmental and critical. I guess I'm frightened."*
- *"Instead of putting words in others' mouths and "fixing," I need to wait until they're finished. I could show them I'm interested."* (I wonder if sympathy would show in your face? Try this. Think of yourself as *gentle* for a moment. How does this make you feel?)
- *"It's reassuring. Trying to comfort. Being patient, concerned."* (What do you think about using the gentle shepherd as a role model? I introduce the idea of God as a serving God, being there to serve us, as well as us serving Him.)
- *"If I take on the serving role, I'm going to have to be there for others without expectations — be patient!"* (Try to free-associate to both the Hare and Tortoise images.)

Hare	Tortoise
rushing	unhurried, slow
out-of-breath	not sweating
on a Gerbil Wheel	lumbering
in a frazzle	time to see things
frantic	methodical, steady
exhausted	relaxed

(That's quite a choice you have there! Which one will get the upper hand, do you think?)

Peter and I could go on indefinitely as we exchange ideas, and "anything goes." I suggest to him that the images of the Hare and the Tortoise might appear to him at the most surprising times!

Step 5. Generosity

This step represents the point in life's journey when the mature individual, with a strong sense of Self and confidence intact, turns outwards to ever-expanding concentric circles, and devotes time and energy towards benefiting others. Knowledge, wisdom, creativity, and joy, acquired from the inwards journey, provide the strength and energy needed for the tasks at hand. Give it away! There is more where that came from, if you use your resources wisely and well.

TOWARDS BALANCE, WISDOM, AND MATURITY

Where does your power come from? The title of Tina Turner's song "What's Love Got to Do with It!" springs to mind. Without the power of love for oneself and others, compassion and the transformation of the Shadow aspects of the Self are not possible. Instead, in individuals whose insight and feeling are missing, shame often invites destructive impulses. When their security or power is threatened, for example, these individuals often are driven towards revenge. They become vindictive towards others, but ultimately punish themselves, too, as the dark Shadow engulfs their own personality. Dr. Jekyll gives way to Mr. Hyde.

Healing solutions come only through understanding and forgiveness. Freeing others by forgiving them for the pain they have caused us is one of the most onerous stumbling blocks to ongoing growth. It helps to remember that through forgiving others, we also free ourselves. Again, there is a choice to be made. Do I remain a bitter, resentful, and angry person, or do I allow my spirituality, the power of love, to work its magic in my life?

Next time some trauma or misfortune strikes, and you feel tremendous discomfort or agonizing pain, instead of reacting immediately, try this exercise.

Look up, and imagine a large stop light flashing a bright neon red. Stop in your tracks! This scene may turn ugly and have dire consequences if you let go and lose control. Or you can choose to learn something new! Try to open up, and allow yourself to remain vulnerable while you get you act together.

STOP........WAIT........WATCH........LISTEN........LAUGH

Your laughter may be fed by pure anxiety, or it may convey surprise and true humility. "What lesson is knocking on my door today?" you might well ask. Or,"How will I transform this lousy state of affairs?" You need time to *think and feel*. It takes time for information to register. Listen to what your Sensation (that is, your sight, touch, taste, smell, and hearing) tells you. What is your gut reaction, your Intuition, shouting out?

Resolve to allow all this information to perk and bubble up over the next twenty-four hours. See what wisdom surfaces from this crazy mixture. You may not be able to understand *why* all this is happening in the "big picture" of your life experience. Trauma tends to make us short-sighted and trigger-happy. Taking time-out before we act is often the wisest decision.

Develop a sense of awe or wonder at such times. Stay free from judgments. Whatever has happened just is! Why it happened may take weeks to figure out, or even months. Sometimes, there is no answer to some questions.

In my practice, I frequently work with families who suffer from depression, anxiety, and physical and psychological signs of stress due to workaholism, alcoholism, or eating disorders. Many of these families are caught in power struggles, in which the husband and wife compete with one another. Greed typically plays a part in all of these traumas. Excesses of anything are rarely healthy, and greed is a recipe for disaster. Just read your newspaper each day for the latest "casualty" — some well-known public figure, business tycoon, or pillar of the community who has fallen from grace. Such scenes are played out at every level of society. None of us is free from the possibility of disaster. God, in His wisdom, left us with the freedom of choice.

Will it be the power of love and transformation, or the power of greed and vindication that shapes your destiny and determines your fate?

THE BALANCED PERSONALITY

Maturity, wisdom, spirituality, creativity, and joy — all are fostered by a balanced life and a well-developed personality.

The doing-performing-thinking side of the personality is capable of changing attitudes, values, and directions. It does so through will and self-determination. We make choices and solve problems that ultimately determine where our energies go. We can choose to invest in a variety of interests and goals. Or we can remain single-minded and restrict our focus to a limited vision or goal. Unfortunately, this goal is often attained at the expense of our family's best interests, and our own health.

Our being-feeling side just is! Although it doesn't *do* anything, it has tremendous influence on determining what choices we make. It is other-directed, open, and vulnerable. Its wisdom, enthusiasm, creativity, humour, and joy influence how we treat ourselves and look out for others.

Purposefully developing your opposite functions, the ones not naturally your best functions, is a useful exercise towards achieving a balanced and mature personality. If you are an Intuitive type, for instance, your balance will come from working on your Sensation side. You might try a process I call "Watching Water." Find a comfortable spot looking out over water. Forget whatever else you might be doing. Concentrate on the surface of the water. Every time the wind changes, look for new patterns. Be alert to shifts in sunlight, and notice the ever-changing hues. Do the clouds form stories in the sky? Do you hear bird sounds? Do you feel the wind on the hairs on your arm? Do the sun's rays make the water shimmer and send arrows across the surface that sparkle and shine luminously?

Because this takes extra effort and patience, you will have to stop to make this happen. However, its rewards are great as you begin to notice small and precious details. It will quiet your restlessness, and ground you in the moment. You will be thoroughly *there,* not wondering where you are going next.

Each one of us can benefit from knowing what our personality type is, and where our direction of growth lies. By entering into the opposite territory, we gain new insights, fresh energy, and enthusiasms that have lain dormant. We discover feelings and thoughts we really never knew existed in us. The Introvert who purposely tries to be more friendly and interested in people, who becomes curious enough to ask questions about others' opinions, will be rewarded with smiles and gratitude by others who wondered if he really cared about them, or if she even noticed they existed. Your world will be *twice* as big, and your adventures surprising! As one of my clients exclaimed, "Something really good happened this week. I decided to take that guy I told you bugged me so much out for coffee. It's hard to believe, but that man is a comedian in his spare time. I guess he exaggerates a lot because that's adaptive when you're telling jokes. We really had quite a fun time! This is great!"

If you take the time and energy to take risks, you, too, will see and feel things that are totally new. This is what real living is all about! Why not start growing and expanding your universe today!

You might start by reminding yourself daily of some of the things you need to work on to get some balance back into your life.

Tips for Living the Good Life

Be open to change. Let the power of love, and your own spirituality, guide you. Growth is never easy, but its rewards are great!

1. Take your empathy-compassion temperature every evening:
   a) How did I interact with each member of my family today?
   b) Was I patient and polite to my colleagues and staff?
   c) Did I remember to take good care of *me*?

2. Do some serious reality-testing of your *honesty*:
   a) Did I say yes when I should have said no?
   b) Did I agree to do something in less time than is realistic?
   c) Did I promise something I can't deliver?
3. Avoid being critical, judgmental, impatient, rigid:
   a) Was I open to different ways of doing the same thing?
   b) Was I able to delegate and really let go?
   c) Did I overreact when others made mistakes?
4. Listen to others:
   a) Did I look for openings in conversations to turn the conversation back to myself?
   b) Did I rehearse what I was going to say, instead of listening?
   c) Did I try to control by "fixing" others, instead of understanding them?
5. No excess adrenalin-pumping please:
   a) Did I overschedule, and find myself rushing from A to B?
   b) Did I try to do two or three things at once?
   c) Did I push myself to play better, go faster, or win, instead of relaxing at "play"?
6. Stop overloading yourself:
   a) Did I deal with each problem, one step at a time?
   b) Did I create artificial, self-imposed deadlines?
   c) Did I try to finish everything before I left work?
7. Make your car a sanctuary:
   a) Did I distract myself with business worries or phone calls?
   b) Was I courteous to other drivers?
   c) Did I enjoy the silence or listen to relaxing music?
8. Avoid business lunches:
   a) Did I talk business during lunch today?
   b) Did I drink to relax?
   c) Did I invite friends who are in different fields to join me?
9. Remember, change involves risk:
   a) Was I prepared to disappoint others and allow them their anger?
   b) Did I leave work on time without apologizing?

c) Did I chat with myself when I started "slipping back" to old ways?
10. Make home a refuge:
   a) Did I leave my briefcase at work?
   b) Have I asked people *not* to phone me about business at home?
   c) Do I protect my family's privacy, free from fax or computer?
   d) If I work at home, do I keep time free for relaxation and fun?
11. Lighten Up:
   a) Did I laugh enough today?
   b) Did I compliment someone, or show my appreciation?
   c) Did I share something interesting or fun with others?
12. Get a life!
   a) Am I fun and interesting to be with, both at home and at work?
   b) Do I truly love people and not use them?
   c) Am I grateful and appreciative of all that I have now?

BON VOYAGE

Good luck on your "Journey from Numbness to Joy." Remember always to love and take care of yourself! Be realistic, not idealistic. You're well on your way when you recognize that half of life is positive, and half is negative. You'll need your sense of humour and your spirituality because there will be detours, distractions, even mountains in your way. Life can be like a bowl of cherries, but cherries do have pits.

Balance and moderation in the external world are crucial for a healthy life-style, and your psyche will remind you of this. It is just a matter of time before people crash when they are spinning out of control on the fast track of the Gerbil Wheel. Esther de Waal, in *Seeking God: The Way of St. Benedict*, speaks of the present-day dilemma in our society of searching for personal fulfilment while admiring expertise, specialization, and professionalism. St. Benedict's dictum that body, mind, and spirit must all command equal respect speaks across the centuries.

Monastery life involves time for prayer, study, and work. De Waal sees the Benedictine life as an equilibrium, a holding together of ultimate values in one centre. Maintaining a balance between polarities, "the monk lives constantly at the point of tension between stability and change; between tradition and the future; between the personal and the community; between obedience and initiative; between the desert and the marketplace; between action and contemplation" (p. 95). Such duality is never simple. Balancing the tugs and pulls we all experience on a daily basis is a demanding and difficult task.

One cautionary note: It is wise to keep in mind that maturity is clearly linked to the ability to produce and appreciate humour. Mature people laugh at themselves, remain flexible, and accept their limitations. They maintain a realistic perspective on life that views situations and personal weaknesses from a humorous standpoint. Harvey Mindess, in *Humour and Laughter: Theory, Research and Applications,* observes that humour highlights an awareness of our common absurdities. It sees that nothing is exactly as it seems or as we claim it to be, that what we profess is at best only partly true. Humour lets us know that "we are all more unreasonable, corrupt and pretentious than we openly acknowledge." This, says Mindess, should leave no cause for alarm or indignation. "The Balancing Act" must be about reality and truth, not idealism and pretension.

Mystery, magic, and joy are as much a part of life as pain, suffering, and guilt. When everything starts to go wrong in your life, *pay attention — it is time to grow again.* No one ever said life was not a challenge. Experience life fully — laugh, cry, mourn, and celebrate, and remember to *feel* it all.

Appendix I
Learn to Internalize
Your Feelings —
A Summary

CHAPTER 7

Step I

Awareness: What emotion are you *feeling* right now? When something happens, immediately tune in to your body.

1. What *physiological* changes (i.e., in your muscles and nerve endings) are occurring that alert you to a shift or change in emotions?
2. What is happening to your *energy* level? Are you pumping excess adrenalin and feeling *light,* or experiencing a decrease in energy and feeling *heavy*?
3. What do you notice about your *body position*?

Practise: Stop a number of times throughout the day, and identify what your body is telling you. Establish which combination of changes typically signals each major emotion. Identify the *earliest* signs.

Labelling: Use your thinking to *name* the emotion. Sometimes you will know the label immediately. Other times, you will need to work backwards from the above information.

Achilles' heel: What are your weaknesses or sore points? Watch for situations that typically trigger feelings that cause you to overreact or be impulsive. Act right away to alleviate stress, and make the situation easier to handle.

Step II

Justification: Test to see if this emotion has validity. Is it based on what is actually happening in your immediate environment? Or is a layering of old feelings over present ones unconsciously heightening your present response?

Conscious data:　　1) *What* just happened?
　　　　　　　　　2) *Who* said what?
　　　　　　　　　3) *What* are you reacting to in the situation?
　　　　　　　　　4) Is a troublesome *dream* still affecting you?
Unconscious data:　5) Are you *overreacting,* or acting *impulsively?*

Stress level: Pay attention to how stressed you are right now. Are you still comfortable? Or are you becoming overstressed? Watch for outward signs of agitation, irritability, frustration, etc.; or inward signs of lethargy, alienation, hopelessness, etc.

Step III

Experiencing: Feel the feeling. Stay with it. Let your emotional reactions be okay, even if they are negative. *Simplify.* Lower your expectations. *Nurture* yourself. Use your senses to feed yourself. Look for humour in the situation!

Exception: Anger, anxiety, fear, pain. Problem-solve as soon as you become aware of the earliest signs of these four feelings.

Defenses: If overstressed, *act immediately* to avoid becoming immobilized by your defenses (i.e., projection of blame, obsessive thinking, rationalization, dissociation, compartmentalization, repression, reaction formation, regression, sublimation).

CHAPTER 8

Step IV

Problem-solving intervention: Take some action to make things better for yourself. Be conscious of your own stress level and aware of what is happening to the other person, before proceeding.

Timing: Are you being sensitive to the other person's well-being, both emotionally and physically. Can that person listen right now? Is he in a mood? Is she unwell, too young, elderly, not very bright? Is he distracted by other problems, etc.?

Time of day may be important. Is this individual a morning or evening person?

Complications must be considered. Are alcohol or drugs involved?

Appropriateness: Do you live or work with this person? Is this really your problem? Is this issue important enough to expend your energy on?

In a group or public setting: Is the setting or situation suitable for your intervention? Is it possible to signal that you are distressed, without embarrassing others? Can you follow through later and discuss your feelings then?

If you are in control of your emotions, proceed to Step VI.
If you are overly stressed, postpone action and take Step V.

Step V

Rescheduling: The boiling point: Let the other person know how you are feeling (i.e., too angry, upset, confused, anxious, etc.).

Set a time to deal with the situation when both parties are free to listen to each other's experience.

Leaving a situation: Take time out to get yourself back in control. You want to be able to think clearly and to experience your feelings fully.

Always say why you are leaving.

Remember to say when you are coming back to talk: Non-verbal communication is ambiguous. It leads to misunderstandings and confusion. No one need feel abandoned.

The triangular pattern:
   1. Make a conscious decision to leave when overly stressed.
   2. Regain your control by performing one or more active or

passive calming techniques (e.g., breathing, meditation, visualization, humour, touch, spirituality).

3.   Follow through on your promise to return, and proceed to
problem-solve.

CHAPTER 9

Step VI

Non-controlling communication: Once you have figured out how you
feel, and you know that you are in control, it is time to communicate your thoughts and your feelings in a responsible manner.

First assumption: You need to take responsibility for informing
others about *what is happening to you.* However, the other person
must be *left free to respond* in his or her own way (i.e., *if* he can,
when he can, and in the *way* he chooses). People have difficulty
hearing when they are being controlled or manipulated.

Second assumption: Neglecting to inform the other person about
your reactions is passive-aggressive behaviour. Others should not
have to "fish," to ask questions about what is going on with you.
Describe your reactions, but *stay on your side of the fence.* Ego boundaries need to be respected if there is to be trust. Responsible communicating includes listening.

"I" messages: Responsible communication informs the other person about what you *feel,* what you *think,* and what your *needs* are.
It is easier to hear if you talk about feelings first. Be careful not to
tell the other person what to *do* about your needs.

Try to be *brief* and to the point. *You do not need to define how
you feel!* No one has to agree with you about *your* feelings.

Stay in your own territory: You have power to change yourself and
your actions. Be clear and succinct. Be firmly assertive, but not
invasive.

A safe atmosphere: There should be no blaming, judging, interfering in others' business, or talk about being "right." The listener has no need to become defensive and launch a counterattack.

Avoid using "you" messages, which cross over to the other's side of the boundary.

"You" messages are controlling. Blatant messages tell the other person what to *do, say, think,* or *feel,* etc. However, covert messages do not necessarily begin with "you." Finger-pointing, non-verbal communication such as sighing or tuning out, as well as expressions such as "Nonsense!" or "You've got to be kidding!" put down or negate the other person's right to have his or her own ideas or feelings.

Name-calling, insulting, interfering, etc. only challenge other people to defend themselves with a counterattack.

The Teeter-Totter power struggle: When someone else has a personal problem, and you offer advice, you are "minding the other person's business." By doing so, you take on responsibility for what happens next. By problem-solving for others, you rob them of their own experiencing. Both parties often end up resenting each other.

Good listening: Do not give advice! Instead, offer empathy and support. Good listeners respect other people's right to solve their own personal problems, or to make mistakes. Listeners need to act as a sounding board for others to bounce off their own ideas as to possible solutions.

Second-guessing is unwise: Second-guessing what is going on with others is disrespectful. A good rule of thumb is to *always ask rather than tell!* If others are present, try to refocus your energy on what you are doing. Plan to check out your perceptions of the situation later. Ask for information so that you can understand the other person's experience. Listen carefully to what is said.

Two-way communication fosters a sharing of information, which will ultimately lead to a better understanding of differences. Friendship and intimacy grow when respect, trust, empathy, and truth are present.

Appendix 2
Additional Functions from Jung's Theory of Psychological Type

During the 1950s and 1960s, two researchers, Isabel Myers and her mother, Katharine C. Briggs, used C. G. Jung's conceptual framework to develop a psychometric questionnaire to determine psychological type. The resultant Myers-Briggs Type Indicator was intended to foster understanding about the similarities and differences among human beings. They discovered that people could be classified into sixteen specific types. Since 1975, the Myers-Briggs has become the most widely used personality measure for non-psychiatric populations.

Along with Jung's four functions — Thinking, Feeling, Sensation and Intuition — and the Introverted–Extraverted attitude, Myers and Briggs added a Judgment–Perception preference for relating to the outer world.

In Chapter 2, we learned about the Thinking and Feeling functions. Here we will discover the roles that the other functions play in our personalities. Each function is greatly influenced by whether individuals, by nature, are Extraverted or Introverted in the way they approach the world. How are people energized, and what conditions restore this energy? We will also learn how different people perceive information, and whether Intuition or Sensation is the dominant function used to perform this processing. Last, we will look at how individuals deal with the world around them. Is Judgment or Perception the preferred function when decisions or plans are to be made? Judgment attitude prefers organizing, making decisions, and reaching closure. Perception attitude chooses to remain open, to postpone closure, to live and let live.

EXTRAVERSION AND INTROVERSION

Jung coined two motivational concepts, Extraversion and Introversion. These terms indicate our psychological modes of adaptation — where our focus lies, and from where we draw our energy and enthusiasm. Introverts derive their motivation from internal or subjective factors. Extraverts are influenced by information from the external world. People and situations affect their judgments, perception, feelings, affects, and attitudes.

All of us turn outwards to take action and go inwards to reflect, but we tend to be more comfortable in the one that is the most natural to us. Although the terms are well used, their meaning is often misunderstood.

As Jung points out in *Psychological Types,* the two types tend to speak badly of one another, and to come into conflict. "The Introvert sees everything that is in any way valuable for him in the subject; the Extravert sees it in the object. This dependence on the object seems to the Introvert a mark of the greatest inferiority, while to the Extravert the preoccupation with the subject seems nothing but infantile auto-eroticism" (p. 517).

Problems arise when the Introvert develops inwardly but remains at a standstill outwardly. Conversely, the Extravert may develop external relations but neglect inner growth. In time, if psychological growth is to take place, both types need to develop their opposite functions to reach an adult, mature level of functioning.

Extraversion

Extraverts are action-oriented, and do their best work externally, preferably with other people. They adapt quickly to their environment because they are curious and directed outwards towards what is going on immediately around them. Consequently, Extraverts pay a great deal of attention to the real outer world of people and things, and to the interaction that takes place between themselves and others. They are attracted to breadth, and are afterthinkers who understand life after they have lived it.

Extraverts are open, confident, assured, trusting, action-oriented people who like to explore and to seek adventure. They enjoy meeting people and travelling to new places. They are challenged by the new and untried. Sociable, friendly, and accessible, they tend to be the centre of attention, even the life of the party. They are talkative, engage others easily in conversation, and are comfortable in new groups. They tend to have many friends and relationships, although they may be fickle or flighty on occasion.

Extraverts expend energy rather than conserve it. They are expansive, and tend to express their emotions as they go along. Early in their development, they take initiative, learn quickly, and play freely with objects because of their risk-taking, optimistic nature. In extreme types, a weakness lies in their tendency towards intellectual superficiality. Also, because they are so other-directed, they tend not to take care of themselves. Their energies are invested in nurturing and caring for others instead. As a result, they are prone to become selfless martyrs who eventually feel taken for granted. They resent the demands others make on them but refuse to see how they contribute to this cycle by not being honest about their own needs and limits. Their ego boundaries may be blurred and enmeshed with those of others.

As Isabel Myers notes in *Gifts Differing,* Extraverts are "The civilizing genius, the people of action and practical achievement, who go from doing to considering, and back to doing" (p. 56).

Whether one is Extraverted or Introverted only becomes apparent when either is coupled with each of the four functions. For example, Extraverted Thinkers have very different personalities from Introverted Thinkers. The former let you know their opinions and thoughts on a subject; while the latter may be churning inside but neglect to tell you about it.

Introversion

In *Gifts Differing,* Myers defines Introverts as "The cultural genius, the people of ideas and abstract invention, who go from considering to doing and back to considering" (p. 56). Introverts are independent because everything they do rests on their own decisions. They are reflection-oriented, and have strong powers of concentration, which they use to focus on their thoughts. Reserved and cautious observers, they pause before new and untried challenges. They tend to stay on the periphery of life's circle, rather than plunge in. Spontaneity is difficult for them.

Because they are slow to take action, Introverts are reluctant to discuss things with others until they have had the opportunity to think them through to a conclusion. Inward-directed, they only trust their inner values, which are based on internal, subjective experience. When reacting to an idea or situation, they turn inwards, and formulate their own unique version of it. This interpretation becomes their reality. Consequently, Introverts often remain oblivious to, or uninterested in, the objective environment that lies outside their experience. Internal reactions are more interesting to them. They are attracted to depth and tend to be intense, so may become passionate about an idea or thing. Introverts are forethinkers who cannot live life until they understand it.

Introverts tend to be closed, timid, cautious, and prone to pessimism. They are reluctant to risk themselves to explore new people, places, or adventure. Energy is cautiously conserved and limited. They prefer the tried-and-true, home turf, predictable food, and familiar customs.

Taciturn and shy, Introverts tend to bottle up their emotions and carefully guard their reactions from others. Sharing and venting feelings are foreign to them unless pressure builds to intolerable levels. A great deal of energy is suppressed simply because they are terrified of strong responses in themselves and in others. Consequently, they remain well-defended against outside influences. Introverts are therefore prone to extreme sensitivity and often suffer from chronic fatigue.

Introverts are often described as reserved, solitary, and private people. They definitely prefer their own way. Therefore, outside influences are met with mistrust and much resistance. Things and ideas must be understood before they are willing to submit to alien rules. Introverted children are often fearful and reluctant to confront unknown objects and people. They want names, meanings, and explanations for things because their defensive attitude makes them question and hold back. They must summon the courage and energy to assert themselves over familiar objects and finally master them.

Introverts prefer a few good relationships, and relate better on a one-to-one basis or in a small group situation. They are able to extravert socially, but tend to become drained easily by too much interrelating. They may leave a party early, and renew their energy by withdrawing into their internal world.

In extreme cases, there is a weakness towards impracticality, being other-worldly and not grounded in reality. Because of their subjective orientation, they are prone to ego-inflation and arrogance, and therefore tend to believe that their way is the best. Introverts are consequently attracted to control and power as a means of getting their own way.

In trying to determine if you are Extraverted or Introverted, think back to childhood. If two young children are playing in a park where there is a new slide, the introverted child will stand watching the other children for some time. Eventually, he will summon up the courage to approach the ladder, and will then climb slowly, pause, and then continue until he reaches the top. After moments of hesitation, he will finally swish down, and look somewhat surprised, but pleased with himself. Remember, Introverts take comfort in conquering something new, in making the unfamiliar familiar!

The Extraverted child, seeing the slide, will rush to the bottom of the ladder, climb eagerly to the top, and triumphantly slide to the ground with great glee. Only then will she think about the experience, and draw her own conclusions. Recall that Extraverts understand life after they have lived it. Life for them is to be experienced and lived fully.

SENSATION AND INTUITION

These are the information-gathering functions that allow us to process information about the world around us. Sensation is a conscious process primarily interested in concrete actualities. Intuition is largely unconscious and concerned with possibilities. Sensation people outnumber intuitives three-to-one,[1] so the interplay between these types is weighted against Intuition.

Sensation

Sensation works on two levels. On one level, Sensation perceives a physical stimulus, such as a person or an object, through information gathered from the five senses (seeing, hearing, touching, tasting, and smelling). Facts, figures, and other details are processed and observed without judgment. On another level, internal bodily reactions to that object or person are conveyed and registered in consciousness. Our psyche seeks the practical, concrete reason for what is occurring or being done.

In other words, sense impressions bring a scene to life, and our faculties respond physiologically. We become aware of our thoughts, feelings, and ideas about the concrete image. As Jung explains in *Psychological Types* (p. 462), a flower is always seen along with its stem, leaves, and its habitat. We experience pleasure or displeasure according to its aesthetic appeal. We smell its fragrance and savour the beauty of its special hue. Going further, we even question the motivation of the gift-giver. Is it an innocent and spontaneous gesture, or one steeped in dubious meaning?

Sensation people are sensible, practical, observant, and realistic. Their energy is directed towards actual here-and-now experience. Their trust is placed in the concrete, that which is accessible and observable.

It is important to note that Sensation people distrust words, spoken or written, that come from others. According to Isabel

---

1. Bradway, K. "Jung's Psychological Types," *Journal of Analytical Psychology,* Vol. 9, Tavistock Publishers, 1964, pp. 129–35.

Myers in *Gifts Differing* (p. 57), words are merely symbolic. They must be translated into reality, and experienced before they mean anything. Therefore, Sensation people often have to bang their heads against a closed door three or four times rather than learn from others' experience.

Sensation types are seen as ploddingly slow because they process data so thoroughly. It takes some time to translate sense impressions into thoughts and feelings. They distrust quick answers because they are not closely connected to their imagination. Sensation types value soundness and a practical approach to learning. For all the facts to be registered, things must be said and read slowly, not skimmed over. They cannot be rushed, or things become a blur. They seldom read just for pleasure, unless the book contains information they are particularly interested in. They learn new skills step by step, and need plenty of practice time to familiarize themselves with all the facts and details.

Sensation types crave enjoyment, and seek pleasure in the art of living the good life. They are reluctant to save for a rainy day, or to protect future security. The saying "A bird in the hand is worth two in the bush" fits their philosophy. They like to imitate. They want what others have, and want to do what others are doing. Physical surroundings are important to their sense of well-being.

Sensation people, Isabel Myers further states, are consumers and natural pleasure lovers. They contribute to public welfare by supporting every form of culture and recreation. Comfort, luxury, and beauty are their aesthetic pleasures. They can become frivolous, self-serving, and greedy for more and more stimulation to fill up an inner emptiness. Sensation alone can resemble a butterfly let loose in a field of daisies, seemingly flitting from one flower to the next without digesting anything. Without the achievement of some goal, and the imagination and vision of Intuition, life can lack meaning and fulfilment. Growth comes through developing their intuitive skills.

It has been my observation that Sensation types tend to terminate the therapeutic process prematurely simply because they are feeling better, and life is more enjoyable. With their focus on the here-and-now, it may be that their imagination does not function well enough for them to see the possibilities for change in the future. "Short-term pain" for "long-term gain" doesn't make sense to them. As we will learn, Intuition introduces goals and guideposts to chart progress, and also provides the drive necessary for growth.

Intuition

Intuition is an instinctive function that gathers information in an unconscious way. Carl Jung in *Psychological Types* explains that Intuition uses a sixth sense to focus its perception on everything — both outer and inner objects and their relationships. The laws of reason, and the process of sifting through all the data, are not involved. Answers pop up unannounced. As Jung further explains, "In intuition a content presents itself whole and complete, without our being able to explain or discover how this content came into existence" (p. 453). This may cause problems, for example, in school when the Intuitive child is certain he knows the answer, yet is unable to justify to his Sensation-type teacher how he got it. This intrinsic knowledge, stated with quiet certainty and conviction, can be quite threatening to others. Therefore, Intuitive people may be accused of guessing or cheating, or of being irrational, opinionated, arrogant, or superficial.

Jung delineates two levels of Intuition. Subjective intuition is a perception of unconscious data that has its origin within the observer. Objective perception of data, on the other hand, depends on subliminal perception of the object along with the feelings and thoughts that object evokes in the person. Jung further distinguishes concrete and abstract forms of Intuition, which differ depending on the degree of sensation involved. Concrete intuition is a reactive process that responds directly to given facts, what is actually there. Abstract intuition involves an act of will, an element of direction, or a goal. It mediates connections between existing ideas, or it creates new ones. Intuition looks at the big picture and seeks to grasp the essential patterns. Brainstorming, for example, is a collective intuitive process used to generate new ideas. Group members pool their information and experience, and new insights emerge.

Intuitives are imaginative, creative, and speculative, especially about their current inspiration. They see meanings, relationships, and possibilities beyond the information presented by the senses. Intuitives tend to day-dream, and to be idealistic. They are restless, and instead of enjoying the present, their energy is directed towards anticipating the future. They are able to delay gratification in the present for future gain or good. They often fail to appreciate and enjoy what is happening around them. At the theatre, for example, the thoughts of an Intuitive may stray. She is off "scriptwriting," anticipating the good time that will be had by all after the show at the local restaurant.

Intuitives love the abstract, the symbolic, the theoretical. Words, metaphors, books, the theatre are therefore fascinating. According to Isabel Myers, Intuitives listen to the enticing vision of possibilities that "vary from the merest masculine 'hunch' and 'women's intuition'; through the whole range of original ideas, projects, enterprises, and inventions; to the crowning examples of creative art, religious inspiration, and scientific discovery" (p. 57).

These people are quick to thought and to action, and therefore often can be impulsive. They rush through things without savouring the experience. I suggest that Intuitives should rely on their gut reaction but wait a day or two to make a final decision. This allows time for their less-developed Sensation to provide the facts and figures to support or reject the quick answer.

Care should be exercised lest these independent and ingenious people get caught in the "bigger is better" and "it's never enough" syndromes, which lead a person from idealism towards workaholism. What is just around the corner is always worth striving for, and this individual may sacrifice everybody and everything that gets in the way of some sought-after goal. There is a strong irony here because the workaholic eventually loses both his Intuition and his Feelings. Negative Sensation, the inferior function, becomes ever more powerful. When this happens, concrete dualistic thinking (right–wrong, black–white, dominant–submissive, etc.) dominates, and the person gets picky and argumentative about what he or she thinks is right. The big picture gets drowned in obsessive detail.

Intuitives, Myers further states, are relatively indifferent to what other people have and do. They are independent of their physical surroundings, and often pay scant attention to the details and facts before them. However, show an Intuitive an empty room, and she will use her imagination to decorate it, set a mood, or even devise a story with a whole cast of characters, in no time at all!

Unless Intuition is tempered by realism, there is danger that idealism and perfectionism will distort reality. Also, Intuitives can be fickle and lack persistence unless a balance is sought through the development of a judging process (i.e., judgment or perception).

JUDGMENT AND PERCEPTION — THE ADDED VARIABLE

Well-balanced individuals must develop perception to support their judgment, and judgment to support their perception.

According to Isabel Myers, Judgment types believe that life should be willed and decided. Closure, achieved through making decisions, reaching conclusions, and settling things, is important for their stability. On the other hand, Perception types regard life as something to be experienced and understood. Their preference is to keep plans and opinions open-ended and subject to review. They make a series of decisions, and even after deciding, they are still reluctant to finalize things in case new information or valuable experiences change their present point of view.

Judgment

Judgment, based on Thinking and/or Feeling, provides a continuity of purpose, and a standard against which one can criticize or challenge one's actions.

People use their Judgment attitude to gather information, form opinions about whether to agree or disagree with the facts, or come up with their own conclusions. For some, being decisive is easy, while others seek closure simply because they dislike having things remain undecided. Their own point of view and being "right" are important.

Judgment people are outcome-oriented. They enjoy settling and finishing things. Upon reaching a conclusion, they take appropriate action to wrap things up. A sense of progress and completion bring them a sense of well-being.

Strong Judgment individuals often make decisions about what others should or should not do simply because they value closure. In order to get things settled, they are prone to freely offer advice and suggestions based on their own experience and information. More timid types think such thoughts and develop expectations for others, but do not speak out publicly.

Judgment people often force a decision because they make the assumption that all the evidence is in. Anything more is considered extraneous and therefore irrelevant and immaterial. In fact, pushing for closure often means that people miss new information or later developments because their perception process is shut off prematurely. This impulsiveness can backfire and result in rigidity and error. There is no give-and-take, no co-operation or consensus. In an extreme case, someone who is caught in the compulsive drive to get from point A to point B will ignore all feedback, sacrificing it to speed. There is no reality-testing along the way. "I'm in an awful rush! Don't confuse me with the facts" might well be his response.

Judgment types like to schedule ahead and organize their lives and their activities well in advance. Sunday night you may find them anticipating their extracurricular activities for the entire week, and planning in some detail how to spend Saturday morning, afternoon, and evening. Often they make decisions impulsively, before it is necessary or even wise to do so. Disappointment over "rained-out" plans is a common complaint among these folks.

Their expertise lies in sorting, ordering, arranging, separating, and listing things. There is a "best" way of doing things, meaning an exact, purposeful, rational way. Judgment people don't handle surprises well and therefore are uncomfortable with unexpected happenings. "Be Prepared" is their motto. Self-discipline and will-power help sustain all their efforts.

Extreme Judgment types with inadequately developed perception (i.e., sensation or intuition) lack the openness, understanding, and experience of life necessary to keep up-to-date and informed. They become narrowly rigid, and thus incapable of adapting or of seeing any point of view except their own. These people fall back on old ways of doing things. Fearful of losing control of their own and others' behaviour, they have problems relating to external control and authority.

Perception

Perception, based on data and impressions gathered by Sensation and/or Intuition, informs our understanding. It opens up our minds to immediate and present knowledge, and provides the details and realities of life as it unfolds. Perception people are process-oriented and prefer to keep their options open. They like to hear about what others are doing, and are more likely to ask *why* questions than to tell others what to do.

Perception types make *series* of decisions based on their personal reactions to ongoing situations and events. Rarely do they make a final decision until forced to do so by a deadline, crisis, emergency, or someone else's ultimatum. Even then, they keep wondering if they have made the right decision. Ideally, problem-solving is achieved simply through understanding and exploring different perspectives. Action is not necessary, and closure is resisted.

Perception people are spontaneous and possess the ability to stay thoroughly in the present moment. They are "here-and-now" people, interested in actualities. Often their intentions to do something in the future are forgotten, and things are left undone. Their well-being depends on being open, curious, flexible, and able to adapt as you go. "Let's wait. Let's see what happens. There's no rush. Something will show up." These are their refrains. This tolerant, live-and-let-live, relaxed attitude fosters an adaptability to handle accidental, unexpected, or unpleasant happenings.

However, this focus on the present means that they are often late and unaware of time. Other people's need to schedule and be on time is lost on them. Perception individuals shun fixed plans and dislike scheduling of any kind. Consequently, they are often unclear about what they want to do next. This makes decision-making difficult. When asked the question "What are you doing on the twenty-fifth, two weeks from now?" their reply takes the form of a protest. "Give me a break! I can't even begin to think that far in advance!"

Starting is easy; finishing is not. Starting something new and fresh is exciting for these people — that is, until the novelty wears off. Finishing is difficult because the discipline to make decisions, organize a plan, and see it through to a conclusion, no matter what, is not their natural expertise.

Extreme Perception types need well-developed judgment processes (i.e., Thinking or Feeling) to give their life direction and structure. Otherwise, they get so caught up experiencing life that they fail to criticize and govern their own actions. What they perceive as necessary freedom can be seen as irresponsible or lacking in purpose by others. They may be all sail and no rudder.

Isabel Myers cautions that it is what we *naturally* tend to do that determines our type. Our natural inclinations, however, may be profoundly affected by others. She states, "A person's idea of what is right may be an acquired ideal, borrowed from another type" (p. 74). A person's actual behaviour may reflect habits or efforts developed to please a parent of the opposite attitude.

Perception types appear lazy and aimless to Judgment types. Conversely, they see Judgment types as driven, set in their ways, and lacking a zest for life. Needless to say, Judgment and Perception types often drive each other crazy! The following story was told to me by Coleen Clark, who introduced me to the Myers-Briggs Type Indicator. Imagine a scenario in which a Perception person, Rose, says to a Judgment person, Sydney, "I think I'd like to go out for a corned beef sandwich tonight."

Sydney gets busy organizing his thoughts about which restaurant has the best corned beef. He goes down his mental list, and makes a decision about which is best. He is about to suggest Ben's, across town, when Rose pipes up, "On the other hand, I wouldn't mind going for a pizza!"

Sydney, in disbelief and annoyance, asks, "Whatever happened to my corned beef sandwich? My mouth was watering!"

Rose quickly recovers, and anxiously begins to offer further suggestions. "Chinese food, Caesar salad, steak" — she goes on and on. Rose really doesn't know what she wants. Making a series of decisions is easy for her. Sydney needs to step in and diplomatically suggest that they try Ben's this time. Rose can make the decision about where they go next week.

A CAUTIONARY NOTE

In this simplified explanation of the different functions, the meaning and effects of coupling the Extraverted-Introverted functions with Thinking, Feeling, Sensation, and Intuition, as well as adding the Judgment-Perception variable, cannot be covered here. The sixteen different personality types are quite distinct, and even one function change transforms the personality type profoundly.

It is important to have a well-trained and qualified practitioner administer and analyse the Myers-Briggs Type Indicator Test to ascertain your true type. In my practice, people often score the opposite on one function from what they really are, the function they were born with. There are a number of reasons this occurs. The individual may have had to adapt in order to survive in a dysfunctional family or in an unhealthy work situation. For example, a workaholic boss or organization does not value people and relationships. Only the bottom line and the productivity of its employees are important. In this setting, it is essential to develop your own objective, impersonal thinking to protect yourself. Goals become all important to you, too. Many people sell their souls to serve the organization. They lose touch with their own values, and therefore with the essence of the Self.

Social pressure in our patriarchal society also makes it difficult for male Feelers and female Thinkers not to follow the traditional, stereotyped roles society tends to impose. To overcompensate, males often strive to be sensitive and nurturing, and females become obsessed with the business world, trying to be better than the men.

Family pressures can often push a child away from his or her best function. I was an extraverted child in a household of Introverts. My parents occasionally let me "get lost" because they worried about my "Curious George" nature. I well remember standing in the entrance to a store and suddenly realizing there was no one in sight whom I recognized. Fears of abandonment are innate, so the child not only experiences fear, but is made to feel "bad" for her natural curiosity.

An Intuitive child, similarly, may distrust his best function when his fantastical ideas cause his other fact-oriented, concrete family members concern. These effects are always most oppressive and damaging when one person in the family is outnumbered by other personality types. The child is often labelled "different," or worse, "weird." I secretly wondered if I had been adopted because my differences were commented on so regularly by both family and visitors.

BRAVE NEW WORLDS

By purposely developing our opposite functions, we enter a new world where our energies can flow into exciting and fresh adventures. The Introvert who challenges himself to introduce himself to others and make new friends will be energized and fulfilled by his efforts. It will become easier each time he makes a friendly gesture. The Intuitive type who learns to truly appreciate small, delicate detail will enrich the way she views her world. She will see beautiful and precious details in paintings she once glanced at only briefly.

People have to learn to appreciate and value their opposite functions, however, before they will give themselves permission to risk such adventures. An admirable goal is to achieve balance in our personality and in our life by developing *all* our functions — the ones we were fortunate enough to be born with, and the ones we ourselves make efforts to develop.

What Is Your Level of Narcissism?

ARROGANCE

1. Do you believe you are "special" and "different" from others?
2. Have you ever been told you are arrogant?
3. Do you tend to exaggerate your own potential?
4. Are your plans overly expansive or diversified?
5. Do you have difficulty accepting your own limitations?
6. Do you think that rules and regulations often don't apply to you?
7. Does your personal well-being override concern for others?
8. Are you entitled to special treatment and privileges?
9. Do you think others have no right to criticize you?
10. Do you fail to appreciate what others do for you?
11. Do you resist asking for help if you have a problem?

CONTROL AND MANIPULATION

1. Do you always like to be "right"?
2. Do you typically arrange things so that you get your own way?
3. Do you sometimes insist on being the centre of attention?
4. Do you find yourself saying things to make people feel sorry for you?
5. Do you think that your spouse should think the same way you do?
6. Are you quite different in public than you are in private?
7. Is being "in charge" very important to you?
8. Can you be cold, calculating, even ruthless, to retain control?

9. Do you make requests of others that take them away from family?
10. Does your family's schedule revolve around your timing, your plans?
11. Is delegating responsibility, without checking up, difficult?
12. Do you find it intolerable if others fail to respect your authority?
13. Do you dismiss others from your life when they challenge you?

DISHONESTY, DENIAL, SECRECY

1. Do you keep your mistakes or failures to yourself?
2. Is privacy extremely important to you?
3. Do you often promise to do things, and then not follow through?
4. Do you tell other people what they want to hear?
5. Do you often neglect to tell the truth?
6. Do you resist asking for help if you have a problem?
7. Do you "forget" your temper tantrums or rages after they occur?
8. Do you sometimes "pretend" you have no money, when this is not true?

FEAR OF AGING

1. Do you pride yourself on your youthful appearance?
2. Do you avoid thinking about your old age, or retirement?
3. Do you hang on to business interests after retirement?
4. Do you try to influence how new management runs things after leaving?
5. Are you able to mourn when someone else dies?
6. Is supporting your spouse difficult when a family member dies?

INSECURITY, LOW SELF-ESTEEM

1. Do you sometimes feel "phony"?
2. Do you distrust words, and emphasize action?
3. Do you watch others to see how you should act in social settings?
4. To avoid crying when things get too emotional, do you laugh instead?
5. Are you fatalistic?
6. Do you ever secretly worry that you are going crazy?
7. Do you find yourself often questioning your own judgments?
8. Would you describe yourself as a loner?
9. Do you sometimes feel empty and emotionally bankrupt?
10. Do you worry that people seem to be avoiding you?
11. Is it difficult to get vicarious pleasure out of others' success?

PERSONAL PERSONA OR IMAGE

1. Is your persona, how the world sees you, very important to you?
2. Is failure one of your deepest fears?
3. Has work become a form of self-aggrandizement?
4. Do you dress to project a certain image?
5. Do you enjoy being recognized by the maître d' at restaurants?
6. Do you neglect to reveal your failures or losses to others?
7. Do you pride yourself on your independence?

POWER

1. Have you always been quite ambitious?
2. Are recognition, praise, and admiration very important to you?
3. When you are succesful, do you still crave more recognition?
4. Do you resent interference, or a challenge to your ideas or plans?
5. Do you sometimes intimidate others to get your own way?

6. Have you become ruthless in your dealings with people or business?
7. Has success in your career become all-important in your life?

PUNISH SELF/AND OTHERS

1. Do you neglect to exercise, or eat properly?
2. Are you smoking or drinking too much, or using drugs?
3. Have you become obsessed with your work?
4. Do you neglect to go for a medical check-up on a regular basis?
5. Can you be vindictive at times?
6. Do you punish others by refusing to do what they want to do?
7. Have you become selfish and self-centred?
8. Do you see others, but not experience them or their point of view?
9. Do you blame others when things go wrong?
10. Do you have temper tantrums or rages when you don't get your way?
11. Do you work to avoid dealing with personal responsibilities?
12. Has your family's welfare become less important to you?

Bibliography

Bandler, R., and J. Grinder. *Frogs into Princes*. Utah: Real People Press, 1979.

Birnbaum, J. *Cry Anger. A Cure for Depression*. Don Mills: General Publishing, 1973.

Bradway, K. "Jung's Psychological Types." *Journal of Analytical Psychology*, Vol. 9, Tavistock, 1964.

Campbell, J. (ed.). *The Portable Jung*. New York: Penguin Books, 1991.

Campbell, R. *Psychiatric Dictionary*. Fifth ed. New York: Oxford University Press, 1981.

Clark, C. "Myers-Briggs Type Indicator." Toronto: 1987.

Davitz, J. R. *The Language of Emotion*. New York: Academic Press, 1969.

de Waal, E. *Seeking God. The Way of St. Benedict*. Minnesota: The Liturgical Press, 1984.

Estes, C. P. *Women Who Run With the Wolves*. New York: Ballantine Books, 1992.

Fox, M. *Creation Spirituality. Liberating Gifts for the Peoples of the Earth*. New York: Harper Collins, 1991.

Fulford, R. "Rediscovering Frank Lloyd Wright." *The Globe and Mail*, January 26, 1994.

Hart, A. *The Hidden Link Between Adrenalin and Stress*. Dallas: Word Publishing, 1991.

Hellmich, N. "When working hard starts to work against you." *USA Today*, August 13, 1992.

Hyder, Q. *The Christian Handbook of Psychiatry*. Old Tappan, NJ: Fleming H. Revell, 1971.

Jung, C. G. *Psychological Types*. Bollingen Series XX. The Collected Works of C. G. Jung, Vol. 6. Princeton, NJ: Princeton University Press, 1971.

Killinger, B. *Workaholics. The Respectable Addicts*. Toronto: Key Porter Books, 1991.

Killinger, B. "A Shift to a New Perspective." (Unpublished paper.)

Killinger, B. *The Place of Humour in Adult Psychotherapy*. Ph.D. Dissertation. York University, 1976. (Unpublished.)

Kintsch, W. *Learning, Memory, and Conceptual Processes*. New York: John Wiley & Sons, 1970.

Kohut, H., and E. Wolf. "The Disorders of the Self and Their Treatment: An Outline." *International Journal of Psychoanalysis,* 59, No. 413 (1978): 413–25.

Krech, D., R. Crutchfield, and N. Livson. *Elements of Psychology*. New York: Alfred A. Knopf, 1974.

Kuerti, A. "All that glitters is not Gould." *The Globe and Mail,* February 12, 1993.

Lasch, C. *The Culture of Narcissism*. New York: Warner Books, 1979.

Lazerson, A. (ed.). *Psychology Today. An Introduction*. New York: Random House, 1975.

Leonard, L. *The Wounded Woman: Healing the Father–Daughter Relationship*. Boston: Shambhala Publications, 1982.

Lowen, A. *Narcissism. Denial of the True Self*. New York: Collier Books, 1985.

Mindess, H. "The Use and Abuse of Humour in Psychotherapy." In T. Chapman and H. Foot (eds.), *Humour and Laughter: Theory, Research and Application*. London: John Wiley & Sons, 1976.

Myers, I. B. *Manual: Myers-Briggs Type Indicator*. Palo Alto, CA: Consulting Psychologists Press, 1975.

Myers, I. B., and P. Myers. *Gifts Differing*. Palo Alto, CA: Consulting Psychologists Press, 1980.

Oates, W. *Confessions of a Workaholic*. Nashville: Abingdon, 1971.

Osborn, A. F. *Applied Imagination*. Rev. ed. New York: Scribner, 1957.

Peck, M. S. *The Road Less Traveled*. New York: Simon and Schuster, 1978.

Pittaway, K. "Overwork: Setting Boundaries in Hard Times." *Pathways,* January/February, 1994.

Sanford, J. *Evil: The Shadow Side of Reality.* New York: Crossroads, 1984.

Sanford, J. *The Invisible Partners.* New York: Paulist Press, 1980.

Schary, D. *Heyday.* New York: Little, Brown, 1981.

Sharp, D. *Personality Types: Jung's Model of Typology.* Toronto: Inner City Books, 1987.

Sharp, D. *The Survival Papers. Anatomy of a Midlife Crisis.* Toronto: Inner City Books, 1988.

Worth, D. "Non-Contact Therapeutic Touch and the Healing of Wounds." *Journal of Subtle Energies,* Vol. 1, No. 1. Colorado: 1990.

Index

abandonment, fear of, 143
abuse, emotional sexual, 99–100
acceptance, unconditional, 74–75
addiction, workaholism and, 43, 44, 46–47
adrenal fatigue, 65
adrenalin, 2, 46, 61, 65, 118
Adrenalin and Stress (Hart), 118
advice, giving, 157, 164–165
aggression. *See* passive aggression
aging, fear of, 89–90, 242
alcohol, 138–139
Alofsin, Anthony, 88
ambition, 45, 53, 59
anger, 2, 3. *See also* passive aggression; rage
    denial of, 77
    fear of, 5
    and Feelers, 20–21, 50
    and guilt, 66
    and Inferior function, 33
    passive-aggressive styles of, 7, 57
anxiety, 2, 3. *See also* panic attacks
    and Feeling function, 7–10, 23, 38,
        49–50, 109
    and narcissistic parents, 95–96
    and physiological change, 116–117
    and Thinking function, 14
    and workaholism, 46, 48, 49, 52, 57,
        59, 66
apologizing, 195
Applied Imagination (Osborn), 205
appreciation, 89, 190–192
arrogance, 46, 53, 55, 84–85, 88, 241
assumptions, 156–157, 188
attention, 82–83
auditory meditation, 146, 147–148
auxiliary function, 35
awareness, 219
    body, 115–119
    diffuse, 181, 182
    of feelings, 108–109
    focused, 17, 27, 181, 182
    and problem-solving, 158

balance, regaining, 34, 211–212

balanced life, loss of, 43–44
balanced personality, 34, 213–214, 239
Bandler, Richard, 146
behaviour, destructive patterns of, 177–178
bitterness, 21
blame, 63, 64, 77
body awareness, 115–119
body language, 174–175, 188
body position, 118–119, 219
boiling point, 142–143
boredom, fear of, 60–61
boundaries, setting, 55
boy craziness, 103
brainstorming, 21, 51, 205–210
breakdown syndrome, 54, 58–68
breathing, stomach, 148
Briggs, Katherine C., 225

Campbell, Robert, 63–64, 131, 145–146
child
    eternal, 94
    idealized, 96–97
    shamed, 96
childhood development
    healthy/normal, 74–76, 78–79
    of narcissists, 76–78, 79–81, 94–95, 96
The Christian Handbook of Psychiatry
        (Hyder), 66
chronic fatigue, 8, 58, 61, 64–66
chronic fears, 59–64. See also fear
Clark, Coleen, 35, 37
claustrophobia, 62
closure statements, 184–185
communication. *See also* conversations;
    interactions
    improving, 182–186
    non-controlling, 155–171, 222–223
    and Thinkers, 17–18, 182
    workaholism and, 67
compartmentalization, 14
competition, 53, 71
compliments, 191–192
compulsions, 56, 131–132
Confessions of a Workaholic (Oates), 44

conflict, 20
conscious data, 121–122
context, 185
control, 2, 3, 69. *See also* non-controlling
    communication
    and breakdown syndrome, 54
    and humour, 149–150
    of information, 156–157
    and meditation, 145–148
    and narcissism, 241–242
    and projections, 187
    regaining, 144–152
    and spirituality, 151–152
    and touch, 150–151
    and visualization, 148–149
    and workaholism, 49, 53, 56, 57, 69,
        70–71
conversations. *See also* communication
    between Thinkers and Feelers, 18, 19,
        22, 28–31
    between two Feelers, 27–28
    between two Thinkers, 26–27
couch potatoes, 61, 65–66
*Creation Spirituality: Liberating Gifts for the
    Peoples of the Earth* (Fox), 200–201
creative problem-solving, 199–217
creativity, 51
criticism, 193–195
crossing the fence, 157, 160
The Culprit, 202, 204. *See also* Shadow
The Culture of Narcissism (Lasch), 94

data, conscious, 121–122
daughter, pedestal, 102–104
death, fear of, 89–90
deceit, and narcissism, 88
decision-making, 15, 16, 20, 51, 200,
    225–226
defense mechanisms, 14, 130–134, 220
delegation, 62
denial, 15, 131
    of anger, 77
    and damaged Self, 77
    and dysfunctional development, 80
        and illusion, 69
    and narcissism, 85–86, 242
    and privacy, 69, 85–86
    and secrecy, 69, 85–86
    and workaholism, 47, 53, 61, 63, 69–70

dependency, 53, 84, 163
depression
    and feelings/Feeling function, 7–10,
        14–15, 21, 23, 49
    and Inferior function, 33
    and rage, 57
    reactive, 7–9, 10
    as sign of imbalance, 14, 49
    and Thinking function, 14, 49
destructive behaviour, patterns of, 177–178
development, early
    healthy/normal, 74–76, 78–79
    and narcissism, 76–78, 79–81, 94–95,
        96
de Waal, Esther, 216–217
diffuse awareness, 181, 182
dignity, 196
diplomacy, 193–195
dirty fighting, 159
discovery. *See also* self-discovery
    fear of, 61–62
dishonesty, 22, 62, 84, 242
dissociation, 14, 132–133
distortion of reality, 52, 79–80
dominance, 57. *See also* control
dominant function, 13, 14, 35, 36
dualistic thinking, 51
duplicity, 84, 242

effective (positive) thinking, 24, 36
ego, 63, 78–79, 85–86
ego boundary, 23, 157, 160
emotion, vs. feeling, 15, 108
empathy, 189, 193–194
energy fields, 151
energy level, 117–118, 219
ENFJ personalities, 35–36
enthusiasm, 21, 185–186, 190–191
envy, 3, 5, 17, 35, 64
Estes, Clarissa Pinkola, 8
eternal child, 94
Evil: The Shadow Side of Reality (Sanford), 75
exercise, 65
exhaustion. *See* chronic fatigue
experiencing
    and defense mechanisms, 130–134, 220
    and internalizing, 113–114, 127–134,
        220
    and nurturing, 128–129, 220

expressions, facial, 196–197
externalizing, 109–112
Extraversion, 226–227
Extraverts, 190, 229–230

facial expressions, 196–197
failure, fear of, 59–60, 81
fairness, 19, 193
family life
    narcissism and, 93–106
    workaholics and, 52, 57
fatigue, chronic, 8, 58, 61, 64–66
fear, 2, 49, 56
    of abandonment, 143
    of aging, 89–90, 242
    of anger, 5
    of boredom, 60–61
    of death, 89–90
    of discovery, 61–62
    of failure, 59–60, 81
    of laziness, 61
    and obsession, 59
    of persecution, 63–64
    of punishment, 66
    of self-discovery, 62–63
feedback, 183–184
Feelers, 20–23. See also feeling; Feeling
    function; feelings
    and anger, 20–21, 50
    and clarification, 28
    and conflict, 20
    and decision-making, 16, 20, 200
    diffuse awareness of, 181, 182
    and enthusiasm, 190
    Extraverted, 21
    and generosity, 29
    and honesty, 22
    interactions between, 21, 27–28
    interactions with Thinkers, 18, 19, 22,
        28–31, 182–186
    and interruptions, 28
    Introverted, 21–22
    jobs suited for, 20
    and marriage, 19, 23
    Myers on, 23
    negative, 38
    and oversensitivity, 22–23, 49
    and personal values, 16, 20, 181
    positive, 38

and resentment, 21, 50
and sacrifice, 20
and self-pity, 21, 50
social skills of, 20, 50
and Terrible Twist, 32–33
feeling. See also Feeling function; feelings
    vs. emotion, 15, 108
    negative, 38
    positive, 38
Feeling function, 3, 14, 20–23. See also
    Feelers; feelings
    and appreciation, 190–192
    best uses for, 16
    and brainstorming, 205
    and criticism, 193–195
    and depression, 14–15, 21, 23, 49
    developing, 181–197
    and diplomacy, 193–195
    and emotion, 15
    and generosity, 190–192
    and harmony, 195–197
    and Inferior function, 34, 35
    key concepts of, 181
    and openness, 186–189
    and sensitivity, 192–193
    and warmth, 192–192
    when dominated by Thinking func-
        tion, 49–50
    when untempered by Thinking func-
        tion, 14–15
    workaholism's effects on, 49–50, 52
feelings, 15–16, 20–23. See also Feelers;
    feeling; Feeling function
    awareness of own, 108–109
    establishing the level of, 126–127
    exceptions to staying with, 129–130
    feeling the, 127–128, 189
    intensity of, 108
    internalizing, 219–223
    labelling, 119–120, 219
    loss of, 47–52, 62, 73
    and narcissism, 78
    playful, 49–50, 68
    projection of, 52, 110
    quality of, 108–109
    telling, 158
    triggering, 120
fence
    as communication tool, 157, 160

crossing the, 157, 160
sitting on the, 200
fight or flight, 118
fighting, dirty, 159
finger-pointing, 161
focused awareness, 17, 27, 181, 182
Fonda, Bridget, 44–45
Fox, Matthew, 200–201
Frank Lloyd Wright: The Lost Years, 1910–1922 (Alofsin), 88
Freeman, Alan, 47
Frogs into Princes (Bandler and Grinder), 146
Fulford, Robert, 88

generosity, 83–84, 190–192, 202, 211
genuineness, 192
Gerbil Wheel, 44, 50, 55, 60, 128
Gifts Differing (Myers), 15, 19, 23, 227, 228, 231
Glenn Gould at Work: Creative Lying (Kazdin), 87
goals, 45, 50, 60, 61
good life, living, 214–216
Gould, Glenn, 87
gratification, delayed vs. immediate, 50–51
gratitude, 190
greed, 51, 58, 71
grieving, 127
Grinder, John, 146
guilt, 2, 49, 56, 58, 66

harmony, 20, 195–197
Hart, A., 118
hate, 5
heaviness, in energy level, 117–118, 219
Hebb, D.O., 123
help, accepting, 104–106
holidays, 61
honesty, 22, 186
hostility, 6
humility, 197
humour, 68, 149–150
Humour and Laughter: Theory, Research and Applications (Mindess), 217
hurt, 2
Hyder, Quentin, 66
hyperactivity, 65

idealized child, 96–97
idealized parent imago, 74–75
identification, 112, 115–121
illusion, 69
image, and narcissism, 80–81, 243
imagination, 51
imago, idealized parent, 74–75
imbalance, identifying, 3–5
"I" messages, 157–161, 162, 170, 171, 187, 222
impression management, 69, 82, 96
independence, 53, 67
individuation, 100–101
Inferior function, 13, 24, 25, 33–39. *See also* Shadow
information
    communicating, 156–157
    gathering/processing, 17, 48. *See also* Intuition function; Sensation function
    storing, 122–124
ingratitude, 84–85
insecurity, 53, 57, 242
insight, lack of, 88–89
integrity, 67–68, 186
intellectualizing, 14
intelligence, 53
intensity, 108, 196
interactions
    between Feelers, 21, 27–28
    between Thinkers, 26–27
    between Thinkers and Feelers, 18, 19, 22, 28–31, 182–186
internalizing, 112–134, 177–178, 220
interruptions, 27, 28
intimacy, 67
INTJ personality, 36
Introversion, 21–22, 226, 228–230
Introverts, 190
Intuition function, 8, 35, 205, 230, 232–234
    and other functions, 15
    workaholism's effects on, 50–51, 52
The Invisible Partner (Sanford), 40
isolation, 133

Japan, workaholism in, 46–47, 68
jealousy, 5, 17, 35, 64
judgment, 34, 182–183, 187

Judgment function, 234–236
Jung, C.G., 94
    and psychological types, 13–14, 17,
        19, 33–34, 225, 226, 230, 232
    on the Shadow, 39, 40
justification, 112–113, 121–127, 219–220

Karoshi: When the Corporate Warrior Dies
    (Kawahito), 47
Karoshi, 46–47
Kawahito, Hiroshi, 47
Kazdin, Andrew, 87
kinesthetic meditation, 146, 148
Kintsch, W., 123
Kohut, Heinz, 74
Kuerti, Anton, 87

labelling feelings, 119–120, 219
Lasch, Christopher, 94
laughter, diabolical, 86
Lazerson, A., 124, 131
laziness, 61, 63
Learning, Memory, and Conceptual Processes
    (Kintsch), 123
leaving situations, 143–144, 221
Leonard, Linda, 103
lightness, in energy level, 118, 219
listening
    and feedback, 183–184
    and Feeling function, 182–186
    and problem-solving, 136–137, 156,
        164–170, 223
    safe atmosphere for, 160–161, 222–223
    second-guessing as part of, 168–170,
        187–188, 223
    selective, 27, 37, 51, 53–54
    and Thinkers, 18
Logical Circle, 201–211
loners, 90–92
love
    loss of, 83
    power of, 71
Lowen, Alexander, 79, 80, 86

manipulation, 241–242
mantra, 147–148
martyr-victim, 7–8
maturity, 15, 40
meditation, 145–148

memory, 18, 123–126
men
    as Feelers, 238–239
    as Thinkers, 19
mental health, workaholism and, 62, 68
Mindes, Harvey, 217
mirroring, 74
moods/moodiness, 15, 38, 49, 188–189
mood swings, rapid/severe, 4, 57
Myers-Briggs Type Indicator, 35, 225–238
Myers, Isabel, 15, 225, 237
    on Extraverts, 227
    on Feelers, 23
    on Introverts, 228
    on Intuitives, 233, 234
    on Sensation people, 231
    on Thinkers, 19

Narcissism: Denial of the True Self (Lowen),
    79, 86
narcissism, 11, 71–92
    and apologizing, 195
    assessing level of, 241–244
    and control, 241–242
    and deceit, 88
    and denial, 85–86, 242
    and dependency, 84
    and development of Self, 76–78, 79–
        81, 94–95, 96
    and family life, 93–106
    and feelings, 78
    and generosity, 83–84
    and image, 80–81, 243
    and loss of Self, 73, 76–78
    and outbursts, 80
    and power, 243–244
    and punishment, 86–88, 102, 244
    and rage, 90
    and secrecy, 242
narcissistic parents, 59, 94–96
narcissistic wounds, 93–97
National Defense Council for Karoshi
    Victims, 47
needs, awareness of, 158
negative feeling, 38
negative sensation, 37, 51–52
negative Shadow, 39
negative thinking, 24, 35–36
negativity, 34, 56

Neuro-Linguistic Programming, 146
non-controlling communication, 155–171,
    222–223
nurturing, 128–129, 220

Oates, Wayne, 44
objectivity, 51
observing, 182–183
obsession
    and chronic fears, 59
    as defense mechanism, 131–132
    and pedestal daughter, 102
    as sign of imbalance, 14
    and Thinking function, 14, 48
    and workaholism, 2, 45, 47, 51, 53,
        55–57
openness, 186–189, 193–194
optimism, 20
Osborn, A., 205
other-directedness, 20, 187
outbursts, 90
overreaction, 124–125, 220
overscheduling, 60
oversensitivity, 22–23, 49

pain, 109
panic attacks, 9, 55, 59, 62, 68. See also
    anxiety
paranoia, 63–64
parent imago, idealized, 74–75
parents, narcissistic, 59, 94–96
passive aggression, 6–7, 57, 111, 143–144,
    160
paths, four spiritual (Fox), 201
Peck, M. Scott, 152
pedestal daughter, 102–104
Penfield, Wilder, 124
Perception function, 234, 236–238
perfectionism, 2, 45, 50, 53–55, 56, 59
performance, 75
persecution, fear of, 63–64
personal balance, loss of, 43–44
personality, workaholic, 43, 44–47
personality type. See psychological type
pessimism, 17, 35
physical health, 62, 68
physiological change, 68, 116–118, 219
Pittaway, Kim, 55
playful feelings, 49–50, 68

positive feeling, 38
positive sensation, 37–38, 51
positive Shadow, 39
positive (effective) thinking, 24, 36
power, 2
    and narcissism, 243–244
    as workaholic trap, 49, 53, 69, 71
power brokers, 91
power struggle, teeter-totter, 162–164, 223
privacy, 62, 69, 85–86
problem-solving
    and alcohol, 138–139
    appropriateness of, 139–141, 221
    assumptions in, 156–157
    and awareness of needs, 158
    complications in, 138–139
    creative, 199–217
    effective, 155–171
    and internalizing, 114
    and listening, 136–137, 156, 164–170,
        223
    with Logical Circle, 201–211
    and openness, 189
    for others (crossing the fence), 157, 160
    and rescheduling, 135–136, 137–138,
        142–144, 221–222
    tools for, 158
productivity, 61
projection(s), 40, 63, 187
    as defense mechanism, 14, 131
    of feelings, 52, 110
    and openness, 188–189
promotions, 60
Psychiatric Dictionary (Campbell), 63–64,
    131, 146
psychological type, overview of, 13–14,
    225–239
Psychological Types (Jung), 13, 226, 230, 232
Psychology Today: An Introduction (Lazerson),
    124, 131
psychotic breaks, 10, 64, 68
punishment
    fear of, 66
    and narcissism, 86–88, 102, 244
purpose, 60

rage(s), 6, 15, 56–57, 64, 90. See also
    anger
rationalizing, 14, 132

reaction formation, 133–134
reactive depression, 7–9, 10
reactors, 111
reality, distortion of, 52, 79–80
reality-testing, 202–204
rejection, 64, 66
relaxation, 61
repression, 133
rescheduling, 135–136, 137–138, 142–144, 221–222. *See also* timing
resentment, 21, 50
resolution, 100–102
respect, 67–68
responsibility, 61, 66
rigidity, 18–19, 34, 51, 64, 67
The Road Less Travelled (Peck), 152

sacrifice, 20
sadness, 21
Sanford, John, 40, 75
second guessing, 168–170, 187–188, 223
secrecy, 62, 69, 85–86, 242
Seeking God: The Way of St. Benedict (de Waal), 216
selective listening, 27, 37, 51, 53–54
Self
    damaged, 76–78
    and ego, 79
    healthy, 74–76
    and narcissism, 73, 76–78, 79–81, 94–95, 96
    and work, 44
self-absorption, 57. *See also* narcissism
self-aggrandizement, 45, 70, 81
self-anger, 66
self-discovery, fear of, 62–63
self-doubt, 60, 63
self-esteem, low, 66, 243
selfishness, 83–84
self-touching, 151
sensation
    negative, 37, 51–52
    positive, 37–38, 51
Sensation function, 36, 230–232, 236
    relationship to other functions, 15
    workaholism's effects on, 51–52
sense of humour, 68, 149–150
sensitivity, 192–193
sex, 102–103

sex drive, 9
sexual abuse, emotional, 99–100
Shadow, 24, 25, 39–40, 63, 69, 170, 178, 211. *See also* Inferior function
    and childhood development, 75, 76
    and Collective Unconscious, 39
    Jung on, 39, 40
    and Logical Circle, 202, 204
    negative, 39
    positive, 39
    and wisdom, 39
shame, 66, 85, 96
shamed child, 96
sharing views, 184, 223
sitting on the fence, 200
"smiling depressives," 21
social isolation, 4, 8
specialness, 81–82
spirituality, 68, 151–152
spiritual paths, 201
stomach breathing, 148
stress, 65
stubbornness, 15, 34, 49, 67
students, workaholic, 59–60
submission, 57
supportiveness, 191, 194–195
survival, 48

tactfulness, 22
takers, selfish, 83–84
tantrums, 15
teeter-totter power struggle, 162–164, 223
temper tantrums, 6, 15
Terrible Twist, 5, 31–33, 70
Therapeutic Touch, 150–151
Thinkers, 16–19. *See also* thinking; Thinking function
    best jobs for, 16
    as communicators, 17–18, 26–31, 182
    competitive nature of, 17
    and decision-making, 16, 200
    effect of on Feelers/feelings, 18, 19, 21, 22
    and enthusiasm, 190–191
    Extraverted, 227
    and fairness, 19
    focused awareness of, 17, 27, 181, 182
    and information processing, 17
    interactions between, 19, 26–27

interactions with Feelers, 18, 19, 22, 28–31, 182–186
and interruptions, 27
Introverted, 227
Jung on, 17, 19
as listeners, 18
and logic and reason, 17
and marriage, 19, 23
Myers on, 19
rigid, 18–19
and selective listening, 27, 37
thinking. *See also* Thinkers; Thinking function
dualistic, 51
negative, 24, 35–36
positive (effective), 24, 36
Thinking function, 16–19. *See also* Thinkers; thinking
and anxiety, 14
best uses for, 15–16
and brainstorming, 205
and communication, 182–186
and depression, 14, 49
and emotion, 15, 27
and externalizing feelings, 110
and Inferior function, 34, 35
and obsession, 14, 48
and survival, 48
when untempered by/cut off from Feeling function, 14, 18–19, 48
workaholism's effects on, 48–49, 52
"3 out of 5" syndrome, 37, 51
time-out, 142–143
timing, 136–139, 220–221. *See also* rescheduling
Touch, Therapeutic, 150–151
transcendental meditation, 146
Transformation Goal, 202, 204–205
triangular pattern, 144, 221–222
Trump, Donald, 46
trust, 20
Type A personality, 90

underlining, 185
university students, 59–60

values, 16
Via Creativa, 201
Via Negativa, 201

Via Positiva, 201
Via Transformativa, 201
visualization, 148–149
visual meditation, 146, 147

Wake-up Call, 202–204
warmth, 192–193
"Watching Water" process, 213
will, 79
wisdom, 15, 39, 114–115
Wolf, Ernest, 74
women, as Thinkers, 19, 238–239
Women Who Run With the Wolves (Estes), 8
Workaholics: The Respectable Addicts (Killinger), 43
workaholics
chronic fears of, 59–64
and family life, 52, 57
personality of, 43, 44–47, 49, 67–68
workaholism
and anxiety, 46, 48, 49, 52, 57, 59, 66
and breakdown syndrome, 54, 58–68
complexity of, 52–72
and control, 49, 53, 56, 57, 69, 70–71
and denial, 47, 53, 61, 63, 69–70
and distortion of reality, 52, 79–80
and Feeling function, 49–50
and Intuition function, 50–51
and narcissism, 53, 57
and obsession, 2, 45, 47, 51, 53, 55–57
and perfectionism, 53–55, 59
and power, 49, 53, 69, 71
and Sensation function, 51–52
and Thinking function, 48–49, 52
work ethic, 59
Worth, Daniel, 150–151
The Wounded Woman: Healing the Father-Daughter Relationship (Leonard), 103
wounds, narcissistic, 93–97
Wright, Frank Lloyd, 88

"you" messages, 161–164, 170, 223
"Yuppie Flu," 66